ELIZABETH
QUEEN & MOTHER

*The story of Queen Elizabeth II
and the British Royal Family*

by GRAHAM and HEATHER FISHER

HAWTHORN BOOKS, INC.

Publishers / NEW YORK

First Edition, October, 1964

H-3412

Contents

DA
590
F52

Illustrations

For our daughters
JANET *and* LINDA

FOREWORD

THIS BOOK STARTED with a telephone call. We were living at the time only a few miles from Sandringham House, the Royal Family's country home on Norfolk's windswept coast. It was February 6, 1952, a gray, wintry day rendered suddenly more so by the telephone call giving news of the King's death. Four thousand miles away in Kenya another telephone call conveyed the same sad news to the young woman who was now, quite suddenly, Queen Elizabeth II.

At Sandringham, so sudden and unexpected was the news, that the flag on the parish church still flapped at full mast. Farmworkers toiled on in the frosty fields unaware that they would see their beloved monarch and squire no more. A few rejected the news as unthinkable. "Don't you go spreading silly rumors like that," said the bluff country policeman who guarded Sandringham's main gates.

But the King was dead and soon a new Monarch was winging her way back from distant Kenya. She arrived at Sandringham late the following day, a small, remote, black-clad figure, her pale face screened from public view.

What was she really like, we wondered, this young woman, wife and mother, now called upon so suddenly and in such sad circumstances to shoulder the burdens of monarchy?

This book is an attempt at answering our own question . . . what is the Queen really like? It is not a biography. Still less could it claim to be an official biography. It is simply the story of twelve years in the life of a young woman who, in addition to being a wife and mother, is also Queen Elizabeth II.

It is the distillation of years of research, thousands of miles of travel, hundreds of interviews. Our research has taken us from a farmworker's cottage near Sandringham to the elegant establishment of Norman Hartnell, where we learned something of how royal clothes are designed and made. It took us to Paris, where we saw a new, fashion-conscious Queen stun the French with her elegance; to Canada, where we sat by a TV screen and watched the Queen undergo her first ordeal by television. We visited the stables at Newmarket where the royal racehorses are trained, interviewed those who know or have met Prince Philip, talked with the boys who have been at school with Prince Charles. We talked with people who, at varying times, have been with the Queen in a dozen different countries, from Australia to Sweden, from India to Jamaica, from New Zealand to the United States of America. We questioned and cross-questioned, delved and checked, endeavoring to sort the wheat from the chaff, fact from fiction, truth from legend. Wherever and whenever possible, we went to firsthand sources for our information. From the late Lord Fermoy we heard how the Queen's father spent his last day at Sandringham. From Mr. Granville Roberts we learned how he received and passed on the momentous message which informed a Princess that she was now the Queen, and to him we are indebted for many of the details of that historic moment. To the many others, who have so willingly helped us and prefer for various reasons to remain nameless, we also express our grateful thanks.

Our task almost completed, the birth of little Prince Edward came as a happy coincidence. Thus, our story, which starts with the sadness of a king's passing, is brought to a happy conclusion with the birth of a fourth royal baby and the completion of the "ideal family" Britain's Queen has so long desired.

CHAPTER ONE

"MY POOR DEAR LADY"

I

IT WAS NOT quite fifteen minutes to two on an afternoon sullen with the menace of an approaching storm. Lieutenant Colonel the Hon. Martin Charteris (now Sir Martin Charteris) entered the Outspan Hotel in Nyeri, the small township overlooked by the snow-capped twin peaks which the Kikuyu call "Kilinyaga," the Masai "Doenyo Egeré" and the British "Mount Kenya." He walked across the lobby to the dining room. It was February 6, 1952.

He was a tall, slim man, clad in jeans and a brightly-checked sports shirt. He was lunching at the hotel on his way to Tree Tops, that lofty perch high in the branches of a wild fig tree from which it was possible to observe the abundant big game of the region as they came, elephant and buffalo, rhino and buck, to drink at the neighboring water-hole.

As he passed the hotel desk Charteris encountered Granville Roberts of the *East African Standard*. It was, as circumstances turned out, a strangely coincidental encounter. The two men knew each other: Charteris was private secretary to the young woman who had gone out to Kenya as Princess Elizabeth; Roberts was a correspondent covering the royal visit. They paused briefly to exchange the time of day.

Roberts was in the middle of sending off some cables for fellow journalists who had already left for Mombasa, where the Princess and her husband would be boarding the liner *Gothic* the following day on the next stage of the long journey to Australia and New Zealand they were undertaking on behalf of her sick father. It was arranged that Roberts would join Charteris for lunch as soon as he had completed his task. The private secretary continued through to the dining room.

Roberts bent again over his cables, the interior of the hotel darkening rapidly as the coming storm built up overhead. Behind him a telephone began to ring in one of the two booths on the far side of the lobby. Roberts turned and crossed the lobby to answer it.

"*Standard* office here," said the voice at the other end of the line, "I want to speak to Granville Roberts, please."

"This is Granville Roberts speaking."

"A flash has just come in from Reuters. It reads: The King is dead. . . ."

Roberts experienced a strange tingling sensation in his scalp.

"Hold on a moment," he said.

He turned and glanced across the lobby of the hotel. There was a girl at the reception desk. He called across to her.

"Call Colonel Charteris, will you, please? He's sitting just in the corner of the dining room . . . and tell him to come running."

He turned his attention again to the telephone in his hand.

"Are you quite sure the message is correct?"

"Quite sure," was the reply. "It's moving on. . . . The King died in his sleep. . . ."

Charteris came out of the dining room at that moment. Roberts caught his eye and beckoned him over.

"Come into the phone booth," he said.

Charteris sandwiched himself inside and Roberts closed the sliding door.

"Martin," he said quietly, "I've just had a message from my office that the King has died."

The tall, slim courtier seemed to sag visibly, his face draining of color. He could utter only four words. . . . "My poor dear lady."

Overhead the threatening storm burst suddenly with all its tropical intensity. Flash after flash of lightning illuminated the dusty sunless streets and darkened hotel. Rain lashed against the windows to the accompaniment of thunder that reverberated like a roll of drums.

Charteris braced himself. "Is the message accurate?"

"It's from Reuters," Roberts replied. "It can't be wrong."

"Then we must phone Royal Lodge immediately."

The Queen as she now was, though she did not yet know it, was staying with her husband, the Duke of Edinburgh, some six thousand feet up the slopes of Mount Kenya in the stone- and cedar-built hunting lodge which had been a wedding present to them from the Kenya Government. They had been there for the past few days, resting, riding, fishing for trout in the ice-cold waters of the Sagana River which ran close by. It was a brief and welcome respite from their packed schedule of public engagements.

Roberts held the telephone towards Charteris. But the private secretary, visibly affected by the grave news which had reached him in such a strange, roundabout fashion, gave a quick shake of his head.

"No, you do it, please."

So it was Roberts who made the telephone call to Royal Lodge, some eighteen miles distant at Sagana.

There was only one telephone at the lodge, in a small room at the rear, linked to a single line strung out across the bush. The call was taken by Lieutenant Commander Michael Parker, the breezy Australian friend of war-time days who now served the Duke of Edinburgh in the capacity of private secretary. Even Parker's exuberance drained from him as he listened to what Roberts had to say. Parker's initial reply was no more than an almost inaudible ejaculation which might have been "Good God."

II

Everyone had thought that the King was recovering successfully, if gradually, from the serious surgery he had undergone the previous September. Even those closest and dearest to him had judged him finally on the road to recovery the day he brought his walking stick up to his shoulder and remarked, "I believe I could shoot again now."

He was out shooting over the frosty acres of his beloved Sandringham the day before he died. Yet as he tramped tiredly uphill, gun in hand and dog at heel, perhaps he sensed that his shooting days were numbered . . . that for him there was to be no real recovery.

Between previous monarchs and their children there had been often a wide gulf of misunderstanding. But George VI was always close to his wife and daughters, as they were to him. He was a simple family man who never coveted a throne, yet with a deep-rooted sense of duty which would not let him dissent when it was thrust upon him. Between him and his elder daughter the link was especially close. They were two of a kind, serious in outlook, conscientious and painstaking in all they undertook, sharing a deep love of country ways and country things.

The King's face was gaunt and haggard that bleak January day when he watched his daughter and her husband fly out from London Airport on the first stage of their long journey. A few minutes before take-off he sought out Margaret MacDonald, the loyal and devoted Scotswoman who had been his daughter's constant companion since the Princess was a baby of no more than a few weeks old.

"Take care of Lilibet for me," he said to her.

No one knows what was in his mind, but in his eyes, as he stood bareheaded in the biting January wind to watch the silvery Argonaut become airborne, was the infinite sadness of a man who senses that he may have looked upon someone he loves for the last time.

Then he went back to Sandringham, to walk, as Sir Winston Churchill so eloquently put it, "with death as if death were a companion, an acquaintance he recognized and did not fear," to enjoy a few more days amid the old familiar surroundings he had known since boyhood . . . and then to die, peacefully, in his sleep. George VI loved Sandringham. He loved the rambling, red-brick mansion with its high-ceilinged rooms, cluttered furnishings and multitudinous chimneys, the farms and heathland around, the villages with their stone-built cottages and warm-colored sand-stone walls, the tall trees where the pheasants roosted, the windswept marshes where the wildfowl flew high. Especially he loved Sandringham at Christmas-time, when the weather was crisply cold, the ground frozen hard underfoot and a man's breath steamed in the frosty air as he tramped the wide acres with dog and gun. Sandringham, he always said, was the one place and Christmas the one time "when I have my family around me and can forget for a little while that I am King."

The King was born at Sandringham. Much of his boyhood was spent there. He climbed the trees, played football with the village lads from neighboring West Newton, roamed the woods and heathland until he knew every stick and stone, nook and cranny. Year after year, whenever opportunity served, he went back there to enjoy, however briefly, its peace and solitude. And always at Christmas.

On February 5, five days after his daughter's departure, a day which sparkled crisply with winter sunshine, he was up at his usual time of half-past seven and out of the house by half-past nine, driving over to Flitcham in a shooting brake for a day's sport in company with his old friend, Lord Fermoy. Wearing the battery-heated boots and gloves which had been specially made for him, the King was out in the open air all day until dusk's probing fingers began creeping across fields and hedgerows. And he was on top of his form. From his manner, there might have been nothing at all wrong with him. He ate a hearty lunch, talking and laughing the whole time. He bagged nine hares and a wood-pigeon which he brought down from a height of eighty to a hundred feet with his twelve-bore shotgun.

Tired, but infinitely content, he sat at the end of the day on a tapestry-covered stool in the front hall of Sandringham House, unlacing his shooting boots.

"The best day's shooting I've had for a long time," he told Fermoy. "We'll go again on Thursday. I shall expect you at nine o'clock."

Then he went along to rest in the small, plainly-furnished ground-floor room which had served him as a bedroom since his illness. Tea was taken in to him on a tray, but he was up again before dinner to bid goodnight to his two small grandchildren, Charles and Anne, and say prayers with them as he did every night during that last stay at Sandringham.

He dined that evening with his wife and daughter, Princess Margaret, back from a drive across Norfolk to visit Edward Seago, the artist, in his Dutch-style home on the Broads. After dinner in the high-ceilinged, tapestry-paneled dining room with its long mahogany table and high-backed chairs, the King strolled briefly in the grounds and stayed up long enough to hear the latest radio bulletin concerning his daughter's tour before going along to his bedroom, a magazine in his hand. It was then a little after ten o'clock.

At half-past seven the following morning, the King's valet, James MacDonald, a short, stocky Scot who now serves Prince Philip in the same capacity, ran the King's bath as usual before going through into the bedroom with his morning pot of tea. He placed the tea-tray on the bedside table and drew back the curtains. But the King did not stir.

MacDonald returned to the bathroom and splashed the bath-water with his hand, a diplomatic trick he employed sometimes to rouse the King from sleep. Still the King did not stir.

Becoming alarmed now, MacDonald left the room in search of

someone with whom to share his concern. He came across Maurice Watts, one of the King's pages.

"I can't seem to wake the King this morning," he told Watts. "Will you come?"

His evident alarm communicated itself to Watts. Together, they hurried back to the King's bedroom and tried again to rouse him until realization dawned that it was something deeper than sleep that kept the King from waking.

A hurried telephone call summoned Dr. James Ansell, the local family physician, from his farmhouse home at Wolferton, three miles away on the edge of the marshes. Arriving at Sandringham the doctor knew at a glance that there was nothing he nor anyone else could do.

The King had been alive at midnight because a patrolling policeman heard him fumble with the catch as he opened his window to let some fresh air into the bedroom. Some time between then and half-past seven in the morning, when MacDonald entered the bedroom with the pot of tea, sleep had graded peacefully into death.

So the girl her father always called "Lilibet" became Her Most Excellent Majesty Elizabeth the Second, Queen of Great Britain and Northern Ireland, Head of the Commonwealth, Defender of the Faith and Sovereign of the British Orders of Knighthood, while wearing brown slacks and an apricot-colored blouse as she perched thirty feet up in the branches of a fig tree in the Aberdare Forest.

III

Along with the Duke of Edinburgh, his secretary, Michael Parker, and her lady-in-waiting, Lady Pamela Mountbatten, Princess Elizabeth, as she still was the previous afternoon of February 5, had driven seventeen miles from Royal Lodge along narrow, dust-red roads to spend a night amid the abounding wild life of the Aberdare Forest. It was to prove an exceptionally enthralling excursion. A herd of wild elephants was trampling around the clearing and the adjoining bush as the Princess got out of her car. There was a furious outburst of angry trumpeting as the boss of the herd, a big bull elephant, clashed with two upstart younger bulls. Rifle in hand, Jim Corbett, the grizzled, veteran white hunter in charge of the Princess's safety, kept constant watch as she crossed the clearing and, with the nearest elephants only a few feet off, climbed the steep, narrow, wooden ladder which led to the tree-top rest-house.

From her perch, thirty feet up, the Princess found that she could look out across the clearing to the lake and salt lick which was a favorite watering place for big game. She put down her handbag, adjusted her movie camera, brought it eagerly to eye level and began filming the herd of elephants below her. Baboons regarded her curiously from the branches of the trees and she managed to tempt one into camera range with a sweet potato and got some excellent close-ups. Two water-buck came leaping out of the forest and again the Princess was busy with her camera as they fought with a clash of horns at the margin of the lake, a briefly violent encounter which ended with the water of the lake stained a dull red where the loser plunged in to die.

She slept that night in the tree, in one of the three small bedrooms of the rest-house, lulled to sleep by the mournful cries of the hyenas and the deeper bass grunt of rhinos as they came down to the lake to drink. But before dawn she was up and about again. From the balcony she saw dawn break across the forest in a burst of rainbow color which stained the mountain peaks beyond. As full light flooded the clearing below she was again busy with her camera, filming the rhinos as they drank at the waterhole.

But the girl whose blue eyes reflected her exhilaration as she watched dawn come to the Aberdare Forest, who pushed her brown hair back from her high forehead as she filmed the wild rhino plodding like old men round the margin of the lake, was no longer Princess Elizabeth. She was, though still unaware of it, now the Queen.

Under the English constitution, the throne is never vacant even for a single instant. So Princess Elizabeth became Queen Elizabeth the Second at the very moment her father died. Now she could enact laws, appoint judges, create peers, confer honors, pardon criminals. She was the owner of Balmoral Castle and Sandringham House, the finest private collection of paintings in the world, a stamp collection running to over three hundred volumes and a string of racing thoroughbreds. A life tenancy of Buckingham Palace, Windsor Castle and the Crown Jewels was now hers. She could in theory, if hardly in practice, disband the army, sell the navy and the air force, declare war or sue for peace. She was not yet twenty-six and of all this she knew nothing

as she ate a breakfast of bacon and scrambled eggs and laughingly
tossed bananas to the chattering baboons in the branches around.

IV

Lieutenant Commander Michael Parker had been on the point
of making his way down to the Sagana River for some trout
fishing when the telephone rang in the small back room of the
Sagana Royal Lodge. All thoughts of fishing vanished instantly
as he listened to the grave voice of Granville Roberts.

After that first muffled ejaculation which escaped him, Parker's
immediate reaction was to ask, "Is the message official?"

In the lobby of the Outspan Hotel Martin Charteris took over
the telephone from Granville Roberts. "No," he told Parker,
"it's not official. But it comes from Reuters and Roberts thinks its
reliable."

But Parker felt uneasy about accepting such grave news from
other than an official source. "We must have confirmation," he
said. "We must check."

"Very well," said Charteris. "I'll do my best to get confirmation
and I'll get back to you as soon as I can."

Totally unaware of all that was going on, the girl who was now
the Queen sat at her desk in the cream-walled sitting room of the
lodge with its floor of warm cedar, curtains of gay chintz and big,
stone fireplace, thinking over the events of the night at Tree Tops
and catching up with her correspondence. In the adjoining bedroom her husband was stretched full-length on the bed, resting.
Tomorrow they would be flying to Mombasa to board the *Gothic*
on the next stage of the long journey eastwards.

Presently the Queen rose from her desk and went outside to
where her personal maid, Margaret MacDonald, and John Dean,
Philip's fair-haired young valet, were cleaning the shoes.

"We shall have to go riding a little earlier than usual tomorrow,"
she told them.

For a few moments more she stayed there with them, enjoying
the feel of the warm sunshine on her face and arms, already tanned
a light gold from her days in the open. Then she went back into
the lodge.

In his small den of an office at the rear of the lodge, Parker
replaced the telephone and immediately switched on the radio.
He was hoping to pick up a news bulletin which would confirm

what he had been told. He tried to put a call through to Nairobi. But the line to Nairobi was busy.

It was busy, though Parker could not know this, because Charteris and Roberts were using it to talk to Government House. Still sandwiched side by side in the telephone booth at the Outspan Hotel, they got through to the Governor's private secretary.

"Nothing has come through here," he told them.

"Is it possible that the Governor has had a message which you haven't seen?" they asked.

"Quite impossible. He's already on the train for Mombasa to see the Princess off."

Charteris said, "Tell him to phone through to Buckingham Palace and ask for confirmation."

"But who do I talk to at the palace?" the Governor's secretary wanted to know.

"Anybody," said Charteris. "Tell him to talk to anybody. Colville . . . anyone he can get hold of."

They ended the call still lacking official confirmation. The thought occurred to them that perhaps the *Gothic*, at Mombasa, could have had an official radio message from London and they decided to call the ship.

Over Nyeri the storm was still raging with all its tropical intensity, the rain drumming like a shower of peas against the hotel windows. Another vivid flash of lightning illuminated the interior of the hotel and, with that, the telephone went completely dead.

Roberts jiggered the instrument up and down. It was no good. That last great flash of lightning has somehow cut the line.

"My car's just outside," Roberts said.

They scrambled into the car and drove post-haste to the town post office. They burst into the postmaster's office without ceremony and hurriedly explained things to him. Then they pushed him out of his own office and along to the telephone exchange, with instructions to cut through all other conversations and connect them with the *Gothic*. In seconds he had them connected. But those aboard the *Gothic* knew nothing.

Government House in Nairobi knew nothing; the *Gothic* at Mombasa knew nothing. They decided to telephone Royal Lodge again to let Michael Parker know that so far their inquiries had drawn a blank.

"It's all right," Parker told them. "I've got confirmation."

It had come in the form of a news bulletin, breaking in on the scheduled programs, while Parker, telephone in hand was still vainly trying to establish contact with Nairobi.

Once there was no longer even the slightest reason to doubt the authenticity of the report, Michael Parker went through to the bedroom where Philip was resting, roused him and gave him the news from London.

Philip was deeply affected by the death of the father-in-law with whom he had been out shooting at Sandringham a week or so before. Between the two men, the work-weary monarch and the breezy young naval officer who was his son-in-law, there had developed an instant liking which deepened rapidly into genuine affection. They had much in common. Both were seafaring men with a sailor's outlook and a sailor's bluntness of speech. They had much the same temperament and shared the same slapstick sense of humor. To the King, Philip was like the son he had never had.

Philip gave Parker a nod of dismissal and went through to break the news to his wife that she was now the Queen.

CHAPTER TWO

THE HOMECOMING

I

IN THAT FIRST moment when she learned of the death of the father she loved so dearly, the Queen felt a need to be alone for a time. She went through to her bedroom in the Sagana Royal Lodge and closed the door behind her.

It was nearly an hour later when she emerged again from the bedroom. Her face was pale and the eyes beneath the strongly-arched brows showed traces of weeping. But her lips were firm and her head was high. She was calm and composed, in command of both her own emotions and the situation in which she so unexpectedly found herself. She talked little.

She was the first Queen to come to the throne for 115 years, and if words did not come readily to her lips in those first moments of grief her heart assuredly echoed what the young Queen Victoria had written in her *Journal* when she had been awakened from sleep to receive the news of her own accession: "I am very young and perhaps in many, though not in all things, inexperienced. But I am sure that very few have more real goodwill and more real desire to do what is fit and right than I have."

Sadly the new Queen glanced round the sitting room of the lodge where she had hoped her father might spend a beneficial holiday the following winter. "I am sure the climate here and these peaceful surroundings would do him good," she had said. Then she sat down again at her desk and began to give her first commands as Queen. Still under great emotional stress, she yet carried herself magnificently. She sent off cables of sympathy to her mother and the aging Queen Mary. She sent off cables to the countries of the Commonwealth. She cabled Australia and New Zealand, postponing her tour. By now there was a deluge of incoming messages from London to keep the solitary telephone line to Sagana incessantly busy. One inquired by what name the new Queen wished to be known.

"My own, of course . . . what else?" she said when Lieutenant Colonel Charteris, who had driven hurriedly back to the Royal Lodge from Nyeri, put the question to her.

In an interval between the incoming calls, Commander Parker commandeered the telephone to contact Nairobi and make arrangements for the new Queen to return to her home and capital. The silver Argonaut which had brought her to Kenya was still standing by at Entebbe to take any surplus baggage back to Britain. The fact was opportune. Now it could fulfill an infinitely more important role.

To get the Queen to Entebbe and the waiting Argonaut, it was arranged that Wing Commander Frankham, perhaps the most experienced pilot then working for East Africa Airlines, should fly a Dakota to Nanyuki, the nearest airfield to the Royal Lodge.

Quickly and methodically, Margaret MacDonald and John Dean began to pack everything. In little more than an hour they had it all done. Inevitably, some things were overlooked in the rush and Philip's field-glasses and a pair of riding spurs were found later in a drawer of the bureau. While the servants packed, the Queen and her husband climbed down the steep, zigzag path which led downhill from the lodge and walked alone with each other by the Sagana River, where only that morning, on their return from Tree Tops, they had laughed and joked happily as they fished for trout.

Despite her personal sorrow, the Queen remained true to her training, remembering even the smaller duties of monarchy. She summoned the Provincial Commissioner and presented him with a pair of cufflinks bearing her personal monogram. She signed photographs of herself for the staff of the Royal Lodge.

It was six o'clock or perhaps a little after—with so many things crowding so quickly one upon the other, no one thought to look at the time—when the royal party left the lodge on the eighteen-mile journey along the dust-red roads to the landing strip at Nanyuki. The short tropical twilight had already set in by the time they arrived there and the weather was building up for a storm. Hurriedly the royal baggage was loaded into the waiting Dakota. With daylight fading fast and a storm blowing up, there could be no delay. The little Dakota, unpressurized and therefore incapable of flying above the weather in an emergency, must be airborne before darkness finally fell.

The Queen boarded the aircraft last. At the final moment of

boarding, she paused briefly, turned as though for a farewell glimpse of Mount Kenya. She turned at that precise moment when the last rays of the dying sun fell aslant the snow-clad peak so that it glinted with wild beauty like a huge diamond rising triumphantly above the encroaching dusk.

The storm held off and the small Dakota reached Entebbe without incident. There the storm broke with all its tropical violence, great gusts of wind threatening to tear down the Union Jack as it flapped at half-mast above the control tower. While the storm raged the royal Argonaut remained motionless on the runway. Just before midnight, with the sky calm again and the stars shining, it soared finally down the runway and became airborne on the long four-thousand mile haul back to London.

The new Queen was coming home to her capital. She was twenty-five years of age . . . exactly the age the first Elizabeth had been when she ascended the throne.

II

All that long day Sandringham was a house of sadness behind its drawn blinds. Uncertain though the King's health had been, his death was a tragic shock to those close to him.

White-faced and drawn, James MacDonald was heard to murmur time and again to himself, "He was alone . . . all alone."

Now, in death, the King was alone no longer. At the Queen Mother's request, a constant vigil was kept.

Princess Margaret, when she learned of her father's death, shut herself alone in her room. Like her sister, the new Queen, she had been close to her father. But it was a different sort of closeness. While the King and the daughter who had succeeded him were linked by their similarity of temperament, the affection between Margaret and her father stemmed from those very facets in which her character contradicted and complemented his. To the King, his younger daughter was the one outstandingly gay but completely unpredictable person in a life of ordered calm. Times there may have been when her chatter and cheerful disregard for punctuality offended his quiet, orderly mind, but there was about her a warmth and impetuousness he could never resist.

The Queen Mother, grief stricken though she was, did her utmost to retain a semblance of outward composure. Characteristically, her thoughts were not for herself, but for the two small grandchildren who had been left in her care while their parents were away about the King's business. Prince Charles, at the time, was just turned three, a sturdy and serious youngster. Princess Anne was a flaxen-topped toddler of only eighteen months.

"Their lives must not be affected by what has happened," said the Queen Mother, and that day, though she took her meals alone in her room, she visited them in the nursery as was her custom.

But she could not bring herself to tell them the sad news and it was left to Nana—the children's nurse, Helen Lightbody—to explain Grandpapa's absence from the nursery that day to little Prince Charles. Anne was still too young to need or comprehend such explanation.

III

For the new Queen, it was a sad and somber homecoming, with the flags at half-mast, church bells tolling to mourn a dead king, shops and factories, movies and theaters closed, with Piccadilly Circus in darkness for the first time since the war.

Her uncle, the Duke of Gloucester, was waiting to greet her at London airport. So was Philip's uncle, Earl Mountbatten of Burma, with the Prime Minister and members of the Cabinet. Winston Churchill, deeply affected by the high emotion of the occasion, could find no words with which to greet the new Queen. So he greeted her in silence, unashamedly in tears. The Queen, too, had difficulty in controlling her emotions and not until she was already some way along the line of waiting dignitaries could she find her first words.

"This is a very tragic homecoming," she murmured.

Yet true to her training, mindful as always of the small things in which monarchy is rooted, she spoke briefly to each member of the crew of the Argonaut before leaving the airport.

"Thank you for making me so comfortable."

The royal standard flew from the car in which she drove into London, while the crowds lining the route stood in sympathetic silence. There was not one of them who did not mourn the King as though a personal friend. The royal standard was run up on the roof of Clarence House as she went inside. A new monarch was in residence.

Waiting to greet her was the aging Queen Mary, whose life span went back through five reigns to the days of Queen Victoria.

Upright and regal as ever at the age of eighty-four, she waited now to be the first to kiss the hand of the new Queen.

"The Queen has a most difficult task and will need all our help," she told those around her.

And when shortly afterwards the Queen put through a call to Sandringham House, it was not the Queen calling the Queen Mother, but a bereaved daughter anxious to console her widowed mother.

IV

For those born royal nothing is their own . . . not even their grief. They must still see and be seen, and the following morning the Queen held her first privy council in the white and gold throne room at St. James's Palace. She looked amazingly youthful, almost too young for the burden sprung so suddenly upon her, as she told members of that ancient assembly in calm, measured tones: "I shall always work, as my father did throughout his reign, to uphold constitutional government and to advance the happiness and prosperity of my peoples, spread as they are all over the world. . . . I pray that God will help to discharge worthily this heavy task that has been laid upon me so early in life."

No one captured the sense of occasion better than Churchill when he said in Parliament: "A fair and youthful figure, princess, wife and mother, is the heir to all our traditions and glories, and to all our perplexities and dangers, never greater in peacetime than now."

London that day witnessed all the pageantry of another proclamation like so many in its long history . . . "the high and mighty Princess Elizabeth Alexandra Mary is now by the death of our late Sovereign of happy memory become Queen Elizabeth II." Four times was the proclamation read in London. At the Palace of St. James's, with the feet of the guards ringing in unison and trumpets shrilling a fanfare from the balcony, at the foot of Charles I's statue where Whitehall runs into Trafalgar Square, at Temple Bar and from the steps of the Royal Exchange.

The King is dead; God save the Queen. The process of change had begun already. The list of cases for hearing that day in the High Court was headed Queen's Bench Division. The black-bordered copy of *Hansard*, which recorded the proceedings in Parliament, bore a new imprint: Her Majesty's Stationery Office. The soldiers of the King were now soldiers of the Queen. King's counsel were Queen's counsel. There were now Queen's scouts instead of King's scouts, Queen's messengers, the Queen's flight, the Queen's peace to be upheld. Official mail would henceforth bear the imprint: On Her Majesty's Service. They were now teaching the Queen's English in the schools and at regimental dinners the toast would henceforth be "The Queen." At the Tower of London the age-old litany of the nightly Ceremony of the Keys underwent like change:

"Who goes there?"

"The keys."

"Whose keys?"

"Queen Elizabeth's keys."

But two things were to remain unchanged . . . the King's Door and the King's Stairs which give access to the royal apartment from the inner courtyard of Buckingham Palace. Royal servants, following the system of change which governed everything else, began calling them the Queen's Door and the Queen's Stairs. But the Queen herself, when she moved from Clarence House into Buckingham Palace, continued to refer to them by their old names . . . and the old names stuck.

As soon as her duty in London was done that day, the Queen left for Sandringham. She traveled by road in a chauffeur-driven Rolls-Royce. But once out of London, she and her husband moved into the front seat and Philip took the wheel.

V

In the privacy of their country home at Sandringham, the two women, mother and daughter, the Queen and the Queen Mother, ceremony forgotten, clasped each other in their arms and shared each other's grief. That night, after sunset, the King's coffin of seasoned oak fashioned by the loyal hands of country carpenters, was lifted on to an old-fashioned wheeled bier and taken across Sandringham Park to the tiny, stone-built church of St. Mary Magdalene.

Moonlight silvered the scene as bagpipes skirled the bitter-sweet strains of *Flowers of the Forest*. Behind the bier, picking their way slowly along the narrow path by the light of torches, came the new Queen and her mother, Prince Philip and Princess Margaret, and a handful of loyal servants who had been closest to the King. Ahead of the cortège a cock pheasant suddenly forsook the sanctuary of the bushes to strut proudly across the path and from high overhead came the mournful honking of wild duck as they scudded across the moonlit sky.

Inside the church, obeying the Queen Mother's injunction that the King must not be alone, gamekeepers in green tweed and estate workers in their Sunday-best suits of blue serge, kept vigil over the coffin, four at a time, one to each corner, throughout the night, while a girl called Lilibet, who had so suddenly and so sadly stepped into her father's shoes, walked slowly back to the lonely house where a devoted and close-knit family had spent so many happy Christmases.

CHAPTER THREE

MOTHERHOOD AND MONARCHY

I

IT WAS BREAKFAST time in the dining room of the royal apartment at Buckingham Palace, a comfortably elegant room of Adam-style sideboards and ladder-backed chairs with an oval dining table of highly polished mahogany dating back nearly two centuries. As the Queen and her husband finished their meal, the dining room door opened and Charles and Anne ran in on their way back to the nursery after their regular early-morning outing in the palace gardens.

There was no bowing or curtseying to their parents, as there had been with earlier generations of royal children. Instead, the two children ran straight to the breakfast table and kissed their parents fondly.

"Morning, Mummy. Morning, Papa," they said.

The Queen had made it plain to the nursery staff that she still wanted her children to look upon her as Mummy. There was time enough when they were older to learn the full significance of their mother's new and important role.

In the days when accession to the throne was still a thing of the shadowy future, the Queen remarked once that her dearest wish was to bring up her children herself. At Clarence House, despite an ever-increasing round of royal duties so willingly undertaken to lighten the heavy burden on the shoulders of her sick father, this wish had been fulfilled to a large extent. Anne's feeding, outings, bath-time . . . the Queen—or Princess, as she then still was—made these things her own particular province. As soon as Charles was old enough to understand, she began teaching him to tell the time, to count from a frame of colored beads, simple spelling with the aid of spelling blocks and picture books. But now, as Queen, with so many more demands on her time, the problem increasingly was to reconcile the new duties of monarchy with the pleasures and responsibilities of motherhood.

The Queen's views on the upbringing of children were given in one of her broadcasts. "A good home," she said, "is the rock upon which a child's future is founded." And in her new home at Buckingham Palace, as at Clarence House, despite all else she now had to do, she set out to make it so.

Adroitly she reconciled the conflicting demands of monarchy and motherhood, splitting her life into separate compartments. The first half-hour of the day following breakfast was meticulously set aside to be spent with her children. So was a further hour and a half in the evening. The hours between were the domain of monarchy. But into these precious periods of family life the demands of monarchy were seldom permitted to trespass. Not even the prime minister's long-standing weekly call upon her at the palace was permitted to invade the sanctity of family life. As soon as she realized that this traditional weekly audience clashed with those precious ninety minutes spent with her children before their bedtime, the Queen asked the prime minister if he would mind delaying it by half-an-hour in the future. He duly obliged.

II

It was three months after her accession to the throne, following an Easter spent at Windsor, when the Queen and her family moved from Clarence House to Buckingham Palace.

The Queen's most treasured furnishings had been moved over during her absence at Windsor . . . her large double bed with its filmy draperies, her Chinese screen, the beautiful chandelier of Waterford crystal from her sitting room at Clarence House, the portrait Edward Halliday had painted of her as a Princess, her favorite chair with its seat of intricate petit-point embroidery, lovingly worked by her grandmother, Queen Mary.

Like any other woman moving house, the Queen took advantage of the move to effect some necessary changes, and the comfortable armchairs and settee which now graced her sitting room had been freshly re-upholstered in a becoming shade of mushroom.

But the Queen's main concern was for her children. She remembered, perhaps, how she herself had felt as a child of ten when it had been necessary to move from the cozy security of her old home at 145 Piccadilly to the vast labyrinth of rooms and corridors which constitute Buckingham Palace.

"I want the children unsettled as little as possible," she told the royal nanny, Helen Lightbody.

For them it was more than a question of moving house. It meant a whole new, strange way of life and she cushioned the upheaval for them as much as possible by surrounding them with the friendly, familiar things they had known since birth.

For the children, it was almost as though they did not move house at all, so cleverly did the Queen arrange things. From Windsor they went straight to Buckingham Palace . . . into a nursery furnished as the nursery at Clarence House had always been, the same applewood table in the middle of the room, the same glass-fronted cabinet to hold their books and playthings, the same gay chintz curtains with the pattern of bowling hoops, parasols and Victorian nursemaids, the same high-backed winged armchairs flanking the fireplace, even the same stout fireguard to keep them from accidently harming themselves.

Links with the earlier occupants of the palace nursery still remained to excite eager questions in the inquiring mind of Prince Charles . . . favorite toys which had once belonged to the Queen and Princess Margaret, the souvenir mugs they had been given when their father was crowned King George VI, the glass and china miniatures they had collected as children, even the old rocking horse, now minus a tail, on which they had once enjoyed endless, exciting rides.

Since her sister's marriage, Princess Margaret had continued to occupy the nursery suite as a small, self-contained apartment of her own. Now she obligingly moved out to make way for her small nephew and niece with their books and toys, pets and playthings . . . Anne's cuddly teddy bear, Charles's toy wheelbarrow, a much-played recording of *The Teddy Bears' Picnic*, and a pet Angora rabbit named Harvey for whom palace carpenters constructed a hutch and run on the back lawn.

Once again, the royal nursery echoed to the laughter and chatter of childish voices. Nor was this confined for long to the nursery. Charles quickly displayed something of his father's inquiring nature and began venturing further afield, lured ever onwards by the seemingly endless vista of red-carpeted corridors and a constant succession of excitingly new faces.

"Hello, I'm Charles," he announced brightly to everyone he met. "Who are you, please?"

III

Now it was half-past nine in the morning and time for the pleasures of motherhood to yield place to the duties of monarchy. Philip had already vanished from his place at the breakfast table, disappearing in the direction of what had hitherto been the King's study. The Queen handed her children back into the safe keeping of their Nana and walked along to her sitting room with its wide bay window and general air of soft femininity.

When she first moved back into the palace, with her mother still living in the traditional royal apartment on the first floor, the Queen had contented herself with the ground-floor Belgian Suite at the rear of the palace, its windows overlooking the gardens. But now that her mother had moved to Clarence House, the Queen transferred her things upstairs into the royal apartment.

She made few changes of any consequence, though she decided against taking over her father's old study with all the sad memories it still held for her. Instead, she moved into her mother's sitting room with its walls of duck-egg blue. It served the double purpose of sitting room and study, and left her father's study free for her husband. But the King's Chippendale desk was moved into the room which was now his daughter's. On its spacious working surface the Queen set out her green leather blotter and gilt-framed engagement card, her stationery rack with its scarlet-crested notepaper and scribbling pads, her paste-pot and sealing wax, scissors and ink-stand, and set about the business of monarchy.

In many ways life was very different . . . even strange. The very atmosphere was different. After the cosy compactness of Clarence House, with its modern central heating and streamlined kitchen, its rooms furnished with wedding presents, the huge hollow square of the palace with its four vast floors and echoing, subterranean basement, its seemingly endless corridors and myriad stairways, seemed immensely strange by comparison, for all that she had known it as a child. A small contingent of personal servants, their faces as familiar to her as those of her own children, were swollen suddenly into a seeming regiment of staff and officials.

So large is Buckingham Palace that to this day there are corners of it which the Queen has never seen. There are long-time servants who do not even catch a glimpse of her from one year to the next.

Along with the move had come the formalities of monarchy. One of the Queen's staff who moved over to Buckingham Palace with her made the mistake, early, of tapping on her sitting room door when he wanted to see her, turning the gilt door-knob and walking straight in, as he had always done. The Queen accustomed to such informality, saw nothing remiss in the action. But others did and subsequently there was a mild rebuke for the erring courtier.

"You must remember that the Princess is now the Queen," he was reminded. "And no one sees the Queen without being properly announced."

This morning, as every morning, the Queen seated herself at her desk in the big recess of the bay window and rang for Sir Alan Lascelles, who had been her father's private secretary and was now, for a time at least, her secretary. Until five o'clock tea brought the children hurrying down from the nursery there would be scarcely a minute to spare. As like as not, lunch would have to be cut to a bare thirty minutes, as had been the case so often of late.

The Queen worked then, as she does still, surrounded by a friendly clutter of family photographs . . . photographs of the children, her husband, her mother and grandmother. The photograph of Philip, which occupied a place of honor on the desk immediately in front of her, was the first he had ever given her. Across the room, on the small antique side table which stood beside her favorite armchair, a folding leather frame . . . still there today . . . held two photographs of her father, constant reminders of all he had taught her and everything he stood for.

From the very moment she seated herself for the first time at her father's desk, the Queen took to the manifold duties of monarchy as a duck takes to water, absorbing herself in an endless round of royal duties, as though seeking comfort from them in her personal sorrow. With her father's trusted and experienced staff around her, Sir Alan Lascelles, Sir Piers Legh, Lord Tryon; with her father's page, Maurice Watts, now her page, she adapted to all the complexities of her new role with a speed and facility that surprised everyone. So quick and firm was her grasp of the job that she was soon getting through things in half the time her father had taken. She had need to. The face of monarchy was changing fast and there was much more to do.

The reason for her aptitude lay in what had gone before. Her father had come to the throne in middle age, suddenly, unexpec-

In 1950 the Royal Family attended the christening of Princess Anne. Seated, from left to right, are Queen Mary (Queen Elizabeth II's grandmother), Queen Elizabeth II holding Princess Anne, and Queen Elizabeth (Queen Elizabeth II's mother) holding Prince Charles. Standing are King George VI, on the left, and Prince Philip, on the right.

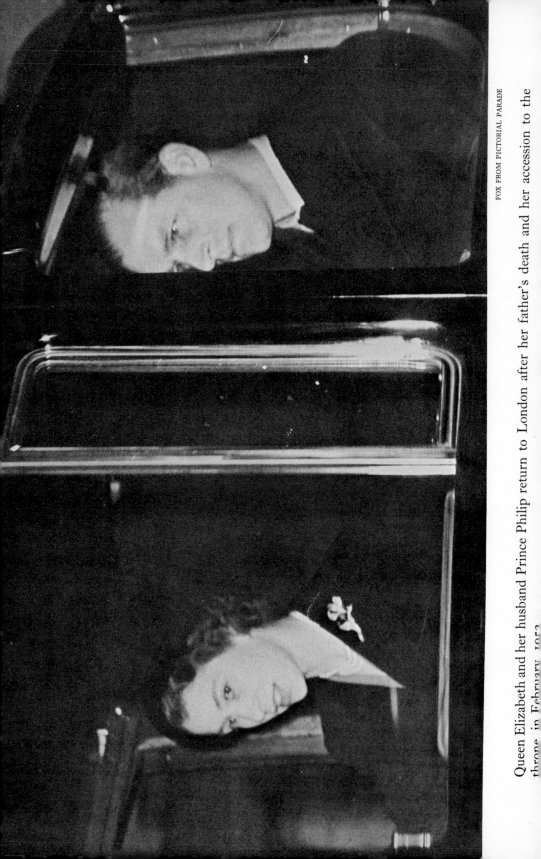

Queen Elizabeth and her husband Prince Philip return to London after her father's death and her accession to the throne in February, 1952.

Queen Elizabeth II, wearing St. Edward's crown and holding the symbols of royal power, sits on King Edward's throne in Westminster Abbey during her Coronation on June 2, 1953, as the Archbishop of Canterbury delivers his benediction.

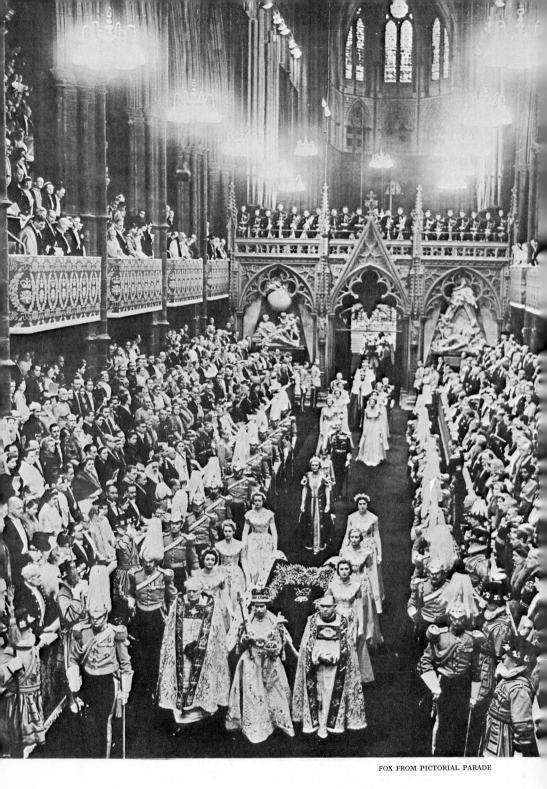

The Queen leads the state procession after the Coronation ceremony in Westminster Abbey.

Queen Elizabeth II poses with her family, foreign royalty, and other dignitaries for a Coronation portrait in the throne room of Buckingham Palace.

The Queen with her maids-of-honor in the throne room of Buckingham Palace. The maids-of-honor, who carried her train, are, from left to right—Lady Moyra Hamilton, Lady Anne Coke, Lady Rosemary Spencer-Churchill, Lady Mary Baillie Hamilton, Lady Jane Heathcote-Drummond-Willoughby, and Lady Jane Vane-Tempest-Stewart. (Photograph by Cecil Beaton)

Queen Elizabeth and Prince Philip with Queen Salote of Tonga during their world tour after the Queen's Coronation.

The Duke of Kent on his twenty-first birthday in 1956. The Duke
wears the dress uniform of the Royal Scots Greys, with whom he
was then serving as a 2d lieutenant. (Photograph by Antony
Armstrong-Jones, now Lord Snowdon)

Princess Margaret on her 29th birthday in 1959. She is standing
by a window that looks out over the garden of the Royal Lodge
at Windsor Castle. The dog is her pet Sealyham terrier, Johnny.
(Photograph by Antony Armstrong-Jones, now Lord Snowdon)

The Queen starts on a floodlit evening cruise along the Seine during her state visit to Paris in 1957.

Accompanied by former President Eisenhower and Lt. Col. Robert Phelps, the Queen reviews the honor guard at National Airport in Washington, D.C., in 1957.

The Queen addresses the United Nations General Assembly in New York. Seated behind her are the late Secretary General Dag Hammarskjold, the former Assembly President Sir Leslie Munro, and the former Assistant Secretary General Andrew Cordier. Prince Philip sits to the left of the Queen.

The Queen poses with Commonwealth Ministers. Left to right, standing—Kawawa of Tanganyika, Williams of Trinidad and Tobago, Margai of Sierra Leone, Balewa of Nigeria, Bustamente of Jamaica, former Premier Welensky of Rhodesia and Nyasaland, Binhassein of Malaya, Goka of Ghana, Fernando of Ceylon, and Archbishop Makarios of Cyprus; seated—Holyoake of New Zealand, the late Premier Nehru of India, former Premier Diefenbaker of Canada, Menzies of Australia, Khan of Pakistan, and former Prime Minister Macmillan of the United Kingdom.

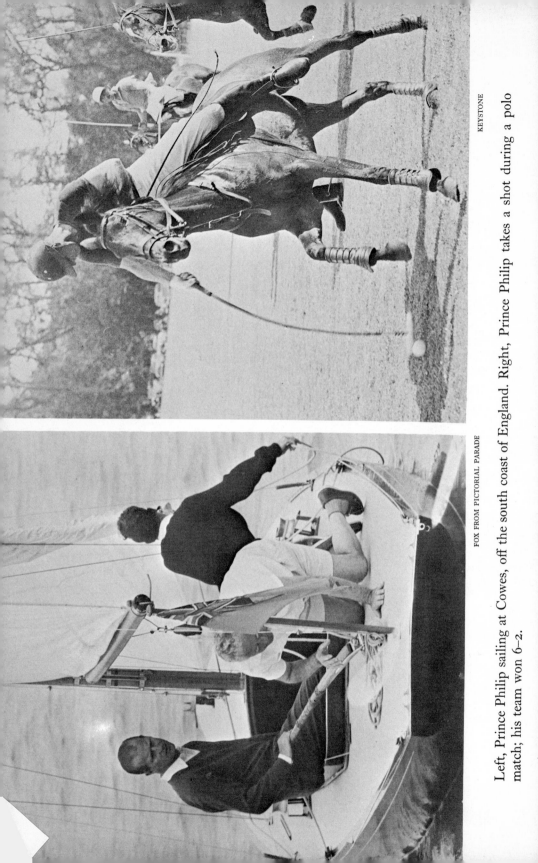

Left, Prince Philip sailing at Cowes, off the south coast of England. Right, Prince Philip takes a shot during a polo match; his team won 6–2.

The Royal Family on holiday at Balmoral Castle. From left to right, Princess Anne, Prince Philip holding Prince Andrew, the Queen, Prince Charles, and one of the royal pet corgis.

Prince Philip and Queen Elizabeth in Buckingham Palace. (Photograph by Antony Armstrong-Jones, now Lord Snowdon)

tedly, largely unprepared. His daughter, by contrast, had spent more than half her young life being coached towards the fact that she would one day succeed him on the throne. Visits to the Old Bailey and the House of Commons, to Westminster Abbey and the National Gallery, the portraits of her ancestors and the speeches of the first Elizabeth painstakingly studied, lessons in constitutional history with colored counters to simplify the complexities of royal lineage, her father's calf-bound volume of coronation ritual, Queen Mary's coronation peepshow . . . all these things, and many more, had played their part over the years in shaping her for her high destiny.

More than anyone else, her father, realizing perhaps the limitation set on his own life, had worked hard and long at the task of training her to succeed him. Conscientious and painstaking in this, as in everything he ever undertook, in long, quiet talks with her he had stressed the importance of royal procedure. Gradually he had initiated her into the innermost workings of monarchy. Carefully he had encouraged her to play her full part in public life, bringing her out more and more as she grew from girlhood to womanhood.

Perhaps the possibility of surrendering the throne to her while he still lived was in his mind the day he confided in a friend, "I hope to give Lilibet another eighteen months of freedom." His untimely death did not permit him to do so, but if he died with his self-imposed task of training his daughter still unfinished there was little sign of it in the serene and serious young woman who sat now at his desk.

She was, as she soon showed, every inch her father's daughter, serious, painstaking and conscientious, gently obstinate if there was something with which she was not entirely in accord, a stickler for punctuality as Britain's monarchs have been for generations past.

Her grandfather, King George V, would order his horses to be brought round at odd times—twenty-two minutes to the hour or seven minutes past—insisting that only in that way could he ensure that they would be ready for him exactly on time. At Sandringham, her great-grandfather, Edward VII, always had the clocks set an hour fast, so that the household was astir that much earlier each morning and there was an extra hour of daylight to be spent out of doors in the shooting field. George V continued this practice of "Sandringham time," and almost the first act of the

Duke of Windsor, when he became Edward VIII, was to order the clocks at Sandringham to be put to the correct time.

The Queen's father disliked being kept waiting. If ever he was, his irritation was revealed in a habit of twisting his signet ring round and round on his finger. Those who served the new Queen soon learned to watch for the same danger signal from her . . . a trick of twisting her engagement ring round and round on her finger if things did not run to schedule.

Things had to go vastly wrong indeed before disturbing the Queen's natural equanimity. Her father had never been slow to convey his displeasure in sharp, heated tones, but that was not the Queen's way. Never once was she known to lose her temper . . . nor has she done so in all the years of monarchy since. There was about her from the start something of the regal and imperious manner of her grandmother, Queen Mary, and royal displeasure could be conveyed by a long, level, silent look, a sudden brittleness of her glance which was more eloquent than words.

Yet some recognized a similarity between the new Queen and the dead King when things were not to their liking. A pale and visibly disturbed courtier, emerging from the Queen's presence one day early in the new reign, could not quite suppress a clearly audible comment as he walked away . . . "And they said the King was dead."

IV

For the new Queen, every day brought its succession of private secretaries and household officials to be seen, consulted, instructed. Twice a day, and sometimes more often than that, the traditional little horse-drawn brougham clip-clopped into the royal mews with dispatch boxes bound in red, green and black leather containing state papers for the Queen to read, study, approve and sign. There was a daily summary of the proceedings in Parliament to be digested, another summary of Commonwealth affairs to be perused. There were requests for the Queen's presence at all manner of public functions to be considered, an endless stream to which the Queen, with the best will in the world, could, and can, only accede to about one in fifty. There were innumerable audiences to be held in the Wedgwood blue-and-white Audience Chamber with its silk-covered gilt furnishings in the style of Louis XV which had been a wedding gift from the Lord Mayor of London.

Not for the first time, the Queen, glancing at the diminutive face of her wrist-watch as she hurried between sitting room and audience room, audience room and sitting room, found herself getting minute by minute further behind schedule. In a single day, soon after her accession, the Queen received, one after the other, the Sheriffs of the City of London, the Lord Provost of Edinburgh, the president of the Royal Society, the president of the Royal Academy, the governor of the Bank of England, the chairman of the London County Council and the new British ambassador appointed to Turkey.

Five o'clock brought its always welcome respite . . . the reappearance of the royal children, a signal to the Queen to put aside monarchy, at least until after the children were in bed, and devote the next ninety minutes to the pleasures of motherhood.

"Where's Papa?" was the first thing Charles wanted to know. A small, sturdy figure in a diminutive dressing gown of brightly colored toweling, he was all set for another swimming lesson in the indoor pool at the rear of the palace.

He collected his father and the two of them went off together, leaving the Queen and her toddler daughter, Anne, to amuse themselves with the royal Welsh corgis, Susan and Sugar.

With the children around, formality and protocol vanished out of the palace windows. Bursts of happy laughter swept the long-silent corridors as children and parents alike dashed about in exciting games of hide and seek or turned the red-carpeted corridor into an improvised field for a boisterous game of football. Time, as it always does on such occasions, passed quickly and all too soon it was time for bed, but not before the children had staged their nightly "raid" on Papa's study for a soft drink each, ice cold from the newly installed refrigerator. Then it was up to bed, with more squeals and laughter as the Queen and the children took the lift while Papa and the corgis bounded up the stairs in an exciting race to see who could be first to the nursery door.

The nursery was a self-contained world of its own presided over by the royal nanny, Helen Lightbody, and later, when she left the palace, by Mabel Anderson, who is still there today. Until they were several years older, the royal children never slept alone. Mrs. Lightbody slept in Charles's room and Mabel Anderson with Anne. Microphones wired to a speaker in the day nursery gave prompt warning if ever the children were restless or fretful during the evening.

The day nursery, a lofty, well-lighted room looking out onto the Mall, was the focal point of nursery life. Here Charles and Anne had their meals, played their games and sometimes (for royal children are no different from any other children) squabbled, until they were old enough to graduate to a governess and the schoolroom along the corridor.

But now, each evening, bath-time and bed-time offered further opportunities for family fun . . . floating toys to be launched on the splashing waters of the bath, boisterous bedroom romps to disarrange the neatness of the bed clothes, bedtime stories read by Mummy or Papa, and, finally, the quietness of prayers . . . "God bless Mummy, Papa, Granny and Aunt Margo." Then the lights would go off and the Queen and her husband would go back downstairs to the workaday world of their own apartment, as like as not to start changing in readiness for some evening engagement.

V

For the Queen, those first twelve months of monarchy were the busiest she had ever known in her life . . . or was to know in the years to come . . . a seemingly endless succession of audiences, state papers and public engagements. There was, on top of all that, the coronation to be planned, though her husband, by taking on the chairmanship of the Coronation Commission, shouldered much of the burden in that direction.

There were, even before the coronation was over, plans to be made for the mammoth royal tour to follow so soon afterwards. There were not enough hours in a day to cope with everything, it seemed. Among other things, the Queen's personal correspondence suffered and letters from friends accumulated on her desk awaiting answers. Official correspondence demanded priority. Yet the Queen was quite obviously enjoying her work and even thriving on it, though weekends at Windsor sometimes found her so tired that she overslept, something she had never done before.

She skipped nothing, avoided nothing, forgot nothing. Surprisingly few details ever escaped her. While she was at the Royal Show at Newton Abbot a pit pony named Dunn was kicked on the leg by another pony and injured. Back at the palace, despite all else that required her attention, the Queen remembered Dunn and told one of her staff to telephone through and find out how he was getting on.

Wherever she went her work pursued here . . . in summer to Balmoral, where, for the first time, she now took her father's place at the head of the table when the family sat down for dinner . . . in December to Sandringham, where, over Christmas, between making up Christmas stockings for her children, distributing gifts to her staff, attending church and joining in a family singsong round the piano, she continued to deal with state papers and official correspondence, decided upon the design for her coronation gown and even found time to select some of the dresses she would be taking with her on her world tour eleven months later.

Inevitably, that first Christmas of monarchy was also a Christmas of sad memories. The Queen Mother walked alone in the grounds where she had once walked so often with her husband. The Queen made her first Christmas broadcast, from the same small room her father had always used, and took over her father's traditional duty of handing gifts to the servants.

And for those servants like James Macdonald who had been especially close to the King there was a gift, too, from the Queen Mother. She summoned them in turn on Christmas Day to her first-floor sitting room with its view across the park and handed to each a small box containing a gold fountain pen. Each pen was engraved with the King's monogram—GRVI.

"I thought you would like this to remind you of the King," said the Queen Mother.

And there was more than one among the recipients of this unexpected gift who found it necessary to blow their noses with unaccustomed vigor as soon as they left her.

CHAPTER FOUR

MAN ABOUT THE PALACE

I

A SURPRISED AND somewhat grimy coal porter looked up from his labors in one of the outsize fuel stores located in the vast basement of Buckingham Palace to find a pair of level blue eyes regarding him quizzically from the half-open doorway.

"Sorry to butt in on you," said the Duke of Edinburgh. "I thought this was the Ministry of Works office."

Philip was by no means the first person, and will doubtless not be the last, to lose his way in the bewildering complexity of rooms, stairways and corridors which make up Buckingham Palace. "I'll never find my way round here," more than one newly engaged servant has wailed, contemplating the seemingly endless vista of red-carpeted corridors.

"You have only to keep going and you will find yourself back at your starting point," they are told.

But it is not always as easy as that. One newcomer to the staff set out from the kitchens with a tray of delicacies intended for an official reception in one of the state rooms, took a wrong turn at the top of one of the staircases and ended up tapping in dismay at the door of a staff bedroom on the topmost floor.

"Please help me," he begged. "I'm lost."

Two days after he and the Queen moved back into Buckingham Palace, Philip, with his insatiable curiosity for knowing what goes on around him, embarked upon a fact-finding cellar-to-attic tour. He inspected the heating unit tucked away beneath the palace forecourt, and was pleased to find it as spotlessly clean as the engine rooms of the naval vessels on which he had once served. He climbed to the topmost floor, taking the stairs two at a time in his long-legged stride, to take a look at the staff quarters. He peeked in at the offices, kitchens, garages, staff canteen, the palace post office and the telephone exchange with its 250 internal lines.

Legend maintains that he even counted the number of rooms in the palace and came up with the figure of 611.

At Windsor, Balmoral and Sandringham during the months to come, he embarked upon the same penetrating, fact-finding tours. "The Duke's naval inspections," they came to be called behind his back. At Sandringham, the staff of the estate office turned up for work one morning to find the Queen's husband already awaiting their arrival. He had some questions he wanted answered about the running of the estate. Another time, the wife of an estate worker, answering a knock at her cottage door, was amazed to find Philip on her doorstep. He had called personally to find out how some repairs to the cottage roof were coming along.

Driving his own Land-Rover, he went from fields to stables, from workshops to dairies, prodding, probing, questioning . . . and his efforts, in the years to come, were to see the royal estate at Sandringham run on strictly economical lines, as a modern, efficient farming estate. Part of the gardens was to be turned over to the growing of soft fruit for the commercial market. Black currants were sold to a jam manufacturer, peas went for canning, sugar beets to a sugar refinery. One of the huge glasshouses, once devoted to the raising of exotic plants, was switched to the cultivation of mushrooms. Old stables were turned into a piggery on up-to-date Scandinavian lines complete with automatic feeding and electric heating.

Every month a report on stock, crops and equipment went off to Buckingham Palace. One month, unavoidably, the report was a day or two late. The result was a telephone call from the palace. Philip wanted to know what had happened to it. Much of the estate was necessarily unsuited to farming. Yet Philip had an answer even to that. "What you can't cultivate—plant," he suggested, and the result, over the years, has been several hundred acres of valuable new timber, oak and poplar, spruce and pine.

Everywhere he went Philip's navy-neat mind made its undeniable impact. At Balmoral he popped into the kitchen to find chips being fried on a day when there was mutton on the staff menu.

"Surely you don't serve chips with mutton?" he queried.

His reaction when it was explained that the chips were being prepared a day ahead was characteristic.

"You can't expect people to eat warmed-up chips with a meal," he protested.

At Sandringham he spotted newly delivered blocks of ice for

the cold store standing on the floor of the yard and promptly gave orders for the construction of a bench where they could be stacked in future. In the carpentry shop he was perturbed by the sight of chippings and shavings littering the floor.

"How about sweeping this place out?" he asked.

When someone murmured diffidently that they were all rather busy, his retort was not only characteristic, but sharp: "You can't tell me there isn't one of you who could spare half an hour with a broom."

Initially, he found his new life as the Queen's husband irksome and restrictive by contrast with what had gone before. At Clarence House, despite an increasing number of royal duties to be undertaken, life for Philip was still relatively free and informal.

Within the limits of public duty, he had still been able to come and go more or less as he pleased. There had been the occasional evening stroll, unrecognized and unnoticed, in St. James's Park, the occasional inclination to send a servant out for fish and chips. But at Buckingham Palace, protocol and tradition began to take over. It was in Philip's nature to chafe and rebel. "Anyone can walk in and see me," he said when he heard that his visitors, like the Queen's, should now be formally announced. But even among his own staff, few accepted the invitation to do so. It was one thing for Philip to rebel; it was quite another for any of his aides to follow suit.

Particularly irritating to Philip's active, urgent nature, as to others who had lived at the palace before him, was the traditional, complex and seemingly long-winded chain of command it was necessary to go through to achieve even the smallest result. If he wanted a few sandwiches left out against his return from a late-night engagement, Philip was horrified to discover that the correct procedure was to ask his page who would inform the Comptroller of Supply who would tell the chef who would let a footman know when the sandwiches were ready. Philip cut straight through this purple tape of palace protocol, picked up the nearest telephone and gave the chef his orders direct.

In a score of different ways he displayed his restless nature. He carried his own cases to and from his car, took the wheel when he and the Queen drove to Windsor for weekends, picked up the telephone to answer it if it chanced to ring in a room where he was, fumed when footmen rushed around opening doors for him. "I can do it myself," he protested, "I've got hands, haven't I?"

Hitherto, royal inhabitants of the palace had always rung for a servant even when requiring so small a thing as a drink. Philip installed his own cocktail cabinet and continued to mix the drinks himself, as he had always done. Previous occupants had instructed a page whenever a car was to be brought round. Philip picked up a telephone, got through to the garage and ordered the car personally. And if he wanted his private secretary, Michael Parker, for anything, sometimes he did not even bother to telephone. He popped along to Parker's office.

From the outset, Philip demonstrated that he was out to modernize and streamline the palace as much as possible. Soon after he and the Queen moved upstairs from the Belgian Suite into the first-floor royal apartment he had a new system of internal communication installed, enabling him and the Queen to talk directly to each other at the flick of a switch, as well as contact the royal nursery, private secretaries, equerries, ladies-in-waiting, the palace superintendent, the palace steward, the royal housekeeper, the head chef or the sergeant footman, as occasion required. The move upstairs also involved a change of dining room. Something like a half-mile of corridors, passages and stairways separated the royal dining room, at one corner of the vast palace, from the lofty kitchens diagonally opposite, and at Philip's suggestion, a smaller, more compact kitchen was installed closer to hand, equipped with all the latest culinary devices from an electric mixer to a revolving spit.

For Philip, in those early days of palace life, to think was to act. Disturbed by the bareness of the corridor walls immediately outside the royal apartment, he suggested that a few paintings might serve to relieve the monotony. His suggestion was promptly carried out, but the Queen, spotting the paintings which now adorned the walls, recognized them as coming from the State rooms.

"If they're seen here we'll all be shot," she said, jokingly. "They're State property."

So back went the State paintings, to their original positions in the State rooms, to be replaced in the royal corridor by pictures from the Queen's own collection.

II

Apart from the odd native tribe hidden deep in the jungles of South America, there can be few people these days who have not heard of Prince Philip, his pungent speeches, his witty asides, his forceful polo playing. It is difficult to imagine a time when he was not part and parcel of Britain's national life, buzzing here and there by car, helicopter and jet plane with his inquiring mind and penetrating vision. Yet even in Britain few people knew of him in the days when he first started driving to Windsor in his little M.G. to woo the girl who was then Princess Elizabeth.

"I've always dreamed of marrying a tall, fair man," the Princess confided once. Philip, when he came into her life, fitted the bill uncommonly well. Tall and slim, blue-eyed and fair-haired, with the well-scrubbed look of an athlete fresh from a shower, he brought with him a refreshing tang of the vast world outside the high walls and railings of Buckingham Palace.

Their first meeting, when the Queen, then a thirteen-year-old princess, accompanied her parents on a visit to Dartmouth Naval College where Philip was a cadet, has been too well documented to need repetition here. Lilibet was impressed to such a degree that afterwards she could have eyes for no other possible suitor; Philip was off-hand in the lofty manner which only a youth of eighteen can adopt towards a small girl. But by the time Philip paid a Christmas visit to war-time Windsor things were vastly different. The Princess who took the role of principal boy in a home-made version of the pantomime *Aladdin* had blossomed into an attractive seventeen-year-old who had left childhood behind. It was Philip's turn to be impressed.

They exchanged Christmas cards, and, later, letters. A photograph of Philip, handsomely bearded in true naval tradition, appeared in the Princess' room. Occasionally, and discreetly, they went to dances and restaurants together. They went to see the American musical *Oklahoma!* and thereafter the strains of *People Will Say We're in Love* were heard issuing over and over again from the Princess' record-player until the recording was in danger of being worn out.

Sometimes during his weekend visits to Windsor Philip would take the Princess for an exhilarating spin in his little sports car. At other times they rode together in Windsor Great Park or swam in the green-tiled pool at Royal Lodge. In the evening, while King George VI tackled state papers, as his daughter was to tackle them in turn, and his wife passed the time playing successive games of patience, the young couple played records or went for a lovers' stroll in the leafy grounds on the pretext of taking the dogs for their evening exercise.

On Sunday evenings, when Lilibet and Margaret returned to Buckingham Palace in one of the royal cars, Philip would shoot on ahead of them in his nippy little M.G., staying to have supper with them before driving back through the night at daredevil pace to his naval base at Corsham. It was on one of these late-night return trips that he skidded into a ditch, overturning his car. Philip was no more than shaken. But the Princess, when told the news, was upset and refused to be satisfied until she had spoken to Philip on the telephone and assured herself that he was all right.

During holiday visits to Sandringham and Balmoral, where Philip was given a tartan-carpeted bedroom and shaved each morning with hot water brought by a servant in a big enamel jug, romance ripened towards fruition. Those were the days when Philip, his scanty masculine wardrobe boasting no such luxury as shooting tweeds, accompanied his prospective father-in-law across the grouse moors in flannel trousers and a polo-necked sweater. "I am one of the generation who started the war in nappies, spent the next eight years in uniform and when peace broke out found myself without any clothes," he once confessed publicly. Even on the day of his official engagement to the Princess the naval-type suitcase he took with him to Buckingham Palace contained no more than the bare essentials of clothing . . . a single lounge suit, a sweater, flannels, spare shoes and socks.

The engagement had been unofficially heralded in the newspapers four times before the official announcement, and as promptly denied. King George VI and his wife thought their daughter still too young for marriage. Besides, there were the complications over Philip's nationality and status to be resolved. Then came four months of parting when the Princess visited South Africa with her parents . . . four months which included that all-important occasion in any girl's life, her twenty-first birthday. She returned from that trip noticeably thinner, overjoyed to be reunited with Philip . . . and eleven weeks after her birthday came the official announcement of her engagement to Lieutenant Philip Mountbatten, as Prince Philip of Greece had become by naturalization.

Her father saw Philip as the sort of son-in-law for whom he had always hoped. "Just the man for the job," the King confided in a friend. "But I'm afraid he doesn't realize yet what he's taking on. Being a consort is much more difficult than being a Sovereign. I'm sure it's the most difficult task in the world."

III

On that February day in 1952 when she succeeded to the throne the Queen was a Mountbatten by marriage. Two months later, acting on what has been referred to as the "formal and insistent advice" of the prime minister, she reverted to the family name of Windsor by an edict which applied also to the small, serious-faced youngster who was now heir to the throne. From Philip, no less than the Queen, monarchy was demanding its own particular type of sacrifice. As the Queen's father had wisely prophesied, marriage to a princess in a modern monarchy does not necessarily accord with the candy-floss tradition of children's fairy tales.

Constitutional demands thus satisfied, there was perhaps considerable personal pleasure for the Queen in a further decree, issued appropriately on her birthday, by which she elevated her husband to the rank of First Gentleman, according him status and precedence second only to herself.

The British constitution does not contain any definition of the duties of a royal consort, which Philip was in fact if not in title. The job is what the man himself makes of it, and from the outset Philip showed that he would mold it in his own forthright fashion, going through life not merely as his wife's shadow, but as a man and a prince in his own right.

In those early days of the new reign he was already the active head of six different organizations and honorary president of some thirty more. Over the next few years this figure was to increase at a prodigious rate until the number of associations, organizations and clubs with which he was connected in one way or another had reached a staggering total in the region of five hundred. Requests for him to go here, there and everywhere were already streaming into his study at Buckingham Palace at a rate of over three hundred a month. Clearly no man could possibly tackle them all, however willing a work-horse he might be. But Philip acceded to as many as possible, once traveling fifteen hundred miles to attend thirty different functions and deliver fifteen different speeches in the course of a single week.

Then, as now, the speeches reflected the man. They were, invariably, larded with wit. One of Philip's early public engagements was to confer a degree on Dr. Kurt Hahn, who had been his headmaster at Gordonstoun. "The hero of Charles Kingsley's *Westward Ho!*," said Philip, the symbolic velvet hat held in his hands, "was expelled for hitting his headmaster over the head with a slate." He held the hat towards Dr. Hahn. "I invite you, sir . . ." The rest of what he intended to say was lost in guffaws of laughter.

He told the Military College of Science: "Throughout history the basic qualification for officers has been the ability to handle men. Modern warfare has added two other requirements—the ability to handle machines and the ability to handle paper."

He told the Chartered Insurance Institute that he doubted if his personal goods and chattels were worth insuring. On the other hand, he added, he might be interested in an insurance covering him against "excessive hospitality."

His speeches were not merely witty. They were also shrewd, forthright, hard-hitting and frequently controversial, and have become even more so over the years.

Of speech-making, Philip has commented that when in doubt it is better to play safe. "People would rather be bored than offended."

He, himself, has rarely practiced what he preaches in this direction. He has seldom played safe; seldom, if ever, bored those who listened to him. Occasionally he has offended people. And always he makes his point. He once coined his own graphic phrase to describe much of his speech-making . . . "dontopedalogy" or "the science of opening your mouth and putting your foot in it."

But whether he put his foot in it or not, he has seldom hesitated to be less than blunt. He called road construction "an absolute paradise for buck-passers." He told the Society of Motor Manufacturers, "It won't be long before it will be quicker to go on foot" . . . and in London, at least, time has since caught up with his words.

The very down-to-earth language of his remarks has upset some people, and delighted thousands more. He compared a Henry Moore bronze to "a monkey's gallstone." He told a factory canteen they were "a bit stingy" with the carrots. Philip has always believed in calling a spade a spade and not merely an agricultural implement. Instead, if he thought it apt, he would doubtless call it "a bloody shovel," just as once, asked what he thought of a plaque of himself hanging on a club-room wall, he rejoined, "You have to live with the bloody thing—not me." Phrases like "fire in the belly" come easily to his tongue. Such phrases are the down-to-earth language of the twentieth century, but not necessarily the sort of speaking everyone expects from a royal prince.

Even in the early days of the new reign, Philip knew what he wanted to say and stood up and said it. A suggested draft for a speech, prepared by one of his aides, was returned with Philip's blunt comment written in the margin: "I don't agree at all!" Those who ventured to draft speeches for him to deliver soon found that they were wasting their time. The speeches Philip delivered bore little or no resemblance to any drafts prepared for him. Then, as now, he preferred his speeches to be entirely his own work and his own thinking. From his study, whenever a major speech was in preparation, would emerge a continuous stream of memoranda. "Get me this, please." "Find out more about this." "Check on this, please." By the time he was through, a single speech could well involve him in a folder of notes, ideas and facts a full two inches thick. Only then does he sit at his desk to write out what he wants to say, often working late into the night.

While he does not believe in learning a speech by heart, fearing to come unstuck should he forget his lines, in the early days he frequently practiced his delivery aloud in the privacy of his study, sometimes listening to the play-back of a tape-recording to judge how he sounded.

The thoroughness with which he researches his subject was never better demonstrated than in the speech he made to the Ramsay Centenary Dinner eight months after the accession. In preparing that speech, he went even to the length of reading the letters which had passed between Sir William Ramsay and Lord Rayleigh concerning the discovery of argon. The result was a speech dealing intelligently with such abstruse subjects as the use of xenon in the field of therapeutics, germanium as a semiconductor in transistors, and the spectographic examination of an argon fraction.

From the outset, he brought his inquiring mind to bear on all manner of contemporary problems—from car production to conscription, from road conditions at home to export sales abroad —with science and technology as his prime interests. He visited the atomic research center at Harwell, the Royal Aeronautical Establishment at Farnborough, the Chemical Research Laboratory at

Teddington. He saw radioactive isotopes being produced, germanium being made, the application of plastics in aircraft construction. Those at the receiving end of such visits were frequently surprised to realize that they had an entirely new type of royal visitor on their hands. Philip was not one to be fobbed off with the meaningless platitudes so often accorded to royal visitors; nor one to rejoice over the pomp and panoply which all too often goes hand-in-hand with a royal visit.

"I am not unaware that special arrangements are sometimes made for my benefit," he commented rather pointedly on one occasion.

There were times when he seemed to take positive delight in circumnavigating such "special arrangements." Attending an army exercise he was informed that tank troops were lined up in a nearby wood awaiting the pleasure of his inspection.

"If they're on exercises they shouldn't be wasting time getting ready for inspections," he rumbled and marched off to take a look at the field kitchens instead.

Inevitably, he upset some people. From time to time he attracted considerable criticism, and has gone on attracting it over the years. He was called a "royal meddler" when he advocated the character-building qualities of conscription by those who sensed a political motive to the remark. He was labeled "ignorant" for trying to urge the military advantages of a new type of vehicle. "It's no good saying a man in his position can play games on Sunday without interfering with anybody else," thundered Dr. Donald Soper. "Whatever he does, however discreet he is, it becomes a public occasion and even a commercial occasion, whether he likes it or not."

Some of it stung, but Philip contrived to shrug it off. "I am one of the most governed people in the world," he said once, and went on speaking his mind, playing his Sunday polo, learning to fly—despite objection to his flying from so lofty a personage as Sir Winston Churchill.

Nor did he take undue notice of mumbled comments that he ought not to drive the Queen and certainly not at the kind of speed he was inclined to favor. In his courting days he reputedly boasted that he could cover the 97 miles from Corsham to London in less than two hours in his little M.G. True or not, it is certainly a fact that he left York on one occasion after an overnight stop and arrived at Balmoral, over three hundred miles away, in time for afternoon tea. "There were times when I thought we were going to sprout wings and take off," said a member of his staff who traveled with him.

At Windsor, where the Queen spent her weekends, royal servants knew they could always expect her some ten to fifteen minutes earlier if Philip was driving. But such trips were not always made without mishap. A motorist, slowing to take a turn at Staines one evening, felt a sudden bump in the rear. Climbing out to inspect the damage—a dent in his own car, a broken spotlight on the other—he realized suddenly that the occupants of the other car were none other than the Queen and her husband, with Philip driving.

"All right—all my fault," said Philip, affably.

IV

Into the King's old study, with its lofty, richly ornamented ceiling and its tall windows from which it is just possible to glimpse the tops of the traffic bowling along Constitution Hill, Philip moved his own leather-topped desk, leather-covered armchairs and massive chesterfield. The Queen had taken over her father's desk, and the rest of the furnishings which the room had originally contained had accompanied the Queen Mother to her new home at Clarence House. Philip hung de Lazlo's portrait of his mother above the marble fireplace, flanking it with portraits of his father and grandfather, the first Marquess of Milford Haven. But one article yet remained in the room from the King's day, the eighteenth-century "synchronizer" clock which stood on the mantelpiece surmounted by the pocket-watch it adjusted automatically with unfailing regularity.

Over the next few years, as the tempo of Philip's workaday life increased, the study underwent considerable change. A fitted work-unit was built in beneath the windows. Within easy reach of his hand as he sat at his desk, Philip had installed an intercommunications system linking him with all parts of the palace. Another system of press-buttons enabled him to operate the radio, television or tape recorder without the necessity for moving from his place at the desk. He could even, by the press of a button, alter the viewing angle of the television screen or cause the green damask curtains to close across the windows. For the hospitality of official visitors who came and went in such a steady stream, he introduced, concealed in the wall alongside the fireplace, a cocktail cabinet complete with its own small refrigerator for cooling beer or manufacturing ice cubes. To give the study a more contemporary and businesslike appearance, he installed a false ceiling which lowered the height of the room and entirely concealed the lavish moulding and gilded ornamentation of the original.

He set about organizing his undefined job as the Queen's husband with all the thoroughness and efficiency a modern business executive brings to bear on the problems of the factory production line. Indeed, visiting the Industrial Efficiency Exhibition, he even acquired an actual production board, had it adapted to show his forthcoming engagements at a glance and hung it on the wall of his private secretary's office. Beside this engagement board multi-colored pins scattered about the surface of a large wall-map marked those spots overseas which he had already visited . . . and the many more he intended to visit in the future. But when he received an offer to demonstrate an electric typewriter for his benefit, he declined with thanks. He already had one, he said.

Then came the day when the first helicopter came buzzing like an angry hornet over the tall trees which screen the rear of the palace. It scattered the ducks in a cloud of feathered alarm as it skirted the lake into which the Queen had once tumbled as a small girl and came to rest, finally, on the velvet lawn which had been the setting for so many royal garden parties. Out of the palace, as the rotor died into silence, came striding the tall figure of the Queen's husband, briefcase in hand, closely followed by his private secretary, Michael Parker, and his personal detective, Frank Kelley. While Parker and Kelley scrambled into the body of the machine, Philip climbed briskly in beside the pilot. The steps were taken away, the rotor whirled again into life and the helicopter hovered upwards, buzzing away over the tall trees in the direction from which it had come. The Queen's husband was going about the Queen's business in the modern manner, and a new streamlined era of monarchy had been installed on the launching pad.

CHAPTER FIVE

CORONATION

I

ONE AFTERNOON NOT long before Coronation Day, a somewhat unusual little procession might have been observed making its way along the wide, carpeted corridors of Buckingham Palace in the direction of the Picture Gallery. The Queen herself led the way. Over one arm, as she walked along, were draped the trailing ends of a long, white sheet pinned to the shoulders of her dress as an improvised train. Accompanying the Queen were the six maids-of-honor who would attend her at her Coronation. Bringing up the rear were two of the royal footmen.

The sheet which trailed from the Queen's slender shoulders represented her coronation robe. As they reached the Picture Gallery, one of the wide green and gilt chairs was lifted from its accustomed place by the footmen, turned round, and, under the Queen's direction, placed in position to represent the royal coach. The Queen was about to rehearse her arrival at Westminster Abbey on Coronation Day.

Gracefully, with the assistance of the two tall footmen, she descended from her imaginary coach while the trailing ends of the make-believe robe were dexterously passed into the hands of the maids-of-honor as they formed up behind her. Slowly the small procession moved off in the direction of the nearest doorway, representing for this occasion the entrance to Westminster Abbey.

Turning in the doorway, her arms now angled as though carrying the orb and scepter, the Queen rehearsed her departure from the abbey while her maids-of-honor practiced the transfer of the "robe" to the footmen whose duty it would be to help her back into the coach.

But the Queen was not yet satisfied. "I'm afraid it's not going to be quite as easy as that," she commented, smiling. "Remember that we shall have His Royal Highness in the coach as well."

Once again they rehearsed the motions of arrival and departure, this time making allowance for the imaginary presence of the Duke of Edinburgh.

For months past, within and without the palace, preparations for the great day had proceeded steadily with mounting momentum. The scarlet and gold state liveries, unworn since pre-war days, were brought from the steel boxes in which they had been so long stored in the livery room in the palace basement, shaken free of mothballs, brushed, pressed, repaired. The steel boxes and the preservative mothballs had done their jobs well. Only the pink silk stockings had perished in the years since state livery was last worn by royal servants. Cotton ones were ordered in replacement.

In the Gold Pantry, the gold plate, much of it unused since pre-war days—candlesticks and vases, trays, plates and cutlery, gold ornaments so heavy it needed four strong men to lift them into place—was fetched from glass-fronted cases to be cleaned with jeweller's rouge and polished with chamois leather.

In the royal mews at the rear of the palace, the state coach, with its lining of quilted satin, was refurbished and fitted with a system of interior lighting worked from batteries tucked away under the seats. Surgeons' scalpels helped in the delicate task of stripping the Cipriani paintings from the weathered wooden panels to be mounted afresh on new panelling. The old iron-shod wheels were replaced with tires of solid rubber to cut down the jolting and give the Queen a more comfortable journey on her Coronation Day. The Queen's great-great-grandmother, Queen Victoria, when told she had to carry the orb, had lamented, "It is very heavy." Now, inside the coach, out of sight, metal brackets were installed to take the weight of orb and scepter and thus ease the strain on the new Queen during the long processional ride back to the palace.

As the great day drew nearer, all the world, it seemed, had succumbed to coronation fever. In New York, a plaster replica of the state coach and Windsor grays drew crowds to the plaza of the Rockefeller Center, with coronation dolls and teenage tiaras selling as readily as hotdogs and hamburgers. Paris, too, developed a sudden rash of coronation fashions and souvenirs. In Singapore a four-hundred-foot carnival dragon was under construction as part of the planned celebrations. Firework displays were arranged in Melbourne and Sydney, Brisbane and Karachi. In South Africa they planned to illuminate the summit of Table Mountain.

In Britain the Ministry of Food, relaxing its customary vigilance, approved seventy-two applications to roast an ox. Souvenir manufacturers who had suffered heavily through Edward VIII's failure to be crowned took out insurance policies to protect themselves against further loss. Britain's premier peer, the Duke of Norfolk, struggled red-faced but unruffled to cope with the task of squeezing 7,600 people into Westminster Abbey, allotting each one a seating space of eighteen inches, with an extra inch for peers on account of the thickness of their robes.

All over London flagpoles sprouted, scaffolding took root, window-boxes blossomed where none had been before. Even chimney-pots developed broad bands of red, white and blue, while a mechanical nightingale trilled its recorded song in Berkeley Square.

The weighty robe of royal purple, which the Queen would wear for part of the Coronation ceremony, was brought from its storage place for her to try on. Even at Buckingham Palace there was nowhere it could be spread out for the velvet to be brushed except on the floor. It was spread out thus when Prince Charles came scampering down from the royal nursery to see his parents one evening.

"What are you doing?" he asked the servant who was diligently brushing the royal robe.

"I'm getting this ready for the Queen."

Charles, now four years old, seemed puzzled.

"Who is the Queen?" he wanted to know.

"Why, your Mummy, of course."

In this way, did the four-year-old heir to Britain's throne first learn that the young woman he called "Mummy" was also the Queen. But to him, Coronation or no Coronation, she was still "Mummy" and not for many years to come did he start using the more formal, "Where is the Queen, please?" when inquiring after his mother's whereabouts.

In preparing herself for Coronation Day, not the least of the Queen's problems was one of cosmetics. Normally, she uses little make-up, usually a peach-colored liquid foundation, a peachy powder, a pinky-red lipstick and a touch of blue-grey eye-shadow to enhance her blue eyes and exceptionally long eyelashes. But the Coronation was no ordinary occasion and the problems were many. Her make-up must look equally well under the yellow lighting of the abbey and the rose-tinted lighting newly installed in the state coach. It must clash neither with the new crimson robe she would wear on her way to the abbey, nor with the regal purple she would wear on the way back. It must photograph as well in color as in black and white. It must show up well on television screens, yet not appear overdone when her face was seen, many times magnified, on the largest of movie screens. Yet with all this, it must not appear even slightly exotic. "Remember, I am not a film star," the Queen said.

A type of make-up used in film studios was tried and discarded. Finally, after many experiments on a young model of similar coloring and bone structure, a satisfactory scheme was evolved . . . the usual peach-tinted foundation, a touch of red-blue rouge, light brown mascara for eyes and eyebrows, and a specially created lipstick, red with blue undertones.

There were rehearsals at Westminster Abbey with the Duchess of Norfolk acting as the Queen's stand-in. At one rehearsal, in which the Queen herself took part, she felt that her husband was treating his share of the proceedings a shade too lightly and had him do it over again. To the Queen, there was nothing light-hearted about her Coronation; it was a most solemn and serious occasion. A suggestion that part of the ceremony should be abridged to ease the strain, accentuated on this occasion by the knowledge that the all-seeing eyes of the television cameras would be watching her every move, brought a prompt inquiry from her, "Did my father do it?"

Told that he had, she said, "Then I will, too."

The overseer in charge of the state coach tramped the processional route to calculate where and when to brake the heavy four-ton coach. Footmen, who would be foot-slogging alongside the coach on the actual day, also went over the route for the two-fold purpose of familiarizing themselves with the various turnings as well as breaking in the brand-new buckled pumps with which they had been issued. And early on Sunday mornings, with the rest of London not yet astir, the whole procession was rehearsed and timed over the coronation route.

Into London poured visitors of every race, creed and clime, in robes, saris and mink wraps. From concrete cities and lonely kraals they came, from Sarawak and Sweden, from Swaziland and the Sudan. Seventy-four foreign states sent official representatives. Australia sent the most sightseers, a staggering 60,000 of them, including a woman from Brisbane who had cheerfully sold her home in order to pay for the trip. The United States, even though it did not belong to the British Commonwealth, sent a further 40,000, ranging from a party of eight hundred and fifty well-to-do Americans who paid a total of £160,000 ($448,000.) for the ten-day visit, not counting their actual air fares, down to the fourteen-year-old youngster from New Jersey who raised £200 ($560.) for the trip by selling newspapers.

As the great day approached, twenty of the world's largest liners converged on Britain while airliners lined up in dizzy circles to land at London Airport. Seven liners were moored in the Thames as floating hotels, and in Madeira, twenty-eight South Africans, realizing belatedly that their boat would not dock in Britain until after Coronation Day, hastily decided to complete the trip by flying boat.

The Imperial State Crown, a glittering confection of diamonds and rubies, emeralds, sapphires and pearls, which the Queen would wear when she left Westminster Abbey after the ceremony, was altered to fit her. Secretly it was taken to the palace in an inconspicuous black wooden box for the Queen to try it for size.

To accustom herself to its weight, shape and balance, she wore it about the palace for the best part of a day. She wore it at her desk as she tackled her correspondence, walked the corridor outside her private apartment with it balanced carefully on her head. And someone who saw her that day swears that the crown, with its great irregularly-shaped ruby which once adorned the helmet of Henry V at Agincourt, glinted from her head when she sat down for her afternoon cup of tea and a quick glimpse of the evening paper.

Into the palace streamed a seemingly endless succession of gifts for the new Queen on her coronation . . . wine from the Rhineland, a necklace of diamonds and aquamarines from Brazil, a silver casket from Malaya, ponies from the Argentine, a floral umbrella from Bombay, a carved wooden drum from the Luvale tribe of Northern Rhodesia. One gift the Queen prized perhaps more than any other—an inscribed silver chest from her family and relatives, surmounting it a magnificent aquamarine, the gift of her grandmother, Queen Mary.

Sadly, that grand old lady did not live to see her granddaughter crowned. She died only ten weeks beforehand, but not before making it plain that neither her failing health nor her death, if it came, must be permitted to interfere with Lilibet's coronation.

II

June 2, 1953 . . . eight o'clock in the morning on Coronation Day. Along the Mall, beneath the festive soaring arches erected for this day of ceremony and pageantry, the best viewing spots were already crowded with families which had camped out all night with their sandwiches and thermos flasks, rugs and radios, playing cards and can openers.

Inside Buckingham Palace, servants, resplendent in their state liveries, came and went endlessly. From the royal mews came the clip-clop of the horses as they were harnessed to coaches. From the front of the palace came the blare of bands, the music amplified over loudspeakers which the Queen, late the previous night, had asked to be quietened a little as she was having difficulty in getting to sleep.

Over it all hung the threat of rain. Yet nothing, not even the overcast sky, could dampen the spirits of the people, or of the Queen herself on this day of days . . . which, for the Queen, had begun with the magnificent news of the conquest of Everest. Years later, the Queen's husband was to describe this news from Everest, coming as it did on the very morning of the Coronation, as "My most unforgettable experience."

The Queen stood at one of the palace windows, gazing out at the weather and preparations . . . just as, years before, she had stood at another palace window to watch the preparations for another Coronation.

The Queen has described her childhood memories of her father's Coronation in the essay she wrote afterwards as a schoolroom exercise set by her governess. Pencilled words in a blue-lined exercise book, written at the age of eleven, recall how she was "woken up" at five o'clock in the morning as the band of the Royal Marines struck up almost beneath the nursery windows. She jumped out of bed and rushed to the window in her dressing-gown and slippers, crouching there to watch all that was going on outside, on a morning so gray and misty that the ever-thoughtful Bobo removed the still-warm eiderdown from the bed and wrapped it carefully round the slender shoulders of her young charge.

Now, on another cold, damp morning, the girl of eleven had blossomed into the woman of twenty-seven, the central figure in her own Coronation, with her beloved Bobo still close at hand.

Just as she had once helped her royal mistress to dress for her wedding, so Bobo MacDonald helped her now to don the bridal-satin gown glittering with pearls, *diamanté* and crystal which Norman Hartnell had created for her Coronation. Eight months of patient research and design, eight months of careful workman-ship and intricate embroidery, had gone into the fashioning of that coronation gown. The order for it had been given as far back as the previous October. "Rather on the lines of my wedding dress," the Queen suggested. "In white satin, of course."

Later, studying Hartnell's eight hand-painted designs, she wondered whether a gown in white and silver might not bear too close a resemblance to her wedding dress. Hartnell pointed out that Queen Victoria had favored a white coronation gown.

"Yes," said the Queen, who had herself been along to Ken-sington Palace in company with Queen Mary to study her great-great-grandmother's coronation robes. "But remember that she was only eighteen at the time and unmarried."

So the original vision of white and silver became a rainbow of glittering color into which was worked, at the Queen's own suggestion, not only the rose of England, the thistle of Scotland, the shamrock of Ireland and the leek of Wales, but the motifs of those other far-off lands of which she was now the Queen . . . Canada's maple leaf, the mimosa-yellow wattle of Australia, the New Zealand fern, South Africa's pink-tinted protea, the lotus of India and Ceylon, and the wheat, cotton and jute of Pakistan.

"Glorious" was the word the Queen used when she first saw the dazzling creation Hartnell had designed.

And "Glorious" was the word used by the privileged few who saw her first on Coronation Day as she descended the wide flights of stairs which led from her private apartment to the Grand Hall of the palace.

As the Queen stood there, framed by the white marble of the floor and columns of the Grand Hall, the gilt balustrading of the staircase and the gold-ornamented ceiling, with the priceless Gobelins tapestries as a backdrop, she looked so radiant and serene that more than one of those who saw her found themselves contending with an unexpected lumpiness in the throat. All the adjectives the newspapers have ever used to describe her were true at that moment in time, as, radiant and smiling, poised and serene, in the glittering coronation dress and heavy crimson robe, the diamond diadem of her great-great-grandmother on her head, she slowly crossed the Grand Hall to where the cumbersome, ornately gilt state coach awaited her coming.

She was handed into the coach with its painted roof on which nymphs and cherubs disported themselves, and the crimson robe was arranged carefully around her. The Windsor grays took the strain and slowly, with the swaying motion of a ship at sea, the great four-ton coach rolled forward across the quadrangle and into the forecourt, across the forecourt and out into the Mall.

At the window of the day nursery the Queen's small daughter knelt on a chair to watch her mother depart. The state rooms and the Queen's private apartment apart, nearly every window of the palace was crowded with faces of friends and relatives of the staff whom the Queen had allowed them to invite. Mindful as always of the well-being of those who work for her, she had arranged a meal of almost Christmas dinner proportions in the Servants' Hall for all of them . . . her own servants, their friends and relatives, as well as the staff from Balmoral and Sandringham for whom a section of one of the stands outside had been specially reserved.

Along the Mall, down Whitehall, into Northumberland Avenue swayed the state coach, borne along on a great, roaring wave of loyal approbation. Out onto the Embankment where thousands of schoolchildren had been assembling since half-past six. As the coach turned the corner on to the Embankment, they let out a wild, loyal yell.

The Queen, at that moment, was completely overcome. For once, emotions which she is so careful to keep in check before the scrutiny of public gaze, got the better of her and as the coach rolled on its ponderous way towards Westminster Abbey the Queen's cheeks were suddenly moist with tears.

Into the abbey, where the Queen Mother curtsied to her daughter for the first time. Slowly and majestically, the solemn rites of Coronation ran their course. Only for one brief moment in all that long ceremony did the Queen let her attention stray, her eyes flickering momentarily towards her small son, Prince Charles. In white silk trousers and frilled shirt, hands and chin resting on the balustrade, he watched wide-eyed the historic proceedings in which he is destined one day to be the central figure.

He had been taken to the abbey by his nanny, Helen Lightbody. But once there, Granny—the Queen Mother—had taken over, providing him with a stool on which to kneel and see better what was going on, her head close to his as she whispered explanations in answer to his childish questions.

The great five-pound Crown of St. Edward was set briefly upon the Queen's head. Her husband knelt on a crimson footstool at her feet to swear allegiance to the woman he had married:

"I, Philip, Duke of Edinburgh, do become your liege man of life and limb and earthly worship; faith and truth will I bear unto you, to live and die, against all manner of folks. So help me God."

III

The ancient ceremony over, the Queen ate a picnic lunch of cold chicken in the royal robing room before leaving for the long, processional drive back to the palace. It was pouring with rain as she left the abbey, her crimson robe now replaced by one of regal purple. Momentarily she surrendered the orb and scepter to one of her aides as she seated herself again in the state coach. The train of her purple robe was coiled up on the opposite seat, its great gold monogram meeting her gaze. Fearing possible travel-sickness from the hammock-like sway of the coach, she asked for the monogram to be covered so that she did not see it.

The Queen, as always, had discerning eyes for everything going on around her, the small details as well as the wider panorama. "Did you see those poor people fainting along the route?" she said, sympathetically, when she was finally back at the palace. "How are your feet?" she asked one of her servants who had toiled manfully through the whole procession at the side of the coach.

For her own part, she emerged as fresh and radiant as ever from what her grandfather, King George V, once described as "the terrible ordeal" of Coronation. Six times that evening, the crown replaced by the magnificent diadem handed down from her great-great-grandmother, Queen Victoria, the new Queen made a smiling appearance on the palace balcony before the floodlights dimmed finally and then went out. It was ten minutes after midnight and the Queen, as she walked away from the balcony for the last time, her tiara now swinging in her hand, was as smiling and serene as she had been when she first came down the stairs from her private apartment in all the splendor of her coronation gown.

CHAPTER SIX

AROUND THE WORLD

I

IN ONE OF the spacious wardrobe rooms on the second floor of Buckingham Palace, immediately above the royal apartment, Bobo MacDonald and her two assistants were busy packing. They had been at it for days past and the landing outside was already piled high with luggage. They would be at it for days to come. The Queen was setting off on the first overseas tour of the new reign. And what a journey it promised to be! A staggering 50,000 mile marathon by land, sea and air, visiting ten countries from the friendly, sleepy little island of Tonga to the vast, sprawling land-mass of Australia. The longest royal tour ever undertaken by any monarch.

For months past the planning and preparation had been going on. Indeed, it had already started long before the Coronation. It was now the November of Coronation year, and as far back as the previous Christmas, when Norman Hartnell had visited Sandringham to show the Queen his proposed designs for her coronation dress, there had also been a private mannequin parade staged in her bedroom to let her select some of the dresses she would be taking on the tour.

Now the time had come for the dresses to be packed . . . from the shimmering coronation gown and other specially designed dresses for state functions to simple cotton dresses for casual wear, costing, some of them, as little as £4 ($11.20). The coronation gown went into a special, strong wooden box of its own. Large wardrobe trunks, each taller than a tall man and mounted on wheels to make for easier handling, held state gowns and evening dresses.

A miscellaneous collection of highly polished trunks, leather suitcases and zipp-fastened holdalls, along with queen-sized hatboxes and shoecases holding up to thirty pairs of royal shoes apiece, contained everything else the Queen might conceivably need at some stage of the long tour which lay ahead of her . . . umbrellas to shield her from rain, parasols to ward off the sun, gloves by the dozen, stockings by the score. There were the Queen's personal jewels to be packed . . . tiaras and necklaces, brooches and bracelets, earrings and watches, a glittering, shimmering mass of diamonds and rubies, emeralds and amethysts, each separate piece snug in its own velvet-lined case. The Queen's own feather-filled pillows would be going along, so would a couple of hot-water bottles in case it was cool at night. There was her gold-backed dressing set to be packed, along with canisters containing her favorite blend of tea, boxes of pine-scented toilet soap and verbena-scented bath salts, bottles of barley sugar to suck to still those "butterflies in the tummy" which still afflicted her on occasion, her cosmetics, shoe polish, even soap powder for rinsing the royal stockings should the need arise.

Nothing must be forgotten; nothing overlooked. Everything must be packed in such a way that the right outfit and the right accessories were always ready for the Queen at the right time and the right place, and Bobo MacDonald, as she supervised the packing, paused from time to time to consult a copy of the half-inch thick itinerary in which the Queen had pencilled brief details of what she proposed to wear for each engagement . . . "red velvet" here, "pink satin" there, "blue lace" somewhere else.

Finally, everything was ready. All the months of complex planning, involving government ministers in more than half-a-dozen different countries, local mayors and private secretaries, dressmakers and drivers, security men and royal physicians, reached their climax in the few moments when the Queen and her husband said good-bye to their small children. It would be six months before parents and children saw each other again, though there would be letters and picture postcards, photographs and round-the-world telephone calls to link them together.

In contrast to the pomp and ceremony of the coronation procession, with its rumbling state coach and liveried grooms, its prancing horses and marching soldiers, the departure from Buckingham Palace was in the new-style pattern of modern monarchy. A gleaming Rolls-Royce swept out through the palace gates with an escort of goggled and gauntlet-wearing police motorcyclists to speed it on its way to London airport. Charles, five years old only a few days before, and Anne, a quicksilver three-year-old, seldom silent, never still, were perched on stools at one of the palace windows to wave to Mummy and Papa as they drove off.

Charles, especially, the Queen realized, was of an age and a nature to miss his parents a great deal during the long months they would be away. To lessen the shock of separation, as well as to ensure continuity of the simple lessons she had already started to give him, she decided that the time had come when he should have a governess. To this end, she engaged Miss Katherine Peebles, a capable young Scotswoman whom Charles and Anne alike soon came to know as "Mispy" (Miss P.).

Each morning while his parents were away, the young prince, after a walk in the palace gardens, went along to the small schoolroom his mother and Aunt Margot had once shared. Here, under Miss Peebles, he continued the lessons in reading, writing and simple sums which his mother had already started. Painting and drawing, for which he displayed a considerable aptitude, scripture and history formed part of the curriculum, while geography became an exciting lesson brought to life by letters and pictures from his parents in far-off places.

Ahead of the Queen, as she waved good-bye to her children, lay a crowded six months of unforgettable experiences, more than two hundred public engagements. By the time it was all over she had been greeted by people wearing everything from saris to swimsuits, been serenaded with everything from hymns to calypsos, been entertained with everything from the wail of conch shells to the rhythmic pounding of war drums. She walked on red carpets and coconut matting, was toasted in champagne and kava, that soapy-tasting concoction peculiar to Fiji, feasted on everything from ham and turkey to raw fish and roast pig.

She watched hula girls and war dances, attended state banquets and official balls, was feted with fireworks, showered with rose petals, and heaped with more than four hundred gifts ranging from a diamond necklace to a barkcloth bedspread, from a nylon nightdress to a collection of leopard skins, boomerangs and native spears.

She was called everything from Lilibet to Liz, while Philip was indiscriminately addressed as both "Your Honor" and "Your Majesty." She was greeted with banners ranging from the sedate "God Bless Her Majesty" to the spontaneous "Welcome Young Mrs. Queen," this last in Jamaica which also bannered "A Big Howdy to Prince Philip."

She endured almost every conceivable degree of rain and shine. In Colombo she endured both extremes at almost one and the same time. A garden party in her honor was flooded out by a torrential downpour and the guests, clutching wet gowns, serenaded her with *Singing in the Rain* as she sheltered under an outsize umbrella. By contrast, she opened the Ceylon parliament in all the glory of her weighty coronation gown on a stifling day when the temperature was ninety in the shade. With everyone around her bathed in pools of perspiration, she contrived, somehow, to look as fresh and cool as on a rainy day in London.

Outside the town hall in Auckland, she stood in the rain wearing only a flimsy summer dress until the deputy mayor passed her his plastic raincoat, a gesture for which she reportedly thanked him with the words, "Thank you, Sir Walter Raleigh." She walked unflinchingly through the swarms of flies which infest the hot, dusty Kalgoorlie goldfields in Australia. For days ahead of the royal visit the whole area has been drenched in insecticide, but still the flies pursued her relentlessly. "They seem to thrive on insecticide," the Queen said.

Everywhere she went, whatever the weather, the crowds flocked to see her. They broke down barriers, penetrated security cordons. If they could get near enough they patted her on the shoulder, plucked Philip by the sleeve. In Panama, which has no connection with either Britain or the Commonwealth, the crowds were so enthusiastic that it was a hard job to prevent them clambering bodily into the royal car, and quite impossible to prevent them invading the grounds of the British Embassy at night in their desire to see her. At a reception in Panama City the invited guests were reinforced by almost as many gatecrashers, and only the Queen's bobbing tiara signalled her movements to her entourage from somewhere in the center of the jittering throng which crowded the dance floor.

Never before in history had there been quite such a royal tour and likely enough there will never be such another . . . so strenuous, boisterous, off-beat, varied and exciting.

II

The very first day gave a clear indication of what a humdinger of a royal tour it was destined to be. From ten o'clock in the morning, when the royal aircraft touched down at Hamilton,

Bermuda, until midnight, the Queen was continuously on the go, even sacrificing her scheduled periods of rest so that everything could be squeezed in. Indeed, her day had started long before that . . . at 3:45 A.M. when her airliner touched down at Gander for a refueling stop which turned into an unscheduled public engagement as the Queen dressed and left the aircraft for the benefit of people who had been waiting at the airport to see her all through the night.

In Hamilton, in a single day, she inspected a guard of honor, visited the historic site of the first British parliament outside Westminster, visited a United States air base and the United States naval base, toured the main island in a small convertible, drove to the House of Assembly in a carriage drawn by two black horses, addressed parliament, went for a boat trip, planted a commemorative tree and attended a garden party with a banquet to follow.

Despite all this, the lights in Government House, where the Queen stayed overnight, came on sharp at quarter-past four the following morning. By half-past five, when it was not yet daylight, she was already on her way to the airfield. By ten minutes past six she was airborne again. And at 9:54 precisely, she was landing at Montego Bay in Jamaica for the whole business to begin all over again.

There was a day in Kingston which started with a military parade staged at quarter-past-eight in the morning to avoid the full heat of the sun and ended with a reception for 1,500 guests which did not commence until half-past nine in the evening. Other engagements so crowded the day that the Queen found herself with only a tight twenty-five minutes in which to wash, change and freshen her make-up for lunch. No wonder she could not quite suppress an audible sigh of relief when bad weather caused the cancellation of a polo game in which she was to have watched her husband take part at half-past seven the following morning.

"I'm so tired I think I'll go back to bed," she said to Lady Hood, the Governor's wife, when she heard that the game was off.

She had slept that night with photographs of her children on the bedside table. Throughout the tour her children were never far from her thoughts. She wrote to them often, sent them picture postcards, talked to them by radio-telephone from aboard the liner *Gothic*.

"We're really looking forward to seeing them again," she confessed in Australia.

"I only hope they'll recognize us when we get home," quipped her husband.

And husband and wife could not resist exchanging warmly affectionate glances in Hobart, Tasmania, when there was an unexpected call of "Three cheers for the royal children."

Motherlike, the Queen made mention of her children in the Christmas Day broadcast she made that year from Auckland.

"Of course, we all want our children at Christmas time—for that is the season above all others when each family gathers at its own hearth," she said. "I hope that perhaps mine are listening to me now."

They were. At Sandringham House, where they were spending Christmas with "Granny," as they call the Queen Mother, it was still only nine o'clock in the morning and Charles and Anne were playing excitedly with the Christmas presents Mummy and Papa had wrapped and left behind for them a full month beforehand. As every year, the Queen had not only picked her own presents for the children, but had personally filled the Christmas stockings which Santa Claus tip-toed in to leave on their beds late on Christmas Eve.

After her broadcast she telephoned Sandringham to talk to her mother and the children, adding the warmth of their laughter and chatter to her own Christmas Day enjoyment in far-away New Zealand. At Sandringham, the children listened with wide-eyed wonder as their mother's voice, coming to them over the telephone, told of quite a different Christmas . . . a Christmas of brilliant sunshine in Auckland as Santa Claus arrived on the lawn of Government House with gifts for the royal visitors. Excitedly they learned that Father Christmas had left more presents for them in New Zealand—a walkie-talkie doll for Anne and a model train for Charles.

At Sandringham, that Christmas, the Queen Mother did everything she could to ensure that the children did not miss Mummy and Papa too much. Like all grandmothers, she spoilt them a little in the process. When Mrs. Lightbody sent word down from the nursery at night that it was time for bed, she invariably begged, "Oh, let them have just a little while longer, please." And, of course, she got her way.

When carol-singers called at Sandringham House as they made

their Christmas rounds she invited them inside so that she and the children could join in the carol-singing with them. When one of the carol party put his fiddle down on an empty chair young Charles promptly went to pick it up. "Now don't touch that, Charles," his grandmother reproved. But a few minutes later she was helping him to hold the fiddle beneath his chin while he drew the bow tentatively across the strings.

III

The long, seventeen-day trip from Panama to Fiji aboard the liner *Gothic*, which was carrying, in addition to its royal passengers, a surprisingly down-to-earth cargo of cars and fire pumps, pianos, wallpaper and brandy, provided the Queen with a welcome respite, enabling her to catch up on the state papers and official correspondence which pursue her relentlessly wherever she goes. She found time also to sunbathe on the privacy of the sundeck, while her husband, more energetically, indulged in boisterous games of deck hockey with no holds barred, cooling himself afterwards with a dip in the ship's pool.

Naturally, he invited others who had been playing deck hockey with him to join him for a dip, among them two sergeants in the Royal Marines. When the two sergeants failed to turn up at the pool, he wanted to know why. It transpired that members of the ship's crew were barred from using the pool. Characteristically, Philip soon cut that bit of red tape.

The swimming pool was the focal point of shipboard life the day *Gothic* crossed the equator. The exuberant Michael Parker was barber for the traditional crossing-the-line ceremony. Philip, his nose reddened with grease-paint, a blue and white butcher's apron flapping about his legs, was the barber's assistant, helping to daub the unfortunate victims with liberal quantities of whitewash, flour and cochineal.

The Queen was not summoned before Neptune, having already crossed the line years before when she journeyed to South Africa with her parents. (Even then, she was let off with no more than a genteel powdering from an outsize powder puff.) But several members of her staff were less fortunate. Lady Pamela Mountbatten, one of the royal ladies-in-waiting, found herself hauled before Neptune, in the person of Inspector Frank Kelley, the Duke's bodyguard, on a charge of "being the daughter of an admiral not appointed by Neptune." Daubed with whitewash and cochineal, into the pool she went. So did the Queen's other lady-in-waiting, Lady Alice Egerton, and the royal page, cherubic Ernest Bennett. The proceedings finally reached a stage of hilarity when everyone was throwing everyone into the pool. The Queen filmed the fun with her movie camera. "I think you're all quite mad," she said, laughingly.

Throughout the whole six months of that fantastic tour, the Queen's cameras were never far from her side. She filmed kangaroos in Australia, flying fish in the Indian Ocean. On Tonga she filmed the giant tortoise which was supposedly taken to the island by Captain Cook. When Viscount Althorp, one of the royal equerries, landed a five-foot shark with rod and line from the stern of the *Gothic* the Queen was there with her camera to film the final tussle.

In New Zealand she filmed the famous hot springs at Rotorua. She was especially keen to get some shots of the famous triple geyser known as the Prince of Wales Feathers. But though she waited patiently for a time, the Feathers seemed disinclined to oblige that day. Finally the Queen moved on. But she had not gone many yards before the chief guide, an old Maori woman named Rangi, called out excitedly, "It's spouting, it's spouting." Turning, her normal regal dignity quite forgotten for once, the Queen literally ran back to the spot in her eagerness to capture this unusual spectacle on film.

The Queen with a camera in her hands is quite a different person from the normally sedate and serious young woman of state affairs. Aboard the *Gothic*, as it sailed through Milford Sound, she darted all over the ship in her determination to get the best possible shots of the fiord-like setting with its snow-capped mountains and tumbling mountain streams. The beauty of the spot quite capti-vated her. "What magnificent scenery," she exclaimed.

She took a film of that amazing armada of small craft which sailed out to welcome her in Sydney harbor, and was dis-appointed the day she visited the Great Barrier Reef, which she had hoped to film from a glass-bottomed boat, to find the normally crystal-clear water clouded from some undersea disturbance.

There were, inevitably, many colorful spectacles the Queen could not film personally for the simple reason that she was playing a leading part in them. On such occasions, she usually entrusted her camera to one of her aides so that she might have as complete a photographic record as possible to show her children when she returned to London. There was, for instance, the ceremonial kava she was given to drink on Fiji. Kava, as anyone who has ever drunk it will tell you, is definitely an acquired taste. The Queen, given only a token tasting, drank it without any change of expression, and possibly the royal camera, in the hands of one of her aides, recorded the quick grin she gave her husband as he manfully swallowed a much more liberal portion.

Then there was that fantastic feast in Tonga to celebrate her reunion with the towering Queen Salote, whose big, beaming smile as she drove through the rainswept streets of London on Coronation Day, captured the hearts of all who saw her. Sitting cross-legged on the ground, eating bare-fingered from plates of banana leaves, the Queen, as the royal camera recorded, was content to merely sample this lavish feast of raw fish and roast pigs, turtles and crabs, water melon and bread-fruit. But Philip, a man who will try anything once—even raw fish—ate heartily.

IV

In New Zealand, in a tight-packed schedule of forty-five days, the Queen visited thirty-nine different places. She saw dairy herds and Maori dances, sheep shearing and sulky racing, the fairy-like glow-worm grotto at Waitomo—"I don't think I've ever seen such a wonderful sight," she said—and the spouting geysers at Rotorua. She was so captivated with the geysers of Rotorua that she insisted on her staff seeing them too, and despite all else she had to do, personally made the arrangements for two cars to take them there.

She stayed at a succession of small hotels and private homes, where the warmth of her welcome more than compensated for the occasional lack of royal facilities. At one hotel the manager loyally yielded up his own dining table to serve as the Queen's desk so that she could tackle her day-to-day paperwork between public engagements. At another, the dressing table mirror in the Queen's dressing room proved far too small for royal purposes. The Queen likes to inspect herself from head to foot before a public function. However, there was a much larger mirror fixed to the wall of one of the staff rooms. It was hastily taken down, carried up to the Queen's room and wedged in place on the dressing table with the aid of books.

At yet another hotel it was the navy-wise Philip who spotted that the bunting which decorated it spelled out the nautical warning: Danger—Am Loading High Explosives. When tackled on the subject, the civic fathers confessed that the bunting consisted of naval signal flags purchased at bargain prices during a sale of surplus stock.

All the royal luggage had been unloaded when the *Gothic* docked at Auckland and now it followed the Queen around New Zealand. At Moose Lodge, on the shores of Lake Rotoiti, where the Queen and her husband stayed for a brief breathing space in all the welter of official engagements, the owner's wife stared in wide-eyed amazement as she saw the royal luggage trundling up the poplar-lined drive—two army lorries piled high with it! "Where on earth are we going to put it all?" she gasped. An answer was found by turning the billiards room into a temporary luggage store.

From this huge stack of luggage, Bobo MacDonald—"My good right hand," the Queen called her—somehow contrived, with the aid of her assistant, Elizabeth MacGregor, always to have the right clothes, pressed and immaculate, ready for the Queen to wear at each stopping place. Not once was there a slip, though the two of them were working in unaccustomed and often confined spaces aboard ship, on the royal train or in small hotels . . . not even on those rare occasions when the Queen exercised the very feminine privilege of changing her mind about what to wear at almost the last moment. It was one such last-minute change of mind by the Queen which caused Philip to say, "Thank goodness I don't have any option in the matter. I've got to wear uniform and like it."

There were, inevitably, the occasional behind-the-scenes flaps and panics of which the Queen was blissfully unaware as she journeyed from place to place. But never on any royal tour before or since has there been such a panic as developed following a night the Queen spent at New Plymouth. The Queen and her husband had already left to visit a local dairy before flying on to Wellington in the afternoon. Behind them, the royal servants—Bobo MacDonald and Elizabeth MacGregor, along with Philip's valet, James MacDonald—got on with the packing. As each trunk and suitcase was packed it was carried downstairs to the army lorries waiting outside to speed it to the local airfield.

Suddenly Bobo popped her auburn head over the banisters.

"Have you seen the jewel case?" she called down to members of the royal staff in the hallway below.

"It's up there, isn't it?"

But it wasn't. A quick, thorough search of the Queen's suite revealed not the slightest trace of the big leather case in which Bobo had carefully packed the Queen's personal jewellery . . . the tiara inherited from Queen Alexandra, half-a-dozen other tiaras, Queen Victoria's diadem, the jeweled Order of the Garter, the flame-lily brooch of 330 diamonds which was a twenty-first birthday gift from the children of Southern Rhodesia, the floral brooch made from the fabulous Williamson diamond, more than a score of other necklaces, brooches and earrings, their intrinsic value alone running into six figures and their historic worth far more than that. In vain, royal servants hunted through the Queen's bedroom, dressing room and bathroom, even looking under the royal bed in case the case had somehow been pushed underneath.

For fairly obvious reasons, the Queen's jewellery does not travel with the rest of the luggage. A member of the Queen's staff conveys it by hand from place to place, never letting it out of sight.

Now it had vanished!

Other servants were sent for and questioned. Yes, one of them remembered just such a case. He had carried it downstairs and stacked it with the rest of the luggage. He was trying to be helpful.

The Queen's staff dashed downstairs. But the rest of the royal luggage was nowhere to be seen. By now, it had been loaded on to the waiting army lorries—and they had already gone while the search for the jewel case was still continuing.

Royal servants immediately set off in pursuit. But fate continued to work against them. A shade too late they arrived at New Plymouth airport. The baggage plane had already loaded and taken off. They boarded another aircraft and followed on. But again they were out of luck. When their aircraft landed they found that the royal luggage was now on its way to Government House.

They piled into a car and drove into Wellington, arriving at Government House to find that the royal luggage had already been unloaded and was standing now in a giant stack on the broad front steps. The staff of Government House were already beginning to carry it inside.

One of the Queen's staff jumped out of the car and dashed over to the huge pile of luggage. His anxious eyes spotted the all-important case right on top of the pile. Hurriedly he intercepted a Government House servant almost in the act of picking it up.

"I'll take this one," he said, reaching for it with a sigh of obvious relief.

V

But the most gruelling part of all this mammoth trip was still to come . . . Australia . . . over fourteen thousand miles of travel, sixty-eight towns and cities to visit, thirty-four processions, twenty-six receptions, six garden parties, six balls, four state banquets and three parliaments to be opened, all in the space of fifty-seven non-stop days. The Queen visited a coal mine and an iron works, watched horse racing and surf riding, sheep shearing and tree felling. She planted trees, made speeches (fifty-eight of them), shook hands . . . and came away from one handshake session with her fingers badly bruised. Normally the Queen contrives to avoid such mishaps, a constant royal hazard, by keeping her hand fairly limp and permitting only the tips of her fingers to be taken. But on this occasion, a hefty backwoodsman, actuated by loyalty, excitement and nervousness, seized her hand so enthusiastically and pumped away at it so vigorously that the Queen was still feeling the effect of the handshake two days later.

The crowds were as dense and excitable as ever. In Sydney, the Queen was fifty-three minutes late visiting a hospital when the million-strong crowd broke through the police cordon nine times. So many of the miniature standards flown from the royal cars disappeared, presumably into the capacious pockets of souvenir hunters, that replacements had to be sent out from London.

Among these extrovert Australians there was little of the restraint that a London crowd normally observes and certainly the uninhibited Australian lasses left little doubt as to their obvious admiration for the Queen's athletic-looking husband. In Sydney he got the feminine version of a wolf-whistle; in Hobart they blew kisses. One young lady who was presented to him took advantage of the occasion to ogle him with so blatant a wink that for once even the normally irrepressible Philip could produce no suitable quip.

Even quite small children seemed no less backward in coming forward. In Brisbane a diminutive four-year-old tried to kiss the Queen. Elsewhere, a still more diminutive toddler, his reins trailing behind him, tried to scramble up the ramp to the royal dais. It was left to Philip to intercept him and hand him back to his mother. "I can see we need nannies instead of security men," he joked.

Philip was constantly at the Queen's side, helping things along with the breeziness of his extrovert personality, bridging the conversation if ever it showed signs of flagging, always ready with a quick joke to ease moments of hesitancy or awkwardness. His best joke, however, was reserved for a dinner at the Australian Club on his return to Britain. It concerned the small Australian boy, who—according to Philip—rushed home excitedly to his mother with word that he had just seen the Queen and a Kingfisher!

If Philip's temper, at times, wore a shade thinner than the Queen's, it was invariably because of his concern for his wife. If the Queen was ever tired she gave little sign of it, though she did confess that Australia's first rumbustious welcome—the combination of excitable crowds and humid heat in Sydney—had made her feel slightly nervous for once.

Even on such packed days as that on which she visited Benalla and Shepperton, Tatura and Echuca, Rochester and Bendigo, Castlemaine and Maryborough—eight stops, eight speeches of welcome and eight royal replies in a whistle-stop tour which started at 10 A.M. and continued until 7:40 P.M.—she could still find time and energy at the end of it all to spend an hour dealing with government papers and correspondence as well as checking through her itinerary for the following day.

She seemed indefatigable as she sat at the window of the royal coach, smiling and waving to the crowds who flocked to see her, and no one who saw her from outside could have guessed that she had slipped off her shoes to ease her aching feet, and was resting with her legs up on the opposite seat.

Even before she arrived in Australia she was already tanned from long days spent in the open air and brilliant sunshine of the southern hemisphere, as she proved by lifting her pearl necklace on one occasion to display the tell-tale white patch which still encircled her throat. The Queen has a fair, though not unduly sensitive, skin, and now, to prevent it becoming too tanned under the glare of the sometimes fierce Australian sun, she resorted to a protective make-up with a liquid powder foundation specially prepared for her by her beauty adviser, Mrs. Thelma Holland, herself an Australian by birth.

The time-honored legend that the Queen's beauty remains

unmarred, come rain, come shine, took a sharp knock in Sydney, where, after one luncheon, she was seen to reach for her handbag, suspended at the table beside her by its special hook, and proceed to touch up her lipstick. Throughout the tour, indeed, she openly employed powder puff, lipstick and comb whenever she deemed it necessary.

In some strange way, the Queen seemed to grow up and mature measurably on that Australian visit. When she opened the Federal Parliament in Canberra, gone from her voice was the slightly high-pitched girlish piping which had long characterized her public utterances. Her voice, as she commanded members of the House of Representatives to wait upon her in the Senate Chamber, was suddenly deeper and more assured, the voice of a true monarch.

She missed little of all that went on around her. At the Military College in Canberra it was the Queen who spotted a small drummer boy clearly on the verge of collapse and drew attention to him so that an ambulance could be summoned. Driving through Melbourne her sharp eyes picked out a familiar face among all those other faces lining the route. It was the face of a man who had been footman at Buckingham Palace before emigrating to Australia. Before moving on from Melbourne, the Queen met him again, along with his wife and daughters, to ask how things were going with them in their new life.

She also proved that her husband was not the only one who could make a joke. Attending a luncheon, she noticed that the time of her departure was down on the itinerary as 2:17. She asked the local mayor who was hosting her why it could not have been quarter-past or half-past the hour.

"You see, Ma'am," his worship explained, "everything has been carefully rehearsed, timed to the minute."

"And what happens if I spill my coffee?" asked the Queen, smiling. "May I have another cup or must I still be away by 2:17?"

With poliomyelitis prevalent in Western Australia, there was considerable concern as to whether or not this part of the royal tour should be abandoned. The Queen herself was not unduly worried. But others were worried for her and it was finally decided that the tour could continue if strict precautions were taken. A demonstration by thirty thousand schoolchildren in Perth was cancelled. It was decreed that the Queen would not shake hands with anyone and that no one should come closer to her than six feet. She would not actually touch any of the bouquets presented to her and would not stay at Government House. Instead, she would continue to live aboard the *Gothic* and the crew of the ship would not be allowed ashore to mix with the local population.

The Queen had been given one anti-polio injection by her physician, Surgeon-Commander D. D. Steele-Perkins, in Canberra, after a woman with whom she had shaken hands was admitted to hospital. Before visiting Western Australia, she had another. When she went ashore, everything needed for her meals, from food and wine down to table napkins, china and cutlery, went with her from the *Gothic*, following her around in a refrigerated van.

Worrying though the situation was for those responsible for the Queen's well-being, it was not without its amusing moments. There was one occasion, as the van was about to set off from the *Gothic*, when it was realized that the cheese with which the Queen sometimes likes to finish a meal had been omitted from the royal picnic hamper. So it was handed to the van driver to take along. But at the end of the meal, when the Queen looked round for the cheese, it was nowhere to be seen. Someone went to ask the driver what had happened to it.

"The Queen's cheese?" he mumbled, noticeably embarrassed. "Why, I thought that was for me. I'm afraid I ate it."

The rule that no one was to approach within six feet of the Queen quickly went by the board. After all, you can't very well pin a medal on someone six feet away. And the Queen herself forgot the advice she had been given not to handle anything when not wearing gloves. At a trotting meeting she asked for a program and accepted it with ungloved hands. Even the ban on hand-shaking was finally forgotten. At a ball at Government House the Queen shook hands with at least three people.

It has often been said that the Queen is a serious, sometimes somber, rather emotionless person. There may be times when she gives that impression. She believes in being serious on serious occasions. But she has an impish sense of humor under it all, and, as we have told, there was a moment on Coronation Day when tears of pride and joy gleamed in her eyes and trickled down her cheeks.

The tears were to come again as she said her last goodbye to the vast land-mass of Australia and the equally vast friendliness

of the Australian people. But a lump in the throat was surely for-
givable at that emotional moment when she stood on the *Gothic*
and heard Sir Eric Harrison, the minister in charge of her visit,
toss protocol to the winds as he sent a final, full-blooded Australian "Coo-ee!" ringing out across the harbor at Fremantle.

VI

The homeward route was by way of Ceylon, Aden and Entebbe,
with its sad memories of that other, more somber homecoming
following the death of the Queen's father. But this time there was
only happiness for the Queen in the prospect of the long-awaited
reunion with her children, sailing to meet her at Tobruk aboard
the newly-completed royal yacht *Britannia*.

For the royal children it was an exciting, adventurous trip, and
not only because they were going to see Mummy and Papa again.
It was their first sea voyage and there were so many new things
for them to see and do. They were accorded an official guard of
honor and duly inspected it after their childish fashion, with
Anne responsible for many a half-suppressed smile as she insisted
on saying a polite "How do you do?" to each seaman.

Some of their toys were taken on the voyage with them as a
nursery precaution against restlessness or boredom, but tricycle
and teddy bear were speedily discarded in favor of such exciting
new games as helping to swab the sun-deck with bucket and mop.
Charles also took along a new box camera, a recent gift, with
which to imitate Mummy and take back memories of seaboard
life.

But even at Tobruk, with her children waiting for her eagerly
aboard the royal yacht only a short distance off-shore, the Queen
refused to skip her royal duty. For four long hours she inspected
guards of honor, watched parades, visited a war cemetery and
met King Idris of Libya before she finally felt free to go out to
Britannia and the long-awaited reunion with her children.

And even that moment, so long awaited, was so nearly dis-
appointing. It was six months since Charles had last seen her, and
six months can be a long, long time indeed in the mind of a five-
year-old whose nursery life must inevitably include a degree of
training along the path of monarchy. Now, confusing Mummy's
return with the sort of greeting he had already been accorded on
official occasions, he extended a small, polite hand.

"Oh, no, darling," said the Queen, and swept both children rapturously into her arms.

Now came the homeward journey aboard the new royal yacht with its air-conditioned cabins and its hushed atmosphere of soft-shoed seamen. On a gray May morning, with the message "Welcome Home" fluttering from the coastguard station on the Needles, and the same message spelled out in giant letters across Tower Bridge, the Queen came home to her capital at the end of the most arduous and fantastic royal tour ever.

In six months she had journeyed 18,850 miles by sea, 19,650 by air, 9,900 by road and 1,600 by rail. She had attended 135 receptions, fifty balls, banquets and garden parties, held eleven investitures, opened seven parliaments. She had opened a new road in Jamaica, and a new school in Fiji, laid the foundation stone for a new cathedral in New Zealand and dedicated a shrine in Australia. She had seen twenty-seven children's displays and seven race meetings, two concerts, a cricket match and a tennis match. She had laid seven wreaths, planted six trees, made four broadcasts, unveiled three memorials. She had sat through 276 speeches, made 157 herself, endured the ordeal of 13,000 handshakes received 468 gifts and bouquets.

Inevitably, there were times when things went wrong, as when Lady Pamela Mountbatten was mistaken for the Queen and accorded a twenty-one-gun salute as she went ashore from the *Gothic* . . . as when a last-minute change of plan at Malta saw the royal party leave from a deserted, derelict wharf littered with broken-down vehicles while a guard of honor waited patiently and uselessly on a quay some distance away.

But even allowing for such occasional mishaps, there can be no denying the success of this tremendous tour with its object of seeing and being seen, cementing old friendships and making new ones. Even Ceylon, where it was said no Union Jack would fly to welcome the Queen and the national anthem would not be played, finally did both and threw in a twenty-one-gun salute for good measure . . . even if the salute was mistakenly accorded the wrong person.

The Queen's homecoming was like Coronation Day all over again, but on a far, far grander scale. The whole of Britain's south coast was turned into one vast grandstand. The little ships went out to bid their Queen "Welcome Home" just as they had once gone forth to Dunkirk on an infinitely grimmer mission. As the first small fishing smack dipped its ensign in salute, the Queen, mindful as always of those things which are the keystone of true monarchy, gave an order aboard the royal yacht. Slowly and majestically, *Britannia* dipped its own ensign in acknowledgement.

And so to that triumphal voyage up the Thames with its flag-bedecked shipping, hooting syrens and cheering crowds, with jets sweeping overhead and church bells ashore pealing "Welcome Back." At nine o'clock that morning, as the bluebottle hull of *Britannia*, a gleaming gold band setting off the snow-white superstructure and yellow funnel, arrived off the Nore, the Queen went up on to the bridge. For the next four-and-a-half hours, until the royal yacht berthed finally at Tower Bridge, she stayed there, continuously smiling and continuously waving. And this was no mere perfunctory royal gesture, but a full-blooded wave high over the head that was to leave her arm and shoulder unexpectedly aching when she arrived back finally at Buckingham Palace. But at the time, in the excitement of her home-coming, the Queen noticed nothing. She was as thrilled to be home again as Britain was to have her safely back.

CHAPTER SEVEN

"WE'VE DONE IT!"

I

THE CLOSING STAGES of this mammoth royal tour coincided with the opening weeks of the flat racing season at home, and cables from the Queen's racing manager, Captain Charles Moore, kept her informed of her successes and disappointments. She was in Uganda when she heard that her chestnut, Corporal, had won at Newmarket. Word reached her at Malta that Biscuit had scored at Kempton Park. And as she drew steadily nearer home a radio message to the royal yacht informed her that Landau had come second in the Derby Trial Stakes.

Ever since she was a small girl the Queen has loved horses . . . horses to be ridden, horses to be raced, horses to be watched. As we have told, even a chance accident to a small pit pony could arouse her interest and sympathy. "Horse mad," her father once termed her, jokingly. "I really think she ought to have been a trainer," he told a friend.

As children, she and Princess Margaret collected toy horses as other small girls collect dolls. At one time they had as many as thirty stabled on the landing of their Piccadilly home, carefully "grooming" them each night at bedtime. One of her favorite books, in childhood, was the story of *Black Beauty*. And one of her earliest requests when she first moved into Buckingham Palace with her parents was to go along to the royal mews and see the horses.

It was on a visit to Newmarket as a girl of twenty that the racing bug really bit her. Watching her father's Hypericum win the 2,000 Guineas Race (worth $5,880.) after a dramatic pre-race incident in which the filly had thrown her jockey, the then Princess Elizabeth was so excited that for a moment or two after the race was over she could scarcely get a word out, though she summoned sufficient breath to beat everyone else in a dash for the unsaddling enclosure.

From that time on her enthusiasm for horse racing was un-
bounded and she was soon so knowledgeable that her father paid
considerable respect to her judgment. But her judgment was not
always infallible. When the King's horse, Above Board, won the
1950 Cesarewitch, father and daughter heard the result over a
car radio on the Balmoral moors where the King was shooting.
The King remarked to a friend, "I'd have gone to Newmarket
today if I'd have thought the filly would win, but Lilibet said it
hadn't a chance."

A gift horse from the Aga Khan on the occasion of her wedding
gave the Princess her first chance of racing a horse of her own.
Deftly she named the filly Astrakhan, displaying an aptitude for
the right name which has revealed itself time and again since, as
when she settled upon Stenographer for the offspring of Fair Copy
and Saucy Lass, and selected Opera Score for the foal of Fair
Copy and Carmen.

But Astrakhan, with weak forelegs and a trick of choking on her
own tongue, was to prove a sad disappointment when raced in the
Princess's newly-registered colors of scarlet with purple-hooped
sleeves and a black cap. Despite electrical therapy and experiments
with a patent bridle, the filly notched only one win in a brief
racing career.

A half-share with her mother in a steeplechaser named Mona-
veen proved a more successful venture. "The milk cart horse," as
he was laughingly referred to because he had drawn a milk float at
one stage of his career, won several races for the joint royal owners
and came close to finishing in the first three in the Grand National.
But unlike her mother, who has been known to seek shelter from
pouring rain under a tree rather than miss a particular race, the
Queen could raise little enthusiasm for steeplechasing. "It's too
unpredictable," she said.

With her father's death, she took over the nine horses he had in
training at the Newmarket stables of Captain Cecil Boyd-Rochfort
as well as a further five National Stud horses at the nearby training
establishment of Noel Murless. She adopted the traditional racing
colors of the Sovereign—purple, gold braid, scarlet sleeves, black
cap with gold tassel—and quickly showed that she was going
racing as an owner and not merely as a monarch.

At Royal Ascot, while V.I.P.'s stood facing the royal box in
which she was expected momentarily to appear after the state drive
along the track, she went straight to the paddock to take a look at

the horses running in the first race. At least one winning owner, whom she entertained to tea in the privacy of her box, could not help noticing that her attention wandered frequently to the window overlooking the unsaddling enclosure.

Her father had always made it a practice to leave after the fifth race. But the Queen, during the whole four days of her first Royal Ascot, stayed enthusiastically each day until the last race had been run.

At Goodwood, not content with watching the racing, she went along to the starting gate to find out exactly how it worked. That veteran racegoer, Lord Rosebery, who accompanied her, confessed later that it was one of the most exhausting day's race-going he had ever experienced. "Her Majesty never stopped," he told an acquaintance. "She was on top of the stand one moment, in the paddock the next and off to the unsaddling enclosure the next."

At Sandringham, on more than one occasion, she was up sharp at six o'clock in the morning to drive the 45 miles to Newmarket in time to watch her horses at their morning gallops. She had breakfast when she got there, and as often as not stayed on the whole day, happily soaking herself in the atmosphere of the training stables, returning to Sandringham only when she had seen the horses finally bedded down for the night.

She subscribed then, as she does now, to a weekly racing report which she reads thoroughly and then files away for future reference. The revolving bookcase which stands close to her desk is crammed with books on racing and breeding. A racing journal is delivered to Buckingham Palace along with the daily newspapers each morning. The Queen belongs also to a subscription service which provides her with a marked selection card whenever she goes to the races. She does not bet and the nearest she comes to "having a flutter" is a ticket in the private sweepstake which members of the Royal Family hold among themselves on Derby Day. The year Crepello won the Derby, the Queen had the winning ticket.

To her betting is unimportant, and racing, for all its momentary excitement, is only part of the wider field of breeding. Her know-ledge of bloodstock is wide and expert, and she has devised her own card index system of the blood lines most suited to successful breeding. There is scarcely a horse running of which the Queen does not know the pedigree by heart, as Australians found out during the course of the Queen's world tour.

She displayed such expert knowledge during a visit to Randwick races that officials responsible for arranging her subsequent visit to Flemington race track sent out a near-panic S.O.S. . . . "For heaven's sake, put someone in the royal box who really knows the form, the stud book and pedigrees right back to Eclipse. Her Majesty has it all pat."

At one race meeting those with her were discussing the next race which was to be run over a mile and a quarter. The name of a particular horse was bandied around as a probable winner. But the Queen shook her head. "Oh, no," she said, smiling, "Its sire was a sprinter and its dam was a sprinter. It can't possibly win over a mile and a quarter." Nor did it.

II

It was two months after the Queen's return from her marathon tour. At Ascot the sky was dull and overcast; it had been raining earlier and would do so again later. In the royal box, the Queen brought her field glasses to eye level as Aureole, her chestnut colt with the three white socks and the distinctive white blaze, went to the starting gate as 9-2 favorite for the King George VI and Queen Elizabeth Stakes.

Ever since she had helped with his feeding when he was no more than a week-old colt in the royal stud at Hampton Court, the Queen had had high hopes that here was a horse to rival her great-grandfather's almost legendary Persimmon, whose larger-than-lifesize statue in weathered bronze overshadows the stables at Sandringham.

But Aureole, as he developed, proved himself an unpredictable animal, so sensitive to the slightest touch that even his royal owner could not approach him with impunity. There was one occasion, visiting the Boyd-Rochfort training establishment at Newmarket to see how her favorite was coming along, when the Queen tried to coax Aureole with an apple . . . and withdrew it hurriedly as he jerked his head and snapped at her. There was another occasion when a timely cry of "Look out, Your Majesty" saw the Queen sidestep just in time as Aureole lashed out with an angry hoof. "A real brute," one stable lad labeled him, and not without a degree of justification.

Aureole's sensitivity was to effect his performances on the race track. The Queen had high hopes that he might provide her with a royal victory in the Derby of Coronation Year. But just as Gay Time had disappointed her in the year of her accession, so Aureole was to disappoint in the year of her coronation. A chance good luck pat from a passing racegoer as Aureole paraded in the paddock before the race had such an unsettling effect that there was considerable difficulty in quietening the animal. The result was a win for Gordon Richards on Pinza by a comfortable four lengths.

"If I had to be beaten, I'm glad it was by you," the Queen said in congratulating the newly-knighted jockey after the race.

At Doncaster the same year in another display of temperament, Aureole cantered away down the course before the start of the race. At Ascot, in this same King George VI and Queen Elizabeth Stakes, he reacted so violently to a chance kick from another horse that his jockey was sent flying.

All in all, Aureole had proved a sad disappointment, but the Queen was not dismayed and not yet defeated. She arranged for a Harley Street physiotherapist to travel to Newmarket and give Aureole a course of treatment designed to offset those failings which prevented him from becoming the wonder horse the Queen was convinced he could be.

The soundness of her judgment was seen in 1954. Victory after victory accrued to Aureole's credit . . . the Coronation Cup at Epsom, the Hardwicke Stakes at Ascot when the Queen, tense and excited, stood on tiptoes with her mother and Princess Margaret as Aureole and Marcel Boussac's Janitor flashed neck and neck past the winning post. Impatiently she shifted from foot to foot as they waited for the camera's verdict. It came at last and tears of pleasure glistened in the Queen's eyes as she heard that Aureole had won. "I've never seen my daughter so excited," the Queen Mother confided in Captain Boyd-Rochfort.

As she watched Aureole go to the starting gate for the year's most valuable race, the King George VI and Queen Elizabeth Stakes with its £23,302 ($65,245.60) prize, the Queen had every reason to feel pleased and confident. Then it happened. Suddenly Aureole shied, unseating his jockey, Eph Smith, and depositing him in the mud.

Smith scrambled to his feet and re-mounted. But that was not the end of his troubles, nor the end of the Queen's worries as she watched anxiously from the royal box. As the starting gate went up and the shout, "They're off!" echoed across the course, Aureole suddenly swerved, losing ground. For three furlongs, while the Queen must almost have resigned herself to defeat, he was last in the field.

Then, with a mile still to go, she saw that he was moving up in a spatter of mud. Her grip on her glasses tightened as he moved into fourth place. So intense was her excitement that her movie camera remained unheeded beside her in the royal box. Always before she had enthusiastically filmed the finish of any major race one of her horses might have a chance of winning, or arranged with a friend or equerry to do the filming for her. But now, as Aureole forged into the lead with a furlong and a half still to go, all thoughts of her camera were momentarily forgotten.

Behind Aureole, Mme. Volterra's Vamos was coming up fast. Was the Queen to be robbed of victory at the very last moment? From foot to foot she hopped in mingled apprehension and excitement, her glasses glued to her eyes.

She could scarcely contain her excitement, for the Queen at the races is a very different person from the serene and serious young woman of public occasions. All at once her own voice mingled with the shouts and cheers of the rest of the crowd as the horses flashed towards the finishing post.

"Keep riding," she cried, excitedly, "Keep riding. Stay in front."

As though her words reached them, the royal horse and jockey stayed indisputably in front as the leaders passed the finishing post. In the royal box, the Queen could not disguise her evident delight, clapping her gloved hands enthusiastically together as she jumped up and down in her excitement.

"We've done it!" she exclaimed, delightedly. "We've done it!" And away she dashed to the unsaddling enclosure.

Aureole's victories that race season contributed more than handsomely towards the total £40,993 ($114,780.40) which saw the Queen at the head of the list of winning owners. And if she did not go as far as having a bronze statue cast to match that of Persimmon already at Sandringham, she did have a small statuette fashioned which still stands in the royal drawing room at Windsor to remind her of Aureole's triumphs. Her one slight regret in all this was her omission to film the exciting finish of that dramatic race, and, sadly, Aureole's greatest victory is missing from the fine collection of her racing films which she shows for the entertainment of friends from time to time.

CHAPTER EIGHT

FAMILY LIFE

I

WITH NO STATE visits or overseas tours to further congest her always crowded schedule in the immediate future, the Queen could feel free, for a time at least, to concentrate her attention on matters closer to home. Not the least of these, perhaps, was the question of Princess Margaret and Group Captain Peter Townsend. It was perhaps more Princess Margaret's problem than anyone else's, but the Queen could not altogether detach herself from it. She was, after all, not only the Queen, without whose consent the Princess could not yet marry, but she was also the elder sister to whom the younger had so often turned in the past for help and advice.

In many ways, the Queen and her sister are strikingly different. There is, admittedly, a recognizable similarity of voice when they speak; there are habitual gestures which are so alike in the two of them as to be virtually identical. But in taste, temperament and personality they are strongly contrasted.

The Queen loves country life and all that it means . . . early morning horse rides while the dew is still fresh on the grass, long brisk walks in the open air, the sighing of wind in the trees, even the exhilarating freshness of a summer shower. Had she not come to the throne, she would almost certainly have let her love of horses, dogs and country life develop to a point where London would have seen her seldom.

Princess Margaret is a creature of the fireside and the concert hall, the dance floor and the box at the theatre, the ski run and the fashionable restaurant.

The Queen is serious, rather aloof, even-tempered, a stickler for punctuality and completely single minded where her royal duty is concerned.

Princess Margaret is impulsive, by no means aloof, sometimes moody, often unpunctual (in which she takes after her mother) and always unpredictable. When her father was alive, her complete disregard for time was the bane of his life. King George VI liked his meals punctually with everyone at the table, and his younger daughter's habit of coming in late at meal-times brought many a reproving frown to his face. But the frown would quickly disappear as Margaret strolled into the room, smiling, unconcerned, cheerfully singing the hit song from the latest musical. No one could be angry with Princess Margaret for long and certainly not her father. "Margaret could charm the pearl out of an oyster," he confided once in a friend.

The Princess's unpredictable personality has many facets. She can be tomboyish, kittenish, sophisticated and completely regal. There was an occasion not long after the accession when she made a passing reference to the Queen in conversation. There seemed some doubt as to whether she was talking about her sister or her mother and the person to whom she was speaking, seeking clarification, was unwise enough to inquire, "Which queen?"

"There is only one Queen," replied the Princess with all the regal dignity for which her grandmother, Queen Mary, was famed.

Despite their differing personalities, the two sisters have always been deeply devoted to each other. "Didn't you know, we're telepathic," Princess Margaret once told a friend jokingly. Throughout childhood and into their teens they were so close as to be almost inseparable. Towards the younger sister, the elder adopted a protective, almost motherly attitude. At their father's coronation Margaret's excited bobbing disarranged her tiny coronet. Lilibet leaned forward and straightened it. Before one of their first royal garden parties she cautioned Margaret not to laugh or point if she saw a funny hat. The younger sister was quite capable of doing both.

"Copy me, Margaret, and you'll be all right," her sister advised her again and again. Always, it seemed, the elder sister was restraining the natural impetuosity of the younger, advising her, helping her, doing things for her.

A tale from their nursery days pinpoints the relationship between them. They had been playing "cooking." Now the game was over and it was time to wash up the dirty dishes.

"Remember, Margaret is to help," said their nanny.

But Margaret promptly disappeared on some childhood errand she found more exciting.

"Only do half the washing up, Lilibet," said their nanny. "Leave the rest for Margaret. She must learn to do her share."

But Lilibet, conscientious as always, did the lot.

Towards this motherly, protective attitude of her elder sister, Margaret responded with complete and utter confidence in everything Lilibet said and did.

At Sandringham, one snowy Christmas years later when both were grown up, they came out of the house together and walked side by side towards the waiting car. The roads around Sandringham that day were deep in snow, icy under the snow, altogether treacherous.

"It's your turn to drive today, Margaret," said her elder sister.

But Margaret responded with a quick shake of her head. "Oh, no—you drive, Lilibet. I'd rather trust your driving than mine in this weather."

Her father's death affected Princess Margaret deeply as it did her mother and sister. The Queen could partly assuage her own grief with all the new responsibilities of monarchy so suddenly heaped upon her. For the younger sister, there was no such antidote immediately available . . . and no elder sister to whom to turn for help and comfort. The Queen was too preoccupied with other things. Margaret felt a deep need of someone with whom to share her grief . . . and suddenly the newspapers were full of rumor and speculation concerning her and Peter Townsend.

Townsend had been at Buckingham Palace since war-time days. He first went there as part of King George VI's plan to surround himself with able young men who had distinguished themselves in combat. With three battle honors and eleven enemy planes to his credit, Peter Townsend was among the first to be selected. His initial appointment at Court was for three months. But the King took an almost instant liking to him and he stayed, finally, for nine years.

When the Queen Mother and Princess Margaret moved from Buckingham Palace to Clarence House following the King's death, Townsend went too. He planned their tour of Southern Rhodesia and was to have accompanied them. But rumors and gossip could no longer be ignored. Almost on the eve of departure came the announcement that Townsend would not be going. Instead, he accompanied the Queen and her husband on their visit to Northern Ireland. By the time Margaret returned from Southern Rhodesia he had gone altogether.

He was now in Brussels as air attaché, but the problem was not yet resolved, and the Queen's concern was twofold: how to help her younger sister as she had helped her with so many smaller things in the past, and how to prevent the possibility of the fabric of monarchy being damaged afresh as it had been at the time of her uncle's abdication.

II

On a happier plane, but none the less important on that account, was the question of the children's upbringing. Charles's upbringing was of particular concern, for he would one day be King Charles III and must be painstakingly coached along the path that leads to monarchy. Indeed, his training for this high station in life had already started. When he was still a babe in arms, his nurse, Helen Lightbody, would take his hand in hers as he sat on her lap in the royal car and encourage him to wave it gently to and fro at the watching crowds. Before he was five years old he had learned how to shake hands with waiting officials, was bidding palace servants a polite and clear "Good morning" when he saw them, doffing his cap politely to the crowds who gathered to see him.

There was a Sunday morning when he was riding his small tricycle along one of the garden paths at Sandringham watched, through the wrought-iron gate let into the high wall, by the few remaining stragglers from the large crowd which had gathered earlier to watch the Royal Family enter and leave church. As he drew near the gate the young Prince halted his tricycle and politely raised his cap. For a few moments, to the great delight of those watching him, he sat there on his tricycle, smiling back. Then his nanny told him it was time to go.

"Do I raise my cap again before I leave?" he asked her, audibly.

The solemn ceremony of his mother's Coronation, and all the preparations that had gone before, had created an awareness in his young mind that he, too, was destined for monarchy. Not long after the Coronation he and Anne were watching from the window of the day nursery as a contingent of guards marched smartly along the Mall and stamped into the palace forecourt for the daily ritual of changing the guard.

"Oh, look," cried Anne, delightedly. "They're having another Coronation."

"There won't be another Coronation for years and years and years," he told her, "and that will be mine."

It was that salt-sea monarch, King George V, who once advised his eldest son, the Prince of Wales, now Duke of Windsor, "Always remember your position and who you are." Charles was perhaps still too young for such plain-spoken advice, but in subtler ways the lessons of future monarchy were imprinted upon his young mind.

He learned quickly, as was shown on the occasion when he was noticeably chewing a sweet as the royal car in which he was riding drew to a standstill. As always, the inevitable small crowd gathered to catch a glimpse of him. Charles, spotting them, hurriedly took the sweet from his mouth and thrust it into the gloved hand of the Queen Mother, who was accompanying him. "Please hold that for me, Granny," he whispered to her.

One of the Queen's main problems at this time was to protect her small son as long as possible from the glaring limelight to which royalty is always subject. On early outings in Green Park and St James's Park, his nurse's instructions were abundantly clear. Individuals might peep at him, but a crowd must never be permitted to gather round. When crowds began to gather, the outings were switched to more out-of-the-way spots like Richmond Park, where the Queen's son, unnoticed, stalked tame deer with a toy gun.

The two children usually enjoyed such outings separately from each other. The Queen reasoned that her children would be much more conspicuous if they were together. At this stage, attempts to enroll the young Prince in juvenile and charitable organizations were tactfully discouraged, and when an innkeeper had the bright idea or re-naming his establishment "The Prince Charles" the Queen quietly let it be known that she did not altogether approve.

In character, temperament and personality, the two children were as different from each other as the Queen and Princess Margaret had been before them. Charles was a shy, serious, thoughtful youngster with his father's insistence upon knowing the why and wherefore of everything he saw and heard. Even Philip, on one occasion, found it necessary to interrupt a boyish spate of words with, "Don't ask so many questions, Charles."

Anne, by contrast, was always laughing, dancing, singing, always on the go, dashing frantically along the palace corridors with shrill little cries of "Wait for me, Charles—wait for me," just as Princess Margaret had once run after her elder sister.

Even when trying on new clothes it was impossible for her to stand completely still and she would hop excitedly from one foot

to the other. Mealtimes were almost the only occasions during
which she could be persuaded to remain in one spot for any worthwhile length of time, as the artist Ludmilla Trapp discovered
when painting her portrait. Each sitting was converted into a sort
of glorified tea-party, with the Princess munching away while Miss
Trapp captured something of her quicksilver personality.

Anne is a born extrovert and soon proved herself a natural
mimic. She was once seen toddling about the palace with her
mouth screwed up in a rather curious fashion. It turned out that
she was imitating one of the servants who had a trick of whistling
silently to himself as he went about his duties.

Just as his mother had once checked the irrepressible Princess
Margaret, so the solemn and serious little Prince Charles now
checked the equally irrepressible Anne with a quick headshake or
a slight frown when it seemed necessary. It was only a reproving
frown from her elder sister which prevented Margaret joining
happily in the applause which greeted the two of them the time
they went to their first pantomime.

Similarly, Charles, though only a very small boy himself, was
quick to call out, "Remember your manners, Anne—come back
and say thank you," on occasions when his little sister omitted to
thank a servant who had performed some small service for her.
The lesson stuck. A passing servant came across the little Princess
struggling to climb on the shiny back of the large bronze deer
which stands in the grounds at Balmoral. She wanted "a ride" and
the man helped her up. Later that day Anne was at some pains
to seek out the servant who had helped her. "I forgot to say thank
you," she told him.

Despite their contrasting, and sometimes conflicting, personalities the two children got along surprisingly well in the royal
nursery. There were, of course, the occasional outbreaks of
childish squabbling. The battered rocking horse inherited from
their mother's days in the royal nursery was sometimes a source
of dispute, ending once in an unexpectedly strong push from
Charles which sent Anne and the rocking horse sprawling. Anne
was in tears and her brother was instantly contrite. "I'm sorry,
Anne," he apologized, helping her to her feet. "I didn't mean to
push you so hard." There was another right royal argument,
coming close to blows, when Anne in the course of a make-believe
washday, hung her doll's clothes across her brother's model railway
layout and obstinately refused to move them.

But dolls were quickly to prove themselves too tame for the quick-silvery Anne. Old ones were relegated to the toy cupboard, while the new ones so frequently received as a result of her parents' travels abroad found a home in a glass-fronted cabinet in the nursery corridor. A similar cabinet housed the collection of model boats which were the most frequent gift her brother received from overseas. But her teddy-bear remained a firm favorite and for years it traveled with her wherever she went—to Sandringham, Windsor and Balmoral, aboard the royal yacht on that exciting voyage to Tobruk—as a source of cuddly comfort when it was time for bed.

Instead of dolls, Anne's inclination was for her brother's toy guns and his working mechanical toys. Cowboys and Indians was a favorite game with the royal children at this stage, the two of them hurtling along the corridors with toy guns clutched in their hot, eager hands. "Stick 'em up or we'll drill you full of lead," they cried at the servants and officials they encountered in the course of the game.

The big dolls' house, nine feet long and three feet high, which Anne was given in Gibraltar on the journey back from Tobruk was to prove less exciting to her than her brother's seven-foot high model of the Rock of Gibraltar with its intricate model railway which sent trains disappearing into small dark tunnels to emerge again at the far end.

Prince Philip shared Anne's enthusiasm and helped the youngsters operate the model. Like so many fathers, Philip derived almost as much fun from his son's toys as the boy did himself. Indeed, the Christmas Charles found an elaborate electrically-operated model railway among his gifts he scarcely had a chance to play with it at all. His father, the Duke of Gloucester and the youthful Duke of Kent all wanted to take turns.

The following morning Charles was up and about unusually early. Asked why, he explained that he wanted to play with his railway before anyone else could get to it first, adding the gloomy proviso, "If it still works."

III

Each morning the two children were awakened promptly at half-past seven. Washed and dressed for the day, they went through to the day nursery, with its ever-fascinating cuckoo clock, to have breakfast. This meal was followed by a short, brisk walk in the palace gardens, often taking along a bag of bread crusts with which to feed the wild duck that frequent the lake. On their way back the children always went to see their parents in the dining room of the royal apartment, where the Queen and Philip would be finishing their own breakfast.

The Queen has always been careful not to spoil her children, and fixed hours and a regular routine were "musts" in the royal nursery. Meal-times seldom varied and few food-fads were ever permitted. Royal or not, the two children had to do as they were told, and the artist Ulrica Forbes has recalled how she suggested to Anne that she should pose for her lying on a settee, only to have the little Princess inform her, "Nanna does not allow us to put our feet on the furniture." Nor would she until a sheet of newspaper had been spread on the settee first.

The Queen seldom interfered in the day-to-day running of the nursery, believing any such parental interference ill advised. She laid down the broad principles along which she wanted her children to be brought up and then left it to the nursery staff to carry them out. And there was no appeal to Mummy against nursery punishments awarded for childish misdemeanors. Nursery discipline was firm, if gentle. Sweets were rationed and none at all were permitted until after lunch for fear of spoiling childish appetites. There was no pampering and the children were taught to do things for themselves instead of merely relying upon the fact that there were servants around them. A request from Anne for a clean handkerchief would be answered with the information that clean hankies were kept in a drawer of her dressing table and she would be sent to fetch one for herself.

Philip was particularly insistent that the children do things for themselves, and nothing irritated him so much as servants who would not let them. Young Charles walked into the dining room one day and left the door open behind him. A servant hurried to close it after him, only to be interrupted by a shout from Philip: "Leave it alone, man. He can do it himself. He's got hands." Charles was sent back to close the door for himself.

The children were never permitted to sit down to meals without first washing their hands and faces and tidying their hair. At Balmoral Anne once came in ravenous after an afternoon spent out of doors, and straightway seated herself at the table. "I'm starving," she said, child-like. But starving or not, she had to go up to the nursery to wash, change into a clean dress and brush her hair before she was permitted to eat. If either of the children omitted to thank anyone who had done some small service for them, the Queen, mindful of her own childhood lessons in politeness ("Royalty is no excuse for bad manners," her own mother impressed upon her) would be sure to prompt them, "Haven't you forgotten something?"

But the two children were not merely royal goody-goodies. They had the same healthy inclination for childhood mischief as any other children. At Windsor Castle one day, after investigating the servants' quarters, they came to a door they had not noticed before. It was, though they did not know it, an emergency exit for use in the event of fire. They tried the handle and found it unlocked. They went through the doorway on to a flat lead roof offering an exciting vista of weathered chimney-pots and stone battlements. For half-an-hour, like children in some dream-like conception of Walt Disney's, they played hide-and-seek among the tall chimney-pots, heedless of the sheer one-hundred foot drop from the battlements. Their mother, when she heard where they had been, was horrified. She gave immediate orders for all doors leading to the castle roof to be locked, with the keys hung where adults could reach them, but the children could not.

On holiday at Balmoral, they loved nothing better than to help in the kitchens, though their childish help was sometimes more of a hindrance. One day the head chef, Ronald Aubrey, to give them something to do, asked them to fetch him some eggs from the store-room. Unfortunately, the eggs, when he got them, were already well scrambled. The children had dropped them on the steps leading up from the store-room.

At Sandringham they invaded the estate fire station several times, clambering excitedly on to the bright red fire tender. Charles would take the wheel, peering with difficulty from under the big fireman's helmet which came down almost over his eyes, while Anne, sitting beside him, clanged the bell enthusiastically as they pretended they were on their way to a big blaze. Nor was this the least of their childish adventures. They helped with counting the pheasants and partridges their father had shot. At least, Charles did while Anne interrupted with teasing remarks. "Every time you start to count your hair stands on end," she teased her brother.

She found a large colored handkerchief fastened with a big knot and wanted to know what was in it. It contained the sandwiches and cake the driver of the game-truck had brought along for a midday snack and, of course, nothing would satisfy the small Princess but that she share it with him. There was another occasion, during the course of a shooting party, when both youngsters mysteriously disappeared at the end of a picnic lunch eaten in the royal waiting room at nearby Wolferton station. A prolonged succession of shrill toots from the engine of a goods train loading sugar-beets in the station siding finally betrayed their whereabouts. They had coaxed the driver into lifting them on to the footplate and letting them play at engine drivers.

Just as Princess Margaret could "charm the pearl out of an oyster," so could Charles and Anne. Charles, on one occasion, talked a policeman patrolling the royal grounds into parting with his helmet and truncheon so that he could play with them. Another time, he persuaded the stationmaster at Wolferton to surrender his flag and whistle, and delighted passengers aboard a London-bound train from Hunstanton saw the young prince give their driver the "right away" . . . three minutes late.

Anne, when she was a little older, returned to Buckingham Palace one day after an educational outing to see how the river police did their work, the proud owner of a shiny new police whistle. Of course, she had to try it out. A succession of shrill blasts on the whistle brought palace police out to search the gardens, while Anne, hidden in one of the shrubberies, lay doubled up with laughter.

Philip, by now, was teaching Anne as well as Charles to swim in the heated indoor pool at the rear of the palace. He was also teaching Charles to handle a car on the private roads around Balmoral while the boy was still too small for his feet to reach the pedals. He would sit on his father's lap, his small hands clutching the steering wheel as the car went along, while Philip operated the clutch and brake pedals with his feet.

Between Philip and his children there existed a warmly companionable parent-child relationship. He taught his son not only to drive a car, but to shoot, fish, sail and play polo, a game Charles learned by maneuvering with his father on bicycles while striking out at a tennis ball with a miniature polo mallet specially fashioned for him. He joined the children in their games of cowboys and Indians, enjoying himself as much as they did as they stalked one another through the shrubberies or charged across the velvety lawns with loud war-whoops; he played hide and seek with them amid the priceless paintings and antique furnishings of Windsor Castle.

Windsor, in those days, could not boast its own swimming pool (though there was one at Royal Lodge), and Philip, on a hot summer's day with the children begging for a swim, saw nothing untoward about changing into swimming trunks and taking them along for a quick dip in the fountain forming the centerpiece of the rose garden. Of an evening, there would be boisterous romps and pillow-fights between father and children in the royal nursery, and it was after one of these bedtime romps that Philip noticed the loss of the signet ring he always wears. It was found between the sheets the following morning by one of the maids as she made the children's beds.

Yet he could be a firm father, too, if the occasion required it. On a holiday cruise aboard the royal yacht, when Anne made something of a show of refusing to put on an extra sweater before going ashore, Philip did not hesitate to spank her.

IV

Life was by no means all play and no work for the royal children. Each morning, following his after-breakfast walk in the gardens, Prince Charles went along to the palace schoolroom to continue his lessons with the recently engaged governess, Miss Peebles . . . lessons in which Anne joined him as soon as her mother felt she was old enough.

For both children there were lessons in dancing, especially Highland dancing, and deportment each Wednesday afternoon under the tuition of Mme. Vacani and her niece, Betty. There were also piano lessons, with Charles showing all the signs of having inherited the family talent for music.

The Queen and her mother, though they play seldom these days, are both able pianists. Princess Margaret is both able and versatile, and at Christmas she will seat herself at the piano in the big main room of Sandringham House, with its Christmas tree and cheerful log fire, switching easily and confidently from carols and old-time favorites to pop songs and beat numbers while the others gather round her for a good old-fashioned family sing-song.

Charles, at this stage of his upbringing, showed all the evidence of possessing a considerable artistic flair, a real feeling for music and painting. He had the patient, serious, painstaking nature such things demand. When both children were given a painting-by-numbers outfit, it was Charles who stuck to it, patiently and perseveringly, until he had executed a very creditable landscape for one so young. Anne, though she started hers, never finished it.

At weekends there were riding lessons at Windsor, with the Queen, herself an expert and experienced horsewoman, usually going along to keep a motherly eye on things, and it was from their mother that the royal children picked up the pleasant practice of rewarding their ponies, Greensleeves and William, with a tasty bunch of well-scrubbed carrots.

Weekends at Windsor became especially exciting the summer the children learned that Sugar, one of the Queen's pet corgis, was expecting puppies. "May I have one, please?" Charles begged. "May I, Mummy?" echoed his small sister.

The first weekend after the puppies were born, and each weekend after that until they went to Balmoral in August for their customary summer stay, the Queen took her children along to the royal kennels to inspect their new pets. There were two puppies which it was decided to name Whisky and Sherry. That November, suitably house-trained, the two pups took up residence in the royal nursery, Sherry presenting a comical aspect at first with her rather floppy ears secured with sticking plaster to encourage them into a more sprightly and corgi-like appearance.

These quaint little fox-like dogs with their penchant for taking a nip at unsuspecting legs have been firm favorites with the Royal Family since the Queen was a small girl. Dookie was the first of the line, followed by Jane, Crackers and Carol, so called because they were born at Sandringham over Christmas, and Susan, a present to the Queen on her eighteenth birthday. Susan became the mother of Sugar and Honey, the Queen Mother's pet, and was now, with the birth of Sherry and Whisky, a grandmother . . . and still the Queen's constant companion, sitting beside her desk as she worked, lying under the dining table at mealtimes. Today, a small white headstone, paying tribute to her as the "beloved companion of the Queen," marks her grave at Sandringham.

But Susan's death, which caused the Queen considerable distress, was still some two years in the future when the antics of her grandchildren, Whisky and Sherry, first brought squeals of childish excitement to the palace nursery. Princess Anne, with all her mother's enthusiasm for dogs and horses, soon set about teaching Sherry all manner of little tricks. She taught her to roll over on the floor, to jump through a hoop, and, her crowning performance, to fetch a ball from the nursery toy cupboard at a word of command from her young mistress.

For royal parents and children alike, it was a happy and contented period of family life. For the Queen, the conflicting demands of monarchy and motherhood had been pleasantly reconciled. Her only concern was lest her children should grow up knowing little of the vast world beyond the palace railings. Philip, too, with an experience of ordinary life gained from his years at Cheam School and Gordonstoun, at Dartmouth and in the Navy, was anxious that his son, in particular, should grow up to learn about life from life itself. Most certainly he did not want to see Charles grow to manhood with only the petticoat influences of the royal nursery and the palace schoolroom as a background.

So was born the great royal experiment which was to lead, in turn, to Hill House, Cheam and Gordonstoun, with the heir to the throne taking his place with other boys in an ordinary schoolroom for the first time in history . . . joining them in their lessons and games, absorbing the give and take of ordinary life.

The experiment had simple enough beginnings . . . outings to museums and art galleries, to the Zoo, the Science Museum and the Tower of London, rides on buses, trips on the Underground. For the Queen, such childhood excursions had been marred by public curiosity and she did not want the same sort of thing happening again where her young son was concerned. To this end, an unusual royal plea came out of Buckingham Palace: "Her Majesty and the Duke of Edinburgh have decided that their son has reached a stage when he should take part in more grown-up educational pursuits with older children. In consequence, a certain amount of the Duke of Cornwall's instruction will take place outside his home. For example, he will attend classes and will visit museums and other places of interest. The Queen trusts that His Royal Highness will be able to enjoy this in the same way as other children can without the embarrassment of constant publicity."

CHAPTER NINE

SEPARATION

I

To the Queen, it must have seemed at one stage as though her entire reign was doomed to be the subject of rumor and gossip, criticism and speculation. Scarcely had the headlines concerning Princess Margaret and Peter Townsend begun to fade than new ones, hinting at a rift between the Queen and her husband, came surging off the presses of the *Baltimore Sun* in America to send a fresh spate of rumor and gossip winging its way round the world.

It was, of course, sheer nonsense. Neither the Queen nor her husband is the type of person to display their hearts on their sleeves. Neither is the sort to make public show of their feelings for the other. The nearest they have ever come to it is the encouraging, half-smiling glance, as though to say, "Buck up, darling," which Philip flashes the Queen when he senses that she is under some strain.

Yet never has he allowed her birthday or their wedding anniversary to pass without marking the occasion with a magnificent all-white bouquet of flowers. Never does he leave the palace, however short the trip he is making, without going along to the Queen's sitting room to say good-bye to her. He is equally prompt to seek her out on his return, and if he should be delayed for any reason he will have someone contact the palace so that the Queen does not worry. He knows she worries if he is late for any reason . . . just as he can look grim if he thinks she is being imposed upon. "You can't expect the Queen to suffer this glare," he rapped out in Sydney as he took in the big lights which had been installed to enable the newsreel cameras film the royal opening of parliament.

Both of them worry if ever the other is ill. When Philip went down with an attack of jaundice, the Queen was in and out of his room to see him every spare moment she could find. When the

Queen was taken ill on the way to Carlisle, Philip looked more anxious than royal aides had ever seen him. "Don't worry—I'll handle everything. You just get back home and get to bed," he sympathized.

The Queen and her husband have always been a loving and affectionate couple, and the world-wide rumors sparked off by the *Baltimore Sun* hurt and puzzled them more than they would perhaps have cared to admit.

The whole business had innocent enough beginnings . . . an invitation to Philip, as the husband of the Queen, to act as host at the 1956 Olympic Games in Melbourne. "It would have been much simpler to have flown out and back," Philip himself said subsequently. Had he done so, there would perhaps have been no rumor of a royal rift. But the invitation to go to Melbourne gave him the idea of visiting some of those isolated communities which could not normally hope to receive a royal visit . . . lonely outposts in the Atlantic, the Pacific and the Indian Ocean.

With the Geophysical Year looming ahead, he conceived also the daring idea of looking in on the Trans-Antarctic Expedition and visiting lonely survey teams in the Falkland Isles. This, then, was the focus and the framework of the four-month, 39,000-mile trip upon which rumor was to feed so avidly. At one time Philip even toyed with the idea of taking the royal yacht, *Britannia*, right into the Ross Sea. Had he done so, and perhaps been iced up for months on end, heaven alone knows what ill-founded rumor and biting gossip would have done to his marriage.

It was perhaps the most un-regal royal tour there has ever been or ever will be. "The idea is not so much for me to be seen as to see for myself," Philip laid down as a maxim, and when he first saw the proposed schedule for his visit to New Guinea he argued that there were too many displays, speeches and guards of honor. While he fully realized that a certain amount of what he knows as "pomping up" was unavoidable, he insisted that full-dress occasions should be kept to a minimum. Speeches likewise . . . and the speech he made in opening the Olympic Games was almost certainly his shortest on record, a mere seventeen words.

In the course of that long, round-the-world trip, ranging from the steam heat of Malaya to the biting winds of Antarctica, Philip certainly saw things for himself. He met and talked with planters and miners, geologists and whalers, ranchers and explorers . . . men doing a real man's job in the great open spaces and remote corners of the Commonwealth. At many of the places he visited there was no traditional red carpet, no official line-up, an absolute minimum of formality. He walked around in slacks and an open-neck shirt, and, later, as *Britannia* sailed southwards into the biting cold, in a duffle coat and beard.

He saw timber mills and cattle stations, the uranium miners of Rum Jungle, the men sweating it out on the great hydro-electric scheme of the Snowy Mountains. At Darwin, after a Government House reception, he changed from dinner suit to bush jacket, donned a waterproof cape as additional protection against the soaking rain squalls, and went crocodile hunting by searchlight far into the night.

In Canberra he dispensed with the services of a driver and took the wheel of his car himself, reportedly clocking seventy-five miles an hour. At Deception Island he insisted upon going ashore in thick fog. At Tristan da Cunha he personally took over the helm of the canvas-skinned longboat sent out to fetch him ashore, and grinned with everyone else when one of his entourage was warned to watch out that the point of his shooting stick did not go through the canvas bottom.

With the exception of two girl secretaries who went along to deal with official correspondence (and at one stage had to be requested to refrain from hula-hooping on the deck because of its unsettling effect on *Britannia's* crew), the trip was an essentially masculine affair. Philip was accompanied by his secretary, Michael Parker, his equerry, Squadron Leader Chinnery, and Dr. Wolf Breitling, an old friend of his Gordonstoun days.

Later he was joined by Sir Raymond Priestley, a one-time member of Scott's expedition and now president of the British Association for the Advancement of Science, and by Edward Seago, the artist. Seago's paintings of whales and icebergs were to provide a colorful record of a colorful royal tour. Philip liked some of them so much that they have since replaced portraits of Queen Victoria's children on the walls at Balmoral.

The trip was sometimes uncomfortable, occasionally dramatic. Michael Parker was underwater swimming in the Maldive Islands when he disturbed three sharks basking on the bottom. Angry at the intrusion, one of the sharks made directly for him. Parker tried to fight it off with a spear-gun with which he was equipped, but the action had no noticeable effect. Conceiving discretion to be the better part of valor, Parker swam quickly round an intervening rock and raced the shark to the beach, which he reached considerably out of breath.

In the mangrove swamps of the Gambia River, where Philip also went crocodile hunting, he and Parker both hammered shots into an extra-large specimen they came across. The croc appeared to be dead and Parker hopped nimbly over the side to secure it with a rope. It was hauled up and lashed to the side of the boat. Then it suddenly came to life again, threshing violently with its tail, doing considerable superficial damage to the boat before it was finally dispatched with a knife.

For Philip, it also turned out to be something of a sentimental journey. In Colombo he saw again the ramshackle little car he had once bought for 450 rupees—half down and half by instalments—when he was serving out there as a young naval officer. "I hope the brakes are better than when I had her," he remarked, grinning.

At Tristan da Cunha he ran across the tracks of his old naval command, *Magpie*, a model of which occupied a place of honor above the electric heater in his study aboard *Britannia*. *Magpie* had visited the island not long before and left its ensign behind as a souvenir.

At Mombasa he had a reunion with another old friend of Gordonstoun days, James Orr, a chief inspector in the Kenya police. When, towards the tail-end of the trip, events in Britain brought about the resignation of Michael Parker, Philip thought again of that meeting with James Orr and invited him to take Parker's place as his private secretary.

II

Whatever criticisms may have been leveled against the royal yacht on the grounds of expense—and there have been many over the years—this one trip surely justified them all. Without "Philip's Folly," as one critic once labeled *Britannia*, the trip could never have been made. The criticism was unfair because plans for the construction of a new royal yacht had already been announced before the Queen came to the throne.

Less harshly, *Britannia* has also been called a "floating palace" and this she is, drawing-room and ante-room forming a vast reception hall, close carpeted and gold curtained, in which as many as two hundred guests have been entertained at a single time. In the ship's dining room, another luxurious setting into which scarcely a nautical note intrudes, the ebony-edged, horseshoe-shaped table can accommodate up to sixty guests. It was originally planned to seat thirty-two, but Philip considered this insufficient and had removable wings added.

Britannia, in short, is as little like an ordinary yacht as Buckingham Palace is like an ordinary house. It is a miniature liner, 412 feet from stem to stern, with a speed of 22.75 knots, a cruising range of 2,400 miles and every conceivable aid to navigation. Part of the deck is strengthened for helicopter landings. There is a garage to house whatever royal car is taken along, and stowed away on board are a whole fleet of smaller craft ranging from the forty-foot royal barge to sailing dinghies and an inflatable rubber raft.

But on this round-the-world trip, with Philip in command, *Britannia* really came into her own. It was as though ship and crew alike felt, with Philip, that they were really doing the sort of task for which *Britannia* was created as they buffeted their way through the Roaring Forties to isolated outposts where a visitor of any sort, let alone a royal visitor, was a distinct rarity. Language took on a rich nautical flavor and Philip, himself, was on the bridge for long hours at a stretch, personally berthing the yacht at Port Moresby, Bathurst and Gibraltar.

On the long haul from Chatham Island to the Falkland Isles, thirteen days covering 3,800 miles of open sea, he passed part of the time painting. An amateur artist of some ability, he executed several portraits and landscapes in oils. He also took up the tricky art of bird photography. His first attempts, on his own admission, were poor, but before the trip was over he had photographed penguin rookeries, seal colonies and whale catching, the mighty wingspan of the albatross and the dive-bombing swoops of the skua gulls.

III

Christmas Day that year found the royal yacht 55 degrees south, 123 degrees west, 1,300 miles from the nearest land as it sailed southeast to the Antarctic. But the Queen's husband, though half a world away from his wife and family, was by no means out of touch with them. One of the bags which brought him his mail also contained a tape recording the Queen had made a week or so before. Listening to it, he heard again the welcome sound of his wife's voice as she wished him a merry Christmas and the cheerful chorus of "Hello, Papa" from Charles and Anne. Even the excited yapping of the royal corgis had been thoughtfully taped by the Queen to bring the atmosphere of family life right into the teak-walled cabin which served Philip as his study.

Philip, broadcasting from aboard *Britannia* as an introduction to the Queen's Christmas Day message, took advantage of the opportunity to include a personal message of his own. "I hope all of you at Sandringham are enjoying a very happy Christmas," he said, "and I hope you children are having a lot of fun."

They were . . . though, inevitably, everyone at Sandringham missed Philip that Christmas. Things seemed somehow a little less gay, and they were certainly a shade less boisterous, without his tall, tireless figure stalking around to organize the big family treasure hunt and other party games which are a feature of the royal Christmas.

Aboard the royal yacht it was seven o'clock in the morning as Philip concluded his broadcast with the touching quotation, "The Lord watch between me and thee when we are absent one from the other." At Sandringham it was already afternoon. The children had had their Christmas gifts, the Queen had been to morning service, Christmas lunch was over, and in her own broadcast which followed the Queen gave expression to her own sense of separation when she said, "Of all the voices we have heard this afternoon, none has given my children and myself greater joy than that of my husband."

She missed Philip a great deal during those long weeks of separation. During the week, of course, her working days were as busy and crowded as ever. But in the evening and during her weekends at Windsor, time seemed to hang a shade more heavily on her hands. From half-past seven on, with the children in bed, was perhaps the loneliest time of the day. To help pass the time, she went several times to the theater in company with such close personal friends as Lord Rupert and Lady Nevill. On other evenings, noticeably at weekends, she retired early to bed. When her husband was at home, the two of them would often stay up, chatting, reading and watching television together, until close to midnight. Now, lacking Philip's company, she often went to her room soon after ten o'clock.

But Philip, for all the vast distance that separated them, was still the thoughtful husband he had always been, and on November 20 the Queen walked into her sitting-room to find a surprise awaiting her—a huge box of flowers, a glorious all-white bouquet of roses, carnations, camellias and lilies-of-the-valley. Her husband, half a world away, had remembered their wedding anniversary.

And on Christmas Day, shortly after the Queen had ended her broadcast, the telephone rang at Sandringham House. It was a radio-telephone call from *Britannia*, somewhere at sea. Philip wanted to talk to his wife and children.

IV

The most adventurous part of his long voyage was still to come . . . and the coldest. As additional protection against the biting cold of Antarctica, those aboard *Britannia* were given permission to grow beards and Philip himself appeared on deck handsomely bearded as he had been in his naval days. In a less serious vein, everyone aboard was presented with a certificate, designed and printed jointly by Philip and Edward Seago, entitling them to "a red nose" for crossing the Antarctic Circle.

Philip transferred briefly to the survey ship *John Biscoe* to visit seven of the eleven isolated survey bases in the Falkland Isles. At Deception Island he found the walls of the mess adorned with lengths of necktie snipped from those who had visited there before them. Philip and others of his party obligingly surrendered their own neckties for similar mutilation, and Michael Parker, who was not wearing a necktie, had the tail of his tartan shirt yanked out and snipped off instead.

Philip invited the survey party aboard *Britannia* to see a film, *Seven Brides for Seven Brothers*, which was perhaps as unsettling for the survey team as the hula-hooping of the girl secretaries had been for the crew of the royal yacht. "I'm not sure whether it was a good idea," Philip confessed, whimsically, later on.

He allowed himself to be slung from the deck of the royal yacht to a whale-catcher in a wicker basket to watch a whale being stripped of its blubber, a process which saw the resulting stench infiltrating the yacht and clinging to it for days after the two vessels had parted company. "The liver of a whale weighs a ton," said Philip in a television talk he gave on his return to Britain. "It must be terrible to wake up with a liver like that."

Entitled *Round the World in Forty Minutes*, Philip's television appearance, in fact, stretched to five minutes short of a full hour. "It's going to be a bit of a rush," he joked at the beginning. "I'm over time, as usual," he grinned at the end.

Without the aid of script-writers, he succeeded in flavoring his talk with enough witticisms to rival Bob Hope. "I'm not surprised it was forbidden," he wisecracked, mentioning the unpleasant taste of the sea coconut which is said to be the original forbidden fruit of the Garden of Eden. "They went on for two days—you can imagine they had stiff necks afterwards," he said of the native dancers he had seen in New Guinea. "They have only recently met white men," he said of a tribe of savages, "and no doubt the surprise was mutual."

But such witticisms had their point and purpose in helping Philip to put across the message he has always been at such pains to drive home: "Remember that all these places and people belong to this great family of nations of ours. And I think it is worth remembering that we stick together not by force, but because we like each other."

V

Whenever possible during the course of that long trip, Philip would put in a radio-telephone call enabling him to speak for a few minutes at least with his wife and children. Such calls were usually timed to reach the Queen, at Sandringham or Windsor as occasion might require, around lunch-time on Sunday. She would take them in the privacy of her sitting-room, with Charles and Anne standing one on either side of her, both eager for their turn to have a few words with Papa.

But the vast distances involved made the timing of such calls not always predictable and there was an occasion when Philip came on the phone at Windsor while the Queen was attending morning service. The call was hastily transferred to the Queen Mother's home at Royal Lodge, where it was known that the Queen would look in on her way back from church.

There was much for wife and husband to talk about during the long weeks of separation, and the future education of their small son must have loomed large in their conversations. The big experiment which had started with visits to museums and art galleries and other places of like interest took another step forward at Sandringham that Christmas with the temporary engagement of a tutor for the young Prince.

The Queen knew that Charles missed his father's companionship while Philip was away and the engagement of a tutor was, in part, intended to offset this. It was, at the same time, another step forward in the gradual chain of upbringing which was to take him as imperceptibly as possible from the ivory-tower atmosphere of the palace schoolroom to the rugged boys' world of Gordonstoun.

Everyone in Britain, it must have seemed to the Queen, knew better than she and her husband how their young son should be raised. The trouble was that few of the voices agreed. Charles, it seemed, was a boy with forty million parents, each urging a different form of upbringing.

But the Queen and her husband knew what they were doing and where they were headed. At the end of January, Charles took his next big step forward when he donned a cinnamon-colored blazer and gray schoolboy trousers and drove in one of the more inconspicuous royal cars to Hill House, Knightsbridge, for his first day at school.

But though it was his first full day at school, it was by no means his first visit to Hill House. He had been there before, exercising in the tiny gymnasium, trotting round the running track, playing football with the other boys. But now, for the first time in history, the heir to the throne was taking his place with other boys in an ordinary schoolroom, and his father, still several thousand miles away, sailing from Ascension Island to Gambia and thence to Gibraltar, eagerly awaited news of how the experiment was working out.

But the royal news ticker-taping out of London around this time was not devoted solely to Charles and his schooldays. To the *Baltimore Sun* in America, early that February, went a message hinting that all was not well between the Queen and her husband. The *Sun* published the story. Other newspapers were quick to pick it up and reprint it, first in America and then elsewhere. Around the world rumors of a royal rift were accorded headlines in newspaper after newspaper.

An understandably terse statement from Buckingham Palace, "It is quite untrue that there is any rift between the Queen and the Duke of Edinburgh," brought hardly any respite, and rumor continued to gain ground steadily as Philip, his long trip over, stayed on in Gibraltar with the royal yacht instead of flying back to join the Queen in London.

Why, then, did Philip stay on in Gibraltar at this particular time?

The reasons were several and varied. For a start, Philip was himself unaware of the extraordinary extent to which rumors of a rift between him and his wife had gained currency. There were no daily newspapers delivered aboard *Britannia*. The only source of news was a crisp twice-daily bulletin prepared by the B.B.C. and radioed to the yacht by the Admiralty.

But he was aware that a state visit to Portugal was imminent for himself and the Queen. Had he flown back to London, to return to Portugal only a day or so later, it is conceivable that criticisms of royal extravagance would again have been heaped on his head. Philip is perhaps more sensitive to such criticisms than he would wish to admit.

Yet perhaps the most important reason of all lay in Philip's own nature . . . the nature of a true seafarer. He had just completed a long, eventful and, at times, arduous voyage with *Britannia*. After months of buffeting by wind and waves alike, the royal yacht arrived at Gibraltar in very obvious need of an extensive overhaul if it was to do justice to the Queen on her state visit to Portugal.

Such overhaul involved a considerable amount of extra and monotonous work for a crew who had already spent long weeks at sea, often in unpleasant extremes of hot and cold. For the crew of *Britannia* there could be no question of simply dropping everything and flying home to Britain to be with their wives and children, sweethearts and mothers. Philip was still at heart very much the naval officer he had once been at sea. In a very real sense, he felt himself to be a member of the ship's company and, for a man of his nature, it would have been tantamount to deserting the ship if he had flown home now while others were compelled to toil on.

Had Philip realized the repercussions that might follow, he might have reconsidered this decision to stick by *Britannia* and her crew until royal duty sent him to Portugal to rejoin the Queen. But he did not realize, and both he and the Queen were hurt and puzzled by the added gossip that resulted. Happy and contented in their private life together, though never unwilling to make sacrifices when necessary for the well-being of monarchy, it eluded their comprehension how rumor could be both so biting and wide of the mark.

VI

As is so often the case, rumor had gotten its facts twisted and its personalities confused, and, as an interlude in the spate of unkind gossip about the Queen and her husband, came the undeniable news that Michael Parker, Philip's personal secretary, was estranged from his wife. It was news, taken in conjunction with all the other headlines, which could have only one outcome and, for Philip, homecoming was marred by the necessity of bidding goodbye to an old and trusted friend.

The two men had known each other since war-time days when they were naval lieutenants together engaged on convoy escort duty out of Scapa Flow. In 1947, on the eve of his engagement to the Princess, Philip sent his old shipmate a characteristically laconic note in which he inquired what he was now doing, how he liked it and whether he would like to switch to being a royal equerry.

At the time he received that letter, Parker had already arranged to take a new job in Australia and was completing plans to return there from Scotland with his family. Meanwhile, he was marking time, working for a rope manufacturing concern. Now, suddenly, his plans were changed. He cancelled his return to Australia, accepted a post as equerry to the Princess, and, in due course, became private secretary to his old friend and naval colleague.

For nearly ten years Michael Parker was Philip's principal trouble-shooter. If Philip wanted more information for one of his pungent speeches, it was invariably Parker who got it for him. If he planned a visit, it was Parker who made the arrangements. Wherever Philip went, the imperturbable, happy-go-lucky figure of Mike Parker was seldom far away, smoothing out unexpected snags, taking some of the stiffness out of royal occasions with his breezy manner and ready wit.

Not even the solemn confines of Buckingham Palace could stem his gusto. Receiving a letter addressed inaccurately and with unintentional humor to Commander Parker, The Royal Seal, Buckingham Palace, he was sufficiently amused to pass the joke on. He went along to Philip's study and made a series of barking noises outside. But the voice which called "Come in" was not Philip's, but the Queen's.

Unabashed, Parker explained that he was fulfilling the function of a royal seal by barking in appropriate fashion. During the royal tour of Australia, he was with the Queen and Philip as they passed through the deserted show-rooms of a departmental store after attending a banquet on the top floor. Irrepressible as always, Parker could not resist the temptation to take over behind one of the counters. "And what can I get for Modom?" he inquired facetiously, sending the Queen into peals of laughter.

In all the years they were together Philip had only one fault to find with his former shipmate. Mike Parker, he explained grinning, was rather inclined to hog the radio-telephone when the two of them were aboard the royal yacht.

But now the laughter and the fun was ended, the long association over. Realizing that, for him, divorce was sooner or later inevitable, Parker tendered his resignation as Philip's secretary. When *Britannia* docked at Gibraltar he went ashore and flew back to London alone. Philip could easily have said good-bye to him in private. Characteristically, he accompanied him to the airport and accorded him a farewell public handshake for all the world to witness.

VII

At Buckingham Palace, as the long-awaited day when she would be reunited with her husband drew ever nearer, the Queen was visibly brighter and gayer than she had been for some time. She returned one afternoon from a busy round of engagements to find her dressmakers awaiting her. The new wardrobe she would be taking with her to Portugal was ready for final fittings.

The Queen seemed tired after all her other engagements and someone suggested that the fittings should wait until she had at least enjoyed her tea. But the Queen would not hear of any such delay. Not pausing for tea, she posed for the fittings. "After all, this is for Portugal," she observed, gaily . . . and saying that, she was surely thinking more of the coming reunion with her husband than contemplating the prospect of yet another state visit.

The laughing, carefree reunion between husband and wife which followed at Montijo airport in Portugal showed the rumors of a royal rift as the nonsense they were. Aboard the royal yacht, earlier, there had been betting as to whether or not Philip would retain his freshly-cultivated blond beard until he again saw the Queen. He didn't. He was again fresh-faced and clean-shaven as he bounded up the steps of the royal air-liner . . . to be greeted by the spectacle of the Queen and her staff laughing at him from behind an assorted array of false beards they had taken out to Portugal with them.

A final knock to the rumors was given twenty-four hours after the royal couple returned from Portugal when the Queen formally accorded her husband "the style and titular dignity of a prince," an official announcement which was also to end the long-

term confusion in the public mind as to whether Philip was or
was not a prince.

Philip himself made what was generally interpreted as an
oblique reference to the rumors at the welcome-home luncheon
which greeted his return to London. "The journey was completed,
against every expectation, to the day of our original estimate,"
he said, adding, "perhaps rather unfortunately as it turned out."

How easily things could have turned out otherwise was shown
by the fact that Philip's visit to Singapore, which was part of the
original planning, was cancelled at almost the last minute when
rioting broke out there. An alternative programme for Malaya
was conceived and planned posthaste while *Britannia* was actually
at sea.

Prince Philip, as he now undisputably was, went on to give
chapter and verse for his long absence. "It would have been much
simpler to have flown out and back," he said. "But if I had done
that I could not have visited several remote communities . . . and
I could not have inspected some of our bases in the Antarctic.

"I might have got home for Christmas, but I could not have
entertained nearly 1,400 people in the Queen's yacht at 26 lunches,
dinners and receptions and thereby strengthened the close links
between the Crown and the people of the Commonwealth.

"For most of my life to be away from home for four months
meant nothing at all. This time, for obvious reasons, it meant
much more to me. But I believe that there are some things for
which it is worthwhile making some personal sacrifice. I believe
that the British Commonwealth is one of those things and I, for
one, am prepared to sacrifice a good deal if, by doing so, I can
advance its well being by even a small degree."

CHAPTER TEN

A BUSY YEAR

I

A BLACK FORD Zephyr, no more conspicuous than any other family-type sedan about the streets of London, picked its way unobtrusively through the rest of the traffic crowding Whitechapel Road one March day in 1957. No crowds gathered to gape as it went by; no traffic policeman gave it special dispensation. Yet inside it, unnoticed and unrecognized, rode the Queen.

The car turned in at the entrance to the London Hospital. The Queen got out clutching a big bunch of freshly-cut flowers and went inside. She was visiting an old friend . . . Bobo MacDonald.

Margaret MacDonald was a girl of twenty when she first left her native Scotland to work for the Royal Family. The Queen was then a baby of no more than a few weeks old, and the affectionate name of Bobo, by which she still calls the now middle-aged Scotswoman, derives from those childhood games of hide and seek when princess and nursemaid would take it in turns to run off and hide round corners, springing out again with laughing cries of "Boo . . . boo."

Throughout the years since, wherever the Queen has been, the neat, unobtrusive figure of this small, auburn-haired, tremendously efficient Scotswoman has never been far away. Officially, she is the Queen's dresser. But, in practice, the role she fulfills goes far deeper than that. She smooths the wrinkles not only from the voluminous royal wardrobe, but to a very considerable extent from the Queen's path through life.

She is a unique combination of servant, personal friend and royal confidante, utterly loyal and wholly devoted to the Queen she serves. It is said that she has been offered a staggering five-figure sum to write her memoirs of her years at Buckingham Palace and turned it down with a scornful shake of her auburn

head. Certainly, if the offer was ever made, that is exactly what
Margaret MacDonald would have done.

Her wage is a modest one. But her position at Buckingham
Palace has long been unique. Alone among royal servants, she can
come and go by any door. A car is always at her disposal if she
wants to go anywhere. She dines not in one of the staff dining
rooms, but in the privacy of her own quarters. She is the proud
holder of the Royal Victorian Order, an honor which only the
reigning monarch can confer for personal services.

Ever since the Queen came to the throne, and long before that,
it has been Bobo who has called her each morning, who has run
her bath for her, tidied her dressing table with its gold-backed
hair brushes and gold-topped bottles. She does much of the
Queen's personal shopping for her, rinses her stockings if they
should need it, attends to a slip that needs shortening or a dress
that needs minor adjustment.

Wherever the Queen goes, there you will find Bobo MacDonald
with her zip-fastened bag containing spare stockings in case
those the Queen is wearing should run, spare shoes in case a
heel should be wrenched, spare white gloves in the event that
those on the royal hands become soiled from too much hand-
shaking.

She goes with the Queen to Balmoral in summer, to Sandringham at Christmas. It was the devoted Bobo who helped the
Queen into her wedding dress and into that other dress on
Coronation Day. She was close at hand, helpful and anxious,
when the royal babies were born. Even at weekends when she is
officially off duty, she frequently spends much of her time ensuring
that the Queen's clothes are ready and immaculate for the following
week's engagements. She has been with her royal mistress on
every major tour and state visit she has ever undertaken . . . to
France and Portugal, Sweden and Denmark, Australia and New
Zealand, Canada and the United States.

The Queen's accession to the throne did nothing to alter the
warm, human relationship that had sprung up between them. At
first, the neat little Scotswoman was careful to address her
mistress by her new title of "Your Majesty." In public she still
does so. But in private they have long since lapsed back into
calling each other Bobo and Lilibet, as they have always done.

Whatever the Queen wants, Bobo does her best to ensure that
it is instantly available . . . a cup of her favorite China tea to revive

her, barley sugar to suck if she has "butterflies in the tummy," a hot water bottle if the nights are cold.

On her first visit to Canada, while still a Princess, the Queen was invited to go square dancing. The difficulty was that there were no suitably informal clothes in the royal wardrobe. Undeterred, Bobo slipped out to a nearby store and was soon back with a suitable skirt and blouse.

Earlier still, in 1947, when the then Princess sailed for South Africa with her parents with a photograph of a young naval lieutenant named Philip beside her bedside in her cabin, the devoted Bobo was ill when the time came for departure. With loyal Scottish obstinacy she insisted upon being carried aboard ship on a stretcher rather than see her beloved Lilibet go without her.

Now ten years later, in 1957, she was ill again, having succumbed to a virus infection following the state visit to Portugal. For three weeks she was in hospital with one of the Queen's own physicians looking after her, and the Queen herself calling with fruit and flowers to speed her recovery.

When Bobo finally came out of hospital again there was only ten days left before the state visit to Paris. In vain did the Queen protest that she was not yet well enough to travel to Paris, that the strain would prove too much for her. But Bobo MacDonald is an obstinate and determined Scotswoman who, like her royal mistress, puts duty ahead of everything else. She listened patiently to the royal protests, turned on her heel and got on with the packing.

II

It was April in Paris. The chestnuts were in blossom and in the Tuilleries Gardens the plane trees and elms shimmered in a fresh green haze. But for the Queen and Prince Philip there was no time to sit and relax at a table under the trees. For them, Paris offered only the usual unremitting timetable of a state visit. In three days the Queen spent 28 hours at luncheons, banquets and other official functions, and a further eleven hours getting from one place to the other. And for nearly seven hours of that time she was under the close scrutiny of televiewers in six countries, with a television camera even pacing the royal car during the state drive along the Champs Elysées.

France accorded the Queen a great welcome. The reception

room at the airport was decorated with Gobelins tapestries, Aubusson carpets and paintings from the national collection. She was given a satin-draped Louis XVI bed in a bedroom with walls of green damask and a ceiling of white and gold. On her dressing table, a gift for the Queen, stood the largest bottle of perfume ever produced, a half-quart of specially-blended jasmine fragrance in a tall, elegant container of Baccarat glass, while beside the bed someone had thoughtfully placed a photograph of the royal children by a young photographer named Armstrong-Jones.

The visit differed only in essentials from the pattern of all such state visits. The Queen laid a wreath on the tomb of the Unknown Soldier, planted a tree, went to the opera, made a speech in her fluent French at a state banquet in the Elysée Palace. An estimated 150,000 eager Parisians struggled to glimpse her as she drove to the opera, climbing lamp-posts, scaling roofs, jumping on cars. One unfortunate car owner returned to find it had collapsed completely under the combined weight of the twenty people who had climbed onto it.

Prince Philip visited the French nuclear research establishment, and was decorated with the Grand Sash of the Legion of Honor. "It is for you, Madame, to bestow the accolade," said President Coty, chuckling. Laughingly, the Queen embraced her husband, according him the traditional kiss on each cheek. She drove to Versailles, where the 18th century Opera House was transformed into life for the first time in nearly 150 years. But one unscheduled item crept into the itinerary. Hearing that she was passing the famed Marcel Boussac stud, the Queen, never able to resist the lure of horses, had her car brought to a brief halt to look at some of the horses. The result was to make her a few minutes late for her scheduled meeting with General Norstadt.

"I see Your Majesty has brought Queen's weather with you from England," an uninhibited American, Major Ann Duffy, remarked when the Queen visited a British sports club in Paris. "I am told you always have it."

"Sometimes I'm not so lucky," the Queen replied, smilingly, doubtless recalling torrential downpours in which she had been caught in Colombo and elsewhere.

During the course of her visit she was presented with a gold-based inkwell, a Renault car, a box of French dolls for Anne and a working model of the Paris Metro for Charles. "I think it will amuse his father very much," she said.

But the gift that delighted her most was a gold and platinum watch. Claimed to be the smallest watch in the world, its face measuring barely three-sixteenths of an inch across, it was intended as a replacement for one she had been given as a small girl and had worn almost continuously for seventeen years until she lost it while out walking at Sandringham.

She had been on her way back to Sandringham House with her dogs when she came to a spot where farmworkers were busy threshing corn. Where there is corn there are inevitably rats and the Queen unleashed her dogs and passed them over the wire-netting fence for a brief bout of catch-as-catch-can with the fleeing rodents. After half-an-hour of this she collected the dogs again and went on her way. But within a few minutes she was back again, rather upset, explaining that she had lost her watch.

"It must have slipped off when I removed my glove," she said.

Aided by the farmworkers, she searched among the chaff and straw until dusk fell. In the days that followed, police, Boy Scouts, estate workers and loyal members of the public from far and near joined in the search. Royal Engineers combed the area with mine detectors. But the Queen's watch was never recovered. Now the French, with a touch of true Gallic inspiration, had replaced it. "One of the loveliest gifts I have ever had," the Queen exclaimed delightedly.

The climax of the royal visit, surpassing all that had gone before and everything that was to come after, was an evening voyage along the Seine when the Queen sat in a glass-walled cabin, high in the stern of a blue and gold river boat, to float through five waterborne miles of floodlit tableaux depicting the beauty, the history and the glory of France. More than sixteen hundred people had worked painstakingly for months past to create these ninety minutes of April-in-Paris magic. Minuets and musketeers, flower sellers and folk dancers, the jesters and jugglers of medieval France, the triumphs of Napoleon . . . all were included in a series of striking tableaux covering hundreds of yards of quayside and river bank, while jets from fire hoses created silvery archways across the Seine and two thousand rockets burst together in the night sky.

But if Paris surprised the Queen with those ninety minutes of waterfront pageantry, the Queen, in turn, made Paris gasp as she boarded the river boat in a Hartnell creation of silver lace over silver tissue embroidered with countless brilliants. Pencil slim, with a low, square neckline, worn with an embroidered stole broadly banded with white fox fur, it was the first truly straight dress the Queen had ever worn. It made her seem, at one and the same time, chic and slender, ravishing and regal, and the Churchillian V-sign she gave to the Paris crowds from her vantage point in the stern of the river boat was perhaps as much a reflection of her joy at this royal fashion revolution as anything else.

Until that evening, the Queen had always been cautious in her selection of clothes, clinging to tradition, declining to experiment. It was not altogether her fault. Many factors must be taken into account in her choice of clothes. To an ordinary girl, a frivolous wind is no more than an annoying or amusing incident, according to her nature.

With the Queen, it becomes headline news, and her dresses must always be designed so that she walks, stands and sits in regal dignity. Hats must be head-hugging or fitted with wire grips to hold them firmly in place in the highest wind. Colors must be easily visible from a distance. There must be no frills or furbelows to catch on snags or projections as she inspects a factory or tours a housing estate.

For a royal tour or state visit the problems are yet more complicated. Her fabulous state gowns, designed afresh for each fresh visit, must never seem too close an echo of anything she has worn before. The time of year and even the vagaries of climate must be taken into account when selecting designs and colors, while colors must never clash with the silken sash of whatever Order the Queen may have to wear on a particular occasion.

To all this must be added the Queen's own nature, her sense of reserve, a dislike of appearing too sophisticated or even slightly exotic. "I couldn't possibly wear that; I'm not a film star," she has said more than once, and when a new hat she had ordered for Ascot arrived with a dashing, dipping brim, she gave immediate instructions for it to be straightened.

It was fashion designer Norman Hartnell who was finally to tempt her into experiment. Among the designs he took along for her approval prior to that state visit to Paris was one for a straight dress in silver lace.

"I was thrilled when she chose it," he said, "and worried as to whether she would really like it when she tried it on. But after the first fitting I knew it was a success."

The French, shunning this British tendency to understatement, went further. They described the new dress as "magnificent" and "ravishing" . . . with the solitary exception of one French designer who enviously insisted that the Queen wore it only because she realized that she would have difficulty negotiating the river boat's narrow gangway in a traditional crinoline.

III

That year of 1957 was a busy and crowded one for the Queen . . . February in Portugal, April in Paris, with visits to Denmark, Canada and the United States still to come. The royal fashion designers, Norman Hartnell and Hardy Amies, worked overtime. The task of creating the Queen's wardrobe for a royal tour or state visit begins far ahead of the actual trip. There are at least six months, and possibly twelve, still to go when the designers sit down at their drawing boards to create the preliminary sketches. Each sketch is a miniature portrait of the Queen showing her exactly how she can expect to look in the finished dress and goes to Buckingham Palace for her approval with samples of the actual materials to be employed. Sometimes the Queen suggests changes; sometimes she asks for a particular color. She so liked the delicate coloring of an Indian sari she had been given that she asked for one of the dresses for Paris to be made in the same shade. The result was the striking gown in kingfisher blue which she wore to the banquet at the Louvre, where elegantly-gowned women so far forgot themselves as to clamber on to priceless Greek statues in their desire to see her.

Designs approved, next comes the task of translating sketches into reality. The state gown the Queen wore for the banquet at the Elysée Palace was more than two months in the making, with nimble-fingered girls working in teams to embroider the intricately lovely design of mother-of-pearl marguerites, cornflowers with gilt stamens, Flanders poppies with gold petals, and pearl and gold buttercups against a background of waving wheat. For a major tour, fittings alone can take up thirty afternoons of the Queen's time as she stands patiently in her white-walled dressing room while the fitters maneuver around her, scattering their pins over the beige carpet, collecting them up again afterwards with the aid of a horseshoe-shaped magnet.

Royal fashions girdle the world with the speed of a bush fire. Princess Marina's pill-box hats, Princess Margaret's ear-of-wheat brooch, Prince Philip's jet-plane cuff-links, Prince Charles's sailor suit, Princess Anne's white muff . . . each, in turn, was copied by the thousand. The famous picture of a happy Queen riding to open Parliament drew attention not only to her laughing face, but also to her earrings. The outcome was a boom in drop earrings on both sides of the Atlantic. Like a woman, the Queen has no desire to be confronted by scores of ready-to-wear copies of her own dress as she walks down the gangway of the royal yacht or descends the steps from the royal aircraft. So sketches for new dresses are kept always in a locked safe by their designers; finished gowns are locked in a special wardrobe pending delivery to Buckingham Palace. For yet greater security, a code system is employed in connection with royal tours so that details of no royal dress are published before the Queen is actually wearing it.

This can occasionally lead to confusion, as when the Queen, attending a banquet at the White House in Washington, was described as wearing the same Hartnell-designed dress in pale green satin garlanded with maple leaves which she had already worn in Canada. In fact, for the White House banquet she wore a dress of gray-blue satin with gold-embroidered autumn leaves which had been designed for her by Hardy Amies.

Washington, indeed, suffered more than its share of confusion in the matter of the Queen's dresses, and driving through the American capital, listening to the car radio, the Queen could not suppress an understandable smile of feminine amusement as she heard the commentator describe the *red* outfit she was supposedly wearing. As it happened, she had had a very feminine change of heart at the last moment and decided to wear green.

The Queen's state gowns, with their lavish jewelled embroidery, defy any attempt at copying. But the technique of copying her less elaborate dresses has been brought to something almost approaching a fine art. Photographs of the Queen in the latest creation are rushed to the copyists and magnifying glasses whipped out to study the essential details. Work continues throughout the night in this cut-throat, competitive world of feminine fashion and in days, sometimes in hours, the first cheap, ready-to-wear copies are being shown to the buyers for the big stores.

Copies of a black and white dress the Queen wore in Paris were selling in London by the following weekend. Copies of an olive-green outfit she wore once in Canada were selling from coast to coast in little more than a week. But the real prize for enterprise—

and sheer downright nerve!—must go surely to the American manufacturer who marketed what were claimed to be copies of the Queen's nightdress, a froth of white satin and misty blue lace retailing at $100.

IV

"You can't visit a friend and ignore a daughter," Canadians rumbled when they learned that the Queen was to visit the United States that autumn of 1957. So arrangements were hastily changed. The Queen would go first to Canada, where she would open Parliament, and then on to the United States . . . as Queen of Canada. Protocol had been observed, and the fourth overseas trip of that busy, bustling year was entered in the Queen's diary with its separate columns for morning, afternoon and evening engagements.

A royal tour is months on the drawing board. Even a short, three or four-day state visit, such as those to Portugal, France and Denmark, can be a full year in the planning from the time the invitation is first issued and accepted. Publicly, the Queen never refuses an invitation to pay a state visit. To avoid the necessity for her ever having to do so, Buckingham Palace is always sounded out privately before an official invitation is issued.

The Queen consults the prime minister, for royal visits always reflect the diplomatic atmosphere, as was seen when Princess Margaret's visit to Paris was cancelled after France had obstinately blocked Britain's entry in the Common Market. She consults her private secretary, Sir Michael Adeane, as to the earliest possible date on which the invitation, if accepted, can be slotted into her already crowded schedule. And doubtless she also talks things over with Philip.

Once the invitation has been accepted and entered in the Queen's diary of engagements, the work of planning starts in earnest, involving people all the way down from the prime minister and foreign secretary to the chauffeurs who will drive the royal cars and the air hostesses who will serve the Queen's meals on the royal aircraft. There must be arrangements not only to rush government papers to the Queen wherever she may be, but also to cope with such mundane problems as the royal laundry and dry-cleaning.

A party of royal officials flies out to travel the proposed route ahead of the Queen, checking every detail from security and overnight accommodation down to such homely points as ensuring that there will be some orangeade for the Queen to drink|if she wants it, and that extra-long beds will be available to accommodate Prince Philip's seventy-three inch frame. One bed suggested for Philip on that 1957 visit to the United States was hailed with immediate approval . . . the eight-footer once used by Abraham Lincoln.

The Queen is consulted at each step of the way. She goes over the proposed itinerary with the aid of maps so large they sometimes overlap the whole of her desk-top and are more conveniently scanned when spread out on the floor carpet.

The Queen is a stickler for detail. Ahead of her visit to Washington, she was quick to spot that it would be after dark when her aircraft landed there. This, she knew, would disappoint thousands of Americans hoping to see her arrive. "Can't we change things so that we arrive in daylight?" she suggested. The change was made.

In Ottawa that autumn, the Queen had her first experience of an American-style press reception. Would the Queen-Mother go to Canada as Governor-General? she was asked, among other things. "Oh, no," she smiled. "We couldn't possibly spare her." She underwent her first ordeal by television, speaking in both English and fluent French. Returning to Britain, she followed up that Canadian telecast by permitting television cameras to invade Sandringham House for her traditional Christmas Day broadcast.

She emerged so triumphant from the ordeal that few who saw her could have guessed that her Christmas lunch was quite spoilt for her by the strung-up state of her nerves, and that she was almost grateful that pressure of time forced her to leave the lunch-table early to change her dress, surrender herself to the attentions of a television make-up expert and rehearse her speech in advance of the actual transmission with the aid of a teleprompter.

In Canada and America, as always, the Queen's own cameras were never far from her side. In Ottawa she was so captivated by the fiery blaze of maple trees donning their autumn garb in the gardens of Government House that she went back for her camera and thereby made herself a few minutes late for a tree-planting ceremony. In New York she filmed the skyscraper skyline, the buzzing helicopters overhead and the criss-crossing jets of the fire floats as she crossed from Staten Island to the Battery on a U.S. Army ferry.

That U.S.-Canadian tour was as crowded and hectic as royal

tours always are. There was one day in which the Queen carried out no fewer than fourteen engagements between the time her aircraft touched down at Patrick Henry Airport at 1:30 P.M. and her arrival at the Williamsburg Inn that evening with only one hour and twenty minutes in which to rest and change before dinner. Yet she could still appear at the dinner looking serene and radiant in a jewel-encrusted dress which so outshone even the lavish gowns worn that evening by the first families of Virginia that one U.S. columnist was moved to comment that it was "as if Marilyn Monroe walked through a roomful of adolescent girls in gym clothes." One wealthy American matron surveying the Queen's jewelled dress, diamond tiara, necklace and earrings, murmured despairingly, "She makes me feel as if my junk comes from a five-and-ten cent store."

The Queen's personal jewel collection is undoubtedly one of the most fabulous in the world. The tiaras alone are worth a queen's ransom. She has a tiara of interlocked diamonds into which either emeralds or pearls can be looped at will which she inherited from Queen Mary, a diamond tiara with matching necklace which was a wedding present from the Nizam of Hyderabad, a diamond and pearl tiara handed down from Queen Victoria, the elegant Russian fringe tiara which she sometimes wears reversed about the throat as a jewelled collar, and several more. She has a pearl and diamond necklace also handed down from Queen Victoria, a necklace of diamonds and rubies which was a wedding present from her parents, a magnificent necklace of fifteen large, perfect diamonds with a matching bracelet of seven more which was a twenty-first birthday gift from South Africa, a three-strand pearl necklace given her in childhood by her grandfather, King George V. She has a necklace of rubies she was sent from Burma, aquamarines and diamonds from Brazil, emeralds and diamonds from British Columbia. She has a flame lily brooch of 330 diamonds which was a gift from the children of Southern Rhodesia, a diamond fern leaf brooch she was given in New Zealand, a wattle brooch of rare yellow diamonds with matching blue-white stones forming the foliage which she received in Australia, and a magnificent brooch made from the huge pink diamond which she was sent from Tanganyika by the late Dr. John Williamson. It took five years of searching to find the right matching pink diamonds to form a setting for this single superb gift.

Desirous of never appearing ostentatious, the Queen normally wears a minimum of jewellery . . . a pearl necklace and matching earrings for her workaday role around the palace, a brooch on her coat when she goes out. Only when the occasion calls for it will she wear more and even then it is sometimes only with difficulty that she can be persuaded to do so. "How can you dance naturally with a tiara perched on your head?" she lamented once as she left the dance-floor anxiously clutching her tiara after taking part in a *palais glide*.

It falls to the loyal Bobo to ensure that her royal mistress presents a truly regal picture on such occasions. "But you must wear them, Lilibet," she was once heard to insist in the matter of jewellery. "It is expected of you."

So much is expected of the Queen in so many different directions. In America, she arrived back at the White House at half-past six one evening following a hectic press reception. She had planned to rest. Instead of which she found a stack of dispatch boxes demanding her attention. She worked away at them for nearly an hour before making a lightning change for dinner. And earlier that day, despite all else she had to do, she had still found time to make a transatlantic telephone call to Buckingham Palace to talk to Princess Anne.

Only once during that whole trip did the Queen show any signs of weariness. Arriving at the White House after visiting Arlington National Cemetery, she sank thankfully into a chair, kicked off her shoes to ease her aching feet and asked for a cup of tea. A near-crisis developed behind the scenes when it was discovered that the cannister containing the Queen's favorite blend of tea had somehow gone astray. Tea-bags were hastily substituted and if the resulting brew was weaker than the Queen normally likes it was none the less welcome.

American security men did their job with characteristic thoroughness. At the White House they were so thorough that a member of the Queen's personal staff was sent back to get his official pass. And that was only to go out! In New York, suspicious of a hold-all which had been hurriedly fastened with string in an emergency when the zipp-fastening came adrift, a conscientious security man insisted on going through the contents in case a bomb had been planted among the royal cameras.

New York quite overwhelmed the Queen with its fire-boat and ticker-tape welcome. "Fabulous," was the word she used to describe it. And later, as she stood at the window of her suite overlooking the city, she remarked, "I could stand here all day."

But time did not permit. In the course of that one crowded day she rode on the Staten Island ferry, drove down Broadway in a bubble-topped limousine under the traditional shower of ticker-tape, attended a civic lunch, addressed the United Nations, soared to the top of the Empire State Building, went to a dinner at the Waldorf Astoria and on to the Commonwealth Ball, where she remained until nearly one o'clock in the morning—half-an-hour later than the time originally scheduled for her departure. And at the end of it all, in the early hours of the morning, she climbed aboard her aircraft at Idlewild Airport looking as fresh and radiant as if the day was only then starting.

CHAPTER ELEVEN

PRINCE OF WALES

I

IT WAS THE Queen's official birthday, the day for Trooping the Color, that traditional ceremony when the Queen, clad in a fitting, feminine version of the scarlet uniform of the Guards, takes the salute at a military march-past on Horse Guards Parade before riding side-saddle back to Buckingham Palace at the head of her troops. As on Coronation Day, her "Queen's weather," which legend insists follows wherever she goes, had again deserted her. It was a June day in 1958, but instead of warm summer sunshine there was only pelting rain. It splattered down on the wooden spectator stands erected for the occasion on Horse Guards Parade, whipped the raincoats and plastic hoods of those who braved the weather to gather along the Mall and in front of the palace.

The rain was still falling in a steady downpour with only an hour to go before the Queen was due to leave for the parade ground. Her aides favored a postponement of the traditional ceremony to a day when the weather might be more favorable. But the Queen, looking out of a window at the rain-washed court-yard and dripping trees, would hear no talk of postponement.

"If those people out there can stand the rain," she said, "then so can I. I won't disappoint them."

Nor did she. Despite the fact that her health had not been good of late, she braved a downpour of almost monsoon proportions to play her traditional role in Trooping the Color . . . just as on another day of pelting rain she insisted upon taking the salute at a march-past in Hyde Park.

Early in her reign, soon after her accession, that authoritative journal, *The Lancet*, had warned the Queen against the dangers of doing too much. "Of late," it stated, "the medical profession has become more and more aware of the physical price paid by those subjected to too frequent or continuous strain of the kind nowadays imposed on royalty. As doctors we should have special reason to welcome an assurance that by deliberate decisions taken in advance Her Majesty's health and vitality will be protected from her hereditary sense of duty."

Yet the Queen is not an easy person to protect from "her hereditary sense of duty." Where royal duty is concerned, she can be gently obstinate. Many times over her years of monarchy she has insisted on sticking to the prescribed schedule when it would perhaps have been wiser, and certainly pleasanter, not to have done so.

She adhered to her schedule during her state visit to Sweden, despite a North Sea crossing so rough that china and phonograph records were broken aboard the royal yacht, members of the royal staff were pitched from their bunks, and her own dressing table was wrenched free of its bulkhead hooks to hurtle across the cabin.

She clung to her schedule in Jersey, despite another bad sea trip and drizzling rain . . . and went on to Sark in steadily worsening conditions. Cancellation of the visit to Sark was suggested, but the Queen would not have it, any more than she would consider postponing Trooping the Color. With the royal barge pitching and rolling in heavy seas, she succeeded in boarding it, whitefaced and tense, at her fifth attempt and so went ashore to fulfill her engagements on Sark.

Since her return from Canada and the United States the previous October, the Queen had been plagued by recurring colds, a form of ill health to which she had long seemed particularly susceptible. As a child, she more than once missed her weekly meeting of the Girl Guides because she was suffering from a cold, and later there was an occasion when she had to forego a visit to the Royal Command Performance with her parents for the same reason. Over the years of monarchy her susceptibility had increased to a degree where head colds so devastated her at times as to force her to take to her bed with a flushed face, streaming eyes and erratic temperature.

In December she had been forced to cancel a weekend she planned to spend with Lord and Lady Brabourn. A few weeks later, during her customary Christmas stay at Sandringham, she was again confined to her room with a feverish chill. In March she visited the Netherlands and in April, after paying a visit to the Staff College at Camberley, she was again taken ill at Windsor with a heavy cold.

A visit by the prime minster and his wife had to be cancelled, as did arrangements for attending the Ascot horse show and a small dinner party planned for the evening. She had arranged to go to Sandringham with her husband, but Philip had to make the trip alone while the Queen stayed indoors on medical advice. She was due to attend that year's Cup Final between Manchester City and Bolton, but on the day of the big game she was still having her meals in her private apartment and still being attended by her physician.

By mid-May she had recovered sufficiently to attend the Windsor horse show, though while there she was observed to resort frequently to the use of a pink handkerchief. In June, defying the weather, she insisted on playing her full part in Trooping the Color, and in July, during a tour of Scotland and the Northeast, she was again taken ill.

At Largs she showed signs of developing another cold and that night as the royal train sped south towards Carlisle, she retired to bed early. But when the faithful Bobo MacDonald went to call her at eight o'clock the following morning she was undeniably worse . . . so much so that it was clearly impossible for her to carry on with her tour. Her voice was hoarse, her eyes swollen and inflamed, and her temperature slightly above the hundred degree mark. Lord Evans was telephoned and advised the Queen's immediate return to Buckingham Palace for treatment and rest.

"You get home and get to bed. I'll handle things in Carlisle," a worried-looking Prince Philip assured her.

And for once the Queen was in no condition to insist upon fulfilling her royal duty. She was far too ill. So it was left to her husband to carry out the various engagements arranged for Carlisle, flying back later in a Heron of the Queen's Flight, while the royal train continued south with the Queen. The train's cooling system picked that particular time to go out of action, which did nothing to lessen the Queen's discomfort.

Despite her condition, she insisted upon getting up later and sat in the royal coach alternately reading and watching the scenery flashing past. She picked at a light lunch of fresh salmon and salad and drank frequent glasses of orange juice to ease her thirst. Arriving at Euston, she walked from the train as usual, though her face was flushed under her make-up. She even managed to chat briefly with the top-hatted stationmaster before going on to Buckingham Palace.

But once at the palace she went straight to bed. She was visited by a trio of royal physicians, Lord Evans, Sir John Weir and Mr. J. Cecil Hogg, the ear, nose and throat specialist who had operated on her cousin, Prince William of Gloucester, not long before. Her immediate engagements were cancelled and for the whole of the week she remained in bed, her condition improving, but her temperature sticking obstinately above normal.

One or other of the royal physicians called daily to see her and portable equipment was brought from hospital for the purpose of an X-ray examination. Outside the palace, as the Queen underwent the X-ray examination, the annual crop of debutantes lined up in cars and taxis in readiness to enter the lofty crimson and gold ballroom where they were received in the Queen's unavoidable absence by Prince Philip and the Queen Mother.

Throughout most of this period of illness the Queen still contrived to carry on with the essential business of monarchy. The inevitable leather-bound dispatch boxes, often arriving several times daily, were taken in to her by the devoted Bobo. Instructions to her private secretaries, as soon as her voice was sufficiently restored, were given over her bedside telephone. As soon as her temperature reverted to normal, she was up and about again, her face paler than usual as she sat at her desk coping with state papers and official correspondence. But she retired to her bedroom early each evening and her dinner was taken in to her on a tray. Whenever opportunity served, Philip would go in to have dinner with her, while Anne came down from the nursery morning and evening as usual to be with her mother.

When she was not working, the Queen passed her time watching television, up-dating the royal stud records and tackling crosswords, one of her favorite forms of relaxation. Normally accustomed to an active life, more than anything she missed her customary exercise and once her health had sufficiently improved she resorted to her former practice of taking a daily walk in the palace gardens. Despite her improvement, however, the basic sinus condition still continued, leaving the physicians no option but to administer a local anesthetic and carry out an operation to irrigate the affected sinuses.

Again the Queen was confined to bed. On the advice of her physicians she cancelled all further engagements to the end of the month, including a tour of Wales and a visit to the Commonwealth Games which were being held that year in Cardiff. Prince Philip went to Cardiff on his own. But he had a big surprise in store to assuage Welsh disappointment.

Up and about once more after her operation, the Queen went along to a seldom-used room at the end of the royal corridor. Here, engineers had installed equipment to enable her to record a speech to be heard at the closing of the Commonwealth Games . . . a speech which was to remain a close-kept royal secret until Philip played the recording in Cardiff.

The Queen, he said by way of introduction, was "determined to have some part in this great occasion." Then followed the surprise recording of the Queen's voice, back to normal again after her lengthy period of ill health.

"By a cruel stroke of fate," said the Queen, "I have been prevented from visiting North and South Wales and seeing something of the British Empire and Commonwealth Games. I regret particularly not being with you in Cardiff today for the closing ceremonies of this great meeting of Commonwealth athletes.

"The British Empire and Commonwealth Games in the capital, together with all the activities of the Festival of Wales, have made this a memorable year for the Principality. I have therefore decided to mark it further by an act which will, I hope, give as much pleasure to all Welshmen as it does to me.

"I intend to create my son, Charles, Prince of Wales today."

Such a burst of tumultuous Welsh applause greeted this unexpected and dramatic announcement that it quite drowned the sound of the Queen's voice and the recording had to be switched off for a full half-minute while the roar died down. Then, in the silence which followed, the Queen was heard to say: "When he is grown up I will present him to you at Caernarvon."

II

The newly-created, nine-year-old Prince of Wales heard his mother's surprise announcement over the radio in his headmaster's sitting room at Cheam School. A message from the huge palace he called home had suggested that he should be listening in.

It was the previous September when Charles first went to Cheam, his father's old school. Before that, to prepare him for the cold-water shock of boarding school life, to accustom him to mixing with other boys, he had passed two terms as a commuter at Hill House, a pre-preparatory school in Knightsbridge.

Until then, the only other youngsters with whom he had mixed had been the small sons of royal relatives like Lord and Lady Brabourne, and of close personal friends of the Royal Family such as Lord and Lady Rupert Nevill. There had, of course, been no opportunity at all of mixing and mingling with such middle-class youngsters as the sons of doctors and diplomats, journalists and civil servants, barristers and army officers, such as he was to encounter at Hill House. By ordinary, everyday standards, his life had been a cloistered one, a nursery world hemmed in by the petticoat influence of nanny and governess, mother and sister, "Granny" and "Aunt Margo." The only male on whom to model himself was his father, and he was all too often away about his royal duties.

Of all this, his father had been only too well aware. More than anything else, Philip wanted to see his son reared in his own breezy, confident image. He, himself, had gone to a kindergarten school in Paris, to Cheam and then to Gordonstoun, and much of the man he was, he knew, was due to this boyhood background. Now he wanted his son to have the same opportunities to stretch himself and flex his muscles in preparation for manhood.

Charles liked the adventure of Hill House and settled down sur-prisingly quickly in this new, rather strange environment of schoolboy life. Each morning he was ready on time, wearing his cinnamon-colored blazer and schoolboy cap, to scramble into the Mighty One—an inconspicuous royal car, so named from its registration plate: MYT 1—for the short drive to his new school.

And soon after starting there, with a schoolboy desire to be just like any other boy, he came out with the request, "Can't I walk to school like the other boys?" There was more than one reason why he could not. He was quite unaccustomed to walking about the streets of London, and several busy junctions lay between Buckingham Palace and Hill House. More importantly, his parents realized that the sight of his sturdy little figure striding along the London pavements could not but attract crowds. Indeed, at the outset of this big experiment in royal upbringing the precincts of Hill House had been thronged with journalists, photographers and eager sightseers and there was one morning when his mother deemed it wise for his departure from the palace to be delayed by three-quarters of an hour to give the crowd around the school a chance to disperse.

At Hill House, Charles learned English and arithmetic, history and geography, botany and elementary science, handiwork and art, scripture and a grounding for languages. He did physical training in the school's diminutive gymnasium with its rope ladders and basketball. He had his free milk at mid-morning with the other boys and ate his midday meal with them in the basement dining hall.

Then he walked in a formation with his new school-fellows to the nearby playing field where he absorbed the rudiments of football and cricket, politely raising his school cap to motorists and taxi-drivers as they halted their vehicles to give the file of boys right-of-way at pedestrian crossings. When the school held its annual field-day, the Queen and Prince Philip were there to watch their small son help manhandle a mock field gun across a make-believe chasm, in imitation of the naval gun-carriage race which is a highlight of the Royal Tournament.

But exposure to schoolboy life inevitably exposed the young prince also to boyhood infection. A week after starting school he was ill with what at first seemed no more than a snuffly cold but later proved to be tonsillitis. He was attended by Dr. (now Sir) Wilfrid Sheldon, physician-in-charge of the children's department at King's College Hospital, and was forced to stay away from school for the next few weeks. The following term he was again forced to stay from school for the better part of a month, convalescing after the offending tonsils had been removed in an operation carried out in the Buhl Room at the palace, the room in which he had been born. Like a boy, he wanted to see the cause of all the trouble for himself. His tonsils, suitably preserved in a proper container, were given back to him after the operation and kept for some time in the nursery toy cupboard to be proudly displayed to the school friends he took home with him from time to time.

Until he went to school, Charles and his small sister, Anne, had been wellnigh inseparable, just as the Queen and Princess Margaret had been in childhood. With Charles at school, the Queen judged that Anne might perhaps feel lost and lonely on her own. To avoid this, she arranged for two other small girls, Caroline Hamilton and Susan Babington-Smith, to visit the palace daily and join the Princess in her own lessons in the palace schoolroom. Each morning the two girls arrived at the palace soon after nine o'clock and went straight up to the nursery to share Anne's lessons under Miss Peebles until lunchtime.

The Queen has always been anxious that her children should

grow up to speak French as fluently as she does herself and she now engaged a teacher from the *Lycées Français* to instruct the three girls in this subject. And that summer, to help Charles brush up on his French before going to Cheam, she had a French girl stay at Balmoral with the family, eating with the children, accompanying them on their outings and talking to them as far as possible in French.

For Princess Anne, there were also piano lessons from concert pianist Hilda Bor, dancing lessons from Mme. Vacani. Schoolroom routine was also varied by physical training in a gymnasium at Chelsea to which she and her two companions were taken each week in one of the royal cars; by outings to the British Museum and the Tower of London, the Tate Gallery and the National Science Museum, traveling sometimes, as Charles had done before her, by bus or Underground. There were meetings of the palace Brownie pack, and, as she grew older, of the Girl Guides, where the Queen's daughter mixed freely with the daughters of royal grooms and chauffeurs, pages and footmen, just as her mother and Aunt Margo had done in their own childhood days.

Gradually and imperceptibly, the Queen was demonstrating in all manner of ways that she could move with the changing times, and not least where the welfare and upbringing of her children was concerned. When Anne's health necessitated the removal of her tonsils the operation took place not at the palace, as had been the case with Charles, but in the Great Ormond Street Hospital for Sick Children. Charles had been the first heir to the throne to go to school; now Anne became the first of the Royal Family to go into a hospital. The Queen wanted all the latest developments of medical science to be available to her children in illness, and later when an urgent telephone call from Cheam informed her that Charles needed an emergency operation for appendicitis, he, too, was rushed into the hospital.

By the age of seven, Anne was already fast becoming an extremely proficient young horsewoman. Every Saturday morning, almost without fail, the Queen and her small daughter would go riding together in Windsor Great Park, sometimes cantering over to the Home Farm for Anne to inspect the young calves and squealing piglets. Charles, before he went to Cheam, always joined his mother and sister for this Saturday morning ride in the park. Initially, there had been half-hour riding lessons with a groom for the children before it was time to go riding with their mother, and if she should be delayed for any reason nothing was more certain than that the two youngsters would fill in time by pitting their ponies one against the other across the castle golf course.

Like her mother, Anne has always been passionately devoted to horses. Even at seven, she was a daring young rider, completely devoid of fear. There was an occasion at Sandringham when she tried to ride her pony up the wide stone steps of the front entrance just as the adjutant at Sandhurst Military College does on the day of the annual graduation parade. When her pony declined to mount the steps, Anne slid from the saddle, took hold of the bridle and tried to lead him up. Had she succeeded, one has visions of her re-mounting and riding him right into the lofty main room of Sandringham House with its big, baronial-style, stone-built fireplace. Fortunately, perhaps, the pony had no intention of mounting the steps, whether led or ridden.

At Balmoral, a year or two later, she came cantering out of a copse of trees to one side of the castle and failed to notice a line which had been strung across the open space beyond for the purpose of airing some of the nursery linen. It caught her across the body, plucking her from the saddle and dashing her to the ground. Shaken, but otherwise unharmed, she scrambled to her feet, brushed herself down and promptly scrambled back on the pony which had come to a well-trained standstill. Quite unperturbed by her mishap, she was later observed cantering her pony bareback round the front lawn, using neither bridle nor saddle, in imitation of a western she had seen on television. But if Anne knew no fear, her mother felt it for her. "Get off that horse at once, Anne," she called from a window, "and take it back to be properly saddled."

III

It was in September, 1957, that Charles, not quite nine, changed from a commuter at Hill House to a boarder at Cheam in accordance with a decision his parents had taken well ahead of Lord Altrincham's much publicized criticisms.

The decision to send the young prince to his father's old school may not have gone as far as Lord Altrincham and others beside him would have wished. "Will she," Altrincham had inquired concerning the Queen in his *National and English Review*, "above all, see to it that Prince Charles is equipped with all the knowledge he can absorb without injury to his health, and that he mixes during his formative years with children who will one day be bus-drivers, dockers, engineers, etc.—not merely with future land-owners or stockbrokers?"

It was, perhaps, expecting too much, and Cheam was a happy compromise between the council school views of some people and the tutor-conscious outlook of some of those closer to the Royal Family.

The boy's parents traveled south with him from Balmoral at the start of the school year and he was duly delivered to Cheam in his father's Lagonda, his leather trunk with its brass label in-scribed "H.R.H. Prince Charles" riding in the car's capacious trunk. If he was initially rather less enthusiastic over boarding school than he had been where Hill House was concerned, at least he took it no better and no worse than any other small boy being wrenched from the bosom of family life for the first time. There was a noticeable lack of appetite during the journey south on the royal train and even a consoling gift of chocolates did not entirely relieve his glumness at the moment of parting.

In the palace nursery he had been largely shielded from the knocks and buffets of everyday life. Servants, naturally enough, had treated him always as the Queen's son and the heir to the throne. Two terms at day school were barely sufficient to toughen him for what was to come and at first he found boarding school a not inconsiderable ordeal.

After the quiet orderliness of palace life, the shouting and scuffling of the other boys with whom he shared dormitory and classes was like a shock of ice-cold water. But boarding school life, as his father had foreseen, was soon to force out the child and replace it with the schoolboy. When Charles returned home at the end of that very first term, the effect of Cheam was already noticeable.

Already he seemed to be growing up, shedding his puppy fat, becoming physically more robust and mentally more assured. In summer, at Balmoral, Anne had seemed on a par with him. Now, at Christmas, she seemed suddenly still a child by comparison. The games of hide-and-seek which still delighted her had become so much "nursery stuff" to her schoolboy brother. Gone was the eager scamper to see his parents each morning and evening. Anne, impetuous as ever, might still dash into the royal apart-ment with an excitable "Hello, Mummy—Hello, Papa," but now her brother followed her more slowly, almost grown-up in his newfound schoolboy dignity.

His appetite, too, had changed. He now ate more heartily, digging into whatever was set before him with schoolboy voraciousness. Playing with toys was fast becoming a thing of the past. Charles was interested now in other things, cricket bats and model boats, cameras and bicycles, eager to be up and doing, out and about.

In sending her son to Cheam, the Queen had emphasized yet again her desire that his upbringing should be as much like that of an ordinary boy as possible. "It is the wish of the Queen and Prince Philip that there shall be no alteration in the way the school is run and that Prince Charles shall be treated exactly the same as the other boys," the school's joint headmasters, Mark Wheeler and F. B. Beck, said in a letter to the parents of their other pupils. "It would be a great help if you would explain this to your boys."

Charles *was* treated like all the other boys. He folded his own clothes at night, had his hands and face scrutinized for cleanliness before being permitted to go through for breakfast in the mornings, and was once reprimanded for nibbling at his fingernails. No longer did he have a room of his own. He shared a dormitory with a number of other boys—"You won't be able to bounce on that," the Queen had said laughingly when she visited the school and sat on one of the beds to test it out—and he ate with the rest of the boys in the school dining hall.

He played cricket and football, demonstrated that he could swim like a fish, got into scraps and scrapes, and took part in schoolboy jokes.

He had the same free Sundays each term as any other boy; no more, no less. On these free Sundays, the Queen willingly allowed him to visit the home of one of his new-found friends at Cheam or bring two or three of them home with him to Windsor. Having associated so much with grown-ups for most of his young life, his outlook tended to be older than his years and the friendships he made at Cheam were usually with slightly older boys.

This by no means prevented frequent outbursts of boyish high spirits. During one Sunday visit to Windsor it was suggested that he should show his school friends round the state rooms with their fine paintings and priceless furnishings. But paintings and furnishings proved a deal less intriguing than cannon and armor, and presently a succession of schoolboy yells accompanied a noisy game of uncertain rules in which the armory became a citadel under attack by a rebel army.

Each new term after his first, Charles traveled back to Cheam with a group of school friends on a train from Waterloo, carrying a small leather case containing the usual schoolboy collection of sweets and comics, handing his ticket to the collector at the end of the journey, and lining up with all the other boys to board the school bus.

The Queen paid no special visits to the school and carefully refrained from telephoning to find out how her son was coming along. Instead, she wrote him a weekly letter on her scarlet-crested notepaper, like any other mother. Even when he succumbed to the flu, she did not go dashing off to Cheam to fetch him home and nurse. One of her ladies-in-waiting telephoned the school to ensure that there was no undue cause for alarm and it was left at that.

Charles settled down quickly to schoolboy life. He pinned a photograph of his pet corgi, Whisky, inside his locker; he wrote home for a model sailing boat on the grounds that all the other boys had one. He had his head ducked under a tap in the wash-room by a bigger and older boy, and spurred on by the school barber, who had witnessed the incident, retaliated by pushing his assailant into a bath of water.

He once excused himself for being late in class with the explanation that he did not have a watch; later he was given one. He was reprimanded by a master for participating in some unexplained schoolboy prank which somehow involved dropping raincoats over the heads of other boys as they entered the cloakroom. He was involved in a classroom incident which resulted in the contents of an ink-pot being spilled on the floor, and dashed off for a cloth with which to clean up the mess.

In short, in no time at all, he was behaving exactly like any other schoolboy at any boarding school.

CHAPTER TWELVE

THE THIRD BABY

I

AT BUCKINGHAM PALACE they were busy packing for yet another
royal tour, the longest and most strenuous tour the Queen had
undertaken since that journey right round the world more than
five years before. This time she was embarking upon the biggest
tour of Canada ever made by a reigning monarch. In forty-five days
she would travel some sixteen thousand miles across Canada, from
the Atlantic to the Pacific, from Newfoundland to British Columbia, as far north as the Yukon. She would see that vast country as
even few Canadians had ever seen it . . . the rolling prairies and
the snow-capped Rockies, the forests and the lakes, the oilfields
and the mineral deposits, the relics of the past and the portents for
the future.

Plans and preparations for this big tour had been in progress
for more than a year. Maps, itineraries and correspondence had
passed between Ottawa, the Canadian High Commissioner's
office in London, the Commonwealth Office and Buckingham
Palace in a steady, seemingly unending stream.

Twice, Canada's Under-Secretary for External Affairs had
flown the Atlantic to consult with royal officials. Palace officials,
in turn, had flown over to Canada to undertake a dummy run
ahead of the Queen, checking on plans, progress and arrangements.
They had little cause for concern. To arrange the Queen's visit,
the Canadian Government had called in a former Chief of Staff,
who, aided by four assistants, a clerical staff of seven and com-
mittees comprising seventy-four members, had planned things
with all the thoroughness of a military operation, not forgetting
an air-lift to leapfrog three shiny, new cars across Canada ahead
of the royal train so that they were ready and waiting for the
Queen at each separate stopping place.

Now, in June, 1959, with her departure imminent, the Queen

had something else to occupy her mind, something all-important and completely personal, the knowledge that she was almost certainly expecting another baby, a happy event for which she had long hoped. "Philip and I have always been anxious to have more children," she was to tell a friend later. But conscientious as always, her principal concern at the moment was to keep her important news to herself so that there might be no undue anxiety concerning her health as she traveled the length and breadth of Canada, no necessity for Canadians to feel they should forego some part of this big royal visit they had so long anticipated.

The Queen flew from London to St. John's, Newfoundland, in a B.O.A.C. Comet 4 which had been specially adapted to provide her with a tiny dining room seating eight, and a sitting room with wheat and turquoise-colored divans, quickly converted into sleeping berths, on either side of the sea-blue carpet of the center aisle. Beyond the divans, silver-gray curtains screened two pocket-sized dressing rooms with built-in wardrobes.

From St. John's the Queen flew to Gander, from Gander to Deer Lake, from Deer Lake to Stephenville, from Stephenville to Schefferville. She tramped round a hot and dusty aluminium works; she trudged round iron ore workings until her hair and eyebrows, coat and gloves alike, were coated with a fine red dust. The temperature that day stood at eighty-two degrees.

No woman in the early stages of pregnancy could possibly maintain such a schedule without it having an effect on her and within three days of the start of her tour the Queen was being examined by Surgeon Captain D. D. Steele-Perkins, the medical officer traveling with her. Inevitably, rumors that all was not well with the Queen's health were quick to start up and as quickly denied.

A week after her departure from Britain, Lieutenant Colonel Charteris, her private secretary when she was a Princess and one of her assistant private secretaries now that she was Queen, flew to Ghana. The Queen had a visit to Ghana scheduled for November. Charteris took news to Dr. Nkrumah that the visit would not be taking place, and whispered the reason why. On the same day that Charteris flew to Ghana, the Queen, opening the St. Lawrence Seaway, confided the happy news of the expected baby to her old friends, President and Mrs. Eisenhower. The time had also come to confide in Mr. Diefenbaker, the Canadian prime minister.

Immediately he was told, Canada's prime minister suggested

cutting the Queen's tour. But the Queen would not agree. To the privileged few to whom she had now confided her happy secret she added a strict injunction that it must stay a secret, for the time being. As a result, in Ghana Dr. Nkrumah maintained a discreet silence while preparations continued for a royal visit which would not now take place. In Canada, French newspaper reports that the Queen was indeed expecting another baby were firmly denied by the Queen's acting press secretary, Esmond Butler, though in doing so he was stating only what he believed to be the actual truth. Back in Britain, the Queen Mother, paying her annual visit to the local flower show at Sandringham, bought a hand-knitted shawl of soft white wool from a stall run by the Women's Institute, of which she is a member.

Despite the hectic pace of that Canadian tour, the Queen's condition and the happiness she felt over the coming baby combined to give her a new, fresh bloom of beauty at first. "My, I've never seen you look so beautiful," Mrs. Eisenhower exclaimed impulsively when the two of them met at the opening of the Seaway.

But, later, as the Queen doggedly insisted on maintaining her tough, rigid schedule without respite, the strain inevitably began to tell on her. In Toronto, on a day when the temperature soared to an enervating ninety-five degrees, with Philip's forehead beaded with sweat and people fainting like fles in the streets as they waited to see the royal party go by, the Queen was continuously on the go for the best part of fourteen hours, carrying out a schedule which began with the inevitable inspection of the inevitable guard of honor, and ended with the equally inevitable banquet.

She looked tense and strung up when she arrived in Chicago on a one-day side trip to the United States. "Relax—they're mad about you," her husband murmured, encouragingly.

America's famed "Windy City," the mayor of which once threatened to bust King George V "on the snoot" if he ventured to show himself there, greeted his granddaughter, Elizabeth II, with cheers and handshakes and a banner which read: "Welcome to the Windy City, Liz and Phil."

Seven American governors, forty mayors, five squadrons of jet aircraft, a water display by the city's fire floats and a two hundred foot barge crammed with flowers and moored near the landing stage helped to swell the welcome. Trumpeters sounded *Rule Britannia*, one hundred tablecloths were dyed gold for a dinner in the Queen's honor, 2,300 feet of red carpet was laid at the

International Trade Fair and even the *Chicago Tribune* building, housing a newspaper not exactly renowned for its Anglomania, flew the Union Jack.

In thirteen hours in Chicago the Queen visited the Trade Fair, the Museum of Science Industry, the Art Institute, inspected a guard of honor, and still found time to purchase a quilted dressing gown and matching slippers which she felt sure would delight Princess Anne. She also found herself spending twenty minutes in the chair of a local dentist undergoing emergency treatment in respect of a lost filling.

As always, wherever the Queen went, she was showered with gifts . . . for herself, for Philip, for the children. She was torn then, as she is now, on this question of gifts. She would be upset if she felt anyone thought she was ungrateful for such gifts; at the same time, she is conscious that there are other uses to which the money could be put.

Before starting her tour she suggested that Canadians, desirous of giving her something, should set up scholarships in her name instead. The Federal Government set the lead with a million-dollar scholarship fund. Individual states, cities and commercial concerns followed suit. Ontario established a half-million dollar scholarship fund, the Hudson's Bay Company launched a million-dollar scheme for a scholarship fund at the University of Manitoba, the International Nickel Company endowed a two-year research scholarship and Newfoundland devised the Queen Elizabeth Assistance Grant for the education of retarded children.

But personal gifts of all sorts and sizes were still heaped upon the Queen. London, Ontario, set up two scholarships in her name . . . and also gave her a pair of bookends. She was given books and paintings, a gold and silver desk set, a buffalo statuette, an Indian totem, a sound movie of Manitoba, a paperweight made from the fossilized bone of a long-dead dinosaur, and a statuette of herself, barefooted, carved in rare green serpentine rock. Altogether, by the time the tour was over, she had been given no fewer than one hundred and twenty gifts.

Normally, the Queen accepts only those gifts of which advance notification has been given. The reason is clear. No one wants to see some astute manufacturer suddenly thrusting something upon her unexpectedly and claiming afterwards that she has his toothpaste or is using his beauty cream. It was this principle which found the Queen declining the various unexpected gifts she was offered at the Chicago Trade Fair. But at Windsor, Ontario, one totally unexpected gift did succeed in penetrating the closely woven web of royal protocol . . . a dappled pony.

"Whatever breed is he?" the Queen asked with obvious interest and delight. "I've never seen one like this before."

She was told that the pony was an appalusa.

"Will the dapple spots spread as he grows?" asked the inquiring Prince Philip. He learned that the pony was already fully grown.

The Queen was asked if she would arrange for the pony to be passed on to some deserving youngster back home in Britain. As a result, children of that other Windsor in Berkshire were later asked to write letters to the local mayor giving their various reasons for feeling that they deserved the dappled pony. The best letter came from Penny Stephenson, a ten-year-old, who wrote that she would share the pony, if she was given it, with her seven-year-old brother and four-year-old sister.

"There is an acre of meadowland at the bottom of our garden," explained Penny in a charming little letter, "and my father says he will make a stable fit for a royal pony. And because it is the Queen's pony, I would let it help out at local fetes for good causes."

More and more the strain of her long and strenuous Canadian tour was beginning to tell on the Queen. In Port Arthur she was drenched by a ten-minute rain squall which blew up so suddenly there was no time even to replace the glass hood of the car in which she was riding. At Vancouver, where she found herself shaking hands three hundred times in non-stop succession, she fulfilled a series of public engagements lasting for more than ten hours with only three brief rests totaling no more than forty minutes in all that time.

It was perhaps concern for his wife, worry over her state of health, which caused Prince Philip, seldom a man to mince his words, to seem even more forthright than usual on that Canadian tour, and sometimes even testy. "I know I have a reputation for being nasty to photographers," he told a gathering of pressmen. "Actually I am not. But if photographers poke a long lens through a keyhole into my private life, then I am bloody nasty."

His reported remark that Ontario's liquor licensing laws were "obsolete and old-fashioned" was hardly calculated to endear him to all Canadians, more particularly those with some knowledge of Britain's own archaic regulations in this direction. In his presidential address to the Canadian Medical Association he had some characteristically frank comments to make concerning the current state of Canadian health and fitness.

"Is the medical profession," he wanted to know, "content only to fight disease and disability and accept the negative definition of health as someone who is not actually ill? Or is it also going to take notice of the state of sub-health which exists?"

Meantime, the Queen's own health continued to give more and more cause for concern. Arriving at Nanaimo in British Columbia, where a colorful ceremony saw her installed as an Indian princess, she was looking as fatigued as she had ever appeared in public. Reaching Whitehorse, two days later, she was clearly exhausted. Her face was lobster-red from the heat she had been forced to endure and there were times when those close to her were frightened that she was going to faint. Next day she was so bad that she was forced to stay in bed. Steele-Perkins was called to see her again and, reluctantly, she agreed to cancel her proposed flight to Dawson City. She was clearly a sick woman, and Philip was a worried-looking husband as he made the trip to Dawson City alone to see the old timber-built saloons, the theater where Diamond Lil once paraded her charms and the cabin which was the home of the author of Dan McGrew.

Pressmen with the royal party were beginning to suspect that the French reports of the Queen's pregnancy were not so wide of the mark. A spate of official statements, many of them contradictory, tried to allay such suspicions . . . the Queen's tooth was still troubling her . . . her old sinus trouble was affecting her again . . . she was tired . . . she was suffering from an upset stomach . . . it was something she had eaten.

Anxious that her mother and Princess Margaret should not be worried by what they might read in the newspapers, the Queen made a transatlantic telephone call to assure them that she was suffering from what all mothers-to-be suffer from in the early stages of pregnancy. She flew to Edmonton while Philip went on alone to Yellowknife and Uranium City. Still wan and tired-looking, she fulfilled her engagements in Edmonton, visiting City Hall, planting a tree and attending a garden party, before embarking on a four-day whistlestop tour of the Prairie Provinces.

From Port Hope, as that long and exhausting tour drew at last to a close, she phoned home yet again to chat with her children. Charles, home from Cheam for the summer holiday, and Anne were spending the weekend with "Granny." The weather was warm and sunny and they told their mother that they had been swimming in the blue-tiled pool at Royal Lodge. But the Queen did not tell them yet of the new baby she was expecting. She was saving that exciting news until she could tell it to them personally.

She had planned a leisurely return trip to Britain in the royal yacht, with an official visit to the Shetlands and Orkneys before going on to Balmoral for her summer rest, never more needed than it was now. But her state of health was such as to necessitate another change of plan. Instead of a leisurely trip by sea, she again flew the Atlantic, looking pale, tired and strained as she arrived at London Airport, where her mother and children were waiting to greet her. From the airport she drove straight to Buckingham Palace where two of the royal physicians, Lord Evans and Sir John Weir, awaited her arrival.

II

Five days after she arrived back in London, the Queen and her family left for a long, restful holiday at Balmoral. During the journey north on the royal train, the Queen confided her exciting news to Mabel Anderson, who had succeeded Helen Lightbody in charge of the palace nursery. This tall, friendly-faced young woman from Elgin would soon have a new charge to look after and she was almost as delighted at the news as the Queen was herself. But at the Queen's request, she did not yet pass the news on to Charles and Anne. Like a mother, the Queen wished to do that herself at an opportune moment.

The opportunity came that first day at Balmoral, over lunch, shortly before the brief, official announcement from Buckingham Palace that the Queen would undertake no further engagements confirmed what so many people already suspected.

Charles and Anne could hardly finish their lunch for their excitement. As soon as the meal was over, they hurried away upstairs to the nursery to tell Miss Anderson, who heard them out as attentively as if she did not already know.

Did they want a baby brother or a sister? the children were asked.

"A brother, of course," Charles declared stoutly.

"Oh, yes—a baby brother," echoed Anne.

Already, that first day at Balmoral, the Queen had lost the signs of strain and fatigue so evident in Canada. Even so brief a rest as those few days in London had enabled her natural powers of recuperation to work wonders. Her joy and happiness at this latest development in her personal life was seen in the dainty pirouette she performed so spontaneously when alighting from the royal train at Ballater station and in the cheerful, white-gloved wave, so different from her normal regal gesture, which she gave to those waiting there to see her.

"She is in the best of health," her physician, Lord Evans, was to announce soon afterwards, and those who saw her inspect the guard of honor which awaited her at Ballater, though the official announcement concerning the new baby had not yet been made, were moved to comment on how well and happy she was looking.

At Balmoral, that summer, the Queen began her preparations for approaching motherhood. Horse-riding is normally her favorite form of outdoor exercise. Now, temporarily, she discontinued her riding. She seldom drinks wine with her meals, except when she has guests. Now she drank none at all; only water. Several times each day she changed from high heels into stout, flat-heeled walking shoes and set off with her dogs for long, healthy tramps across the heather-clad moors.

There were several occasions when she and Philip and the children packed themselves into a Land Rover and drove off to a hideaway spot in the hills for a family picnic. To parents and children alike, picnics had long been a popular form of outing. Now they took on a new excitement with the unpacking of a portable barbecue outfit Philip had brought back with him from Canada. Philip thoroughly enjoyed this transatlantic form of outdoor cookery. He would go along personally to the kitchen to select the food—chicken, steaks, sausages, as the fancy might take him—and would carefully supervise the glowing charcoal chips as the meal sizzled succulently in the open air, while Charles and Anne, eager to help, mixed the batter for scones and pancakes.

For the Queen, there was further health-giving exercise in accompanying Philip when he went out over the grouse moors. As though that was not sufficient, there was one day when she donned her specially-made knickers and tweed jacket, took a packed lunch of sandwiches and fruit with her, and set off with her rifle and a guide to stalk stag in the hills. She was gone from nine in the morning until close to tea-time, returning peat-streaked, healthily tired and buoyantly triumphant with the news that she had brought down a royal, a stag with twelve-point antlers.

Returning to Buckingham Palace at the end of the summer stay at Balmoral, the Queen continued her no-nonsense approach to the business of motherhood. At no time did she regard herself as sick or any form of an invalid, and for her there was no question of an afternoon nap. Instead, most afternoons found her taking a brisk walk in the palace gardens. Right up to the day her baby was born she continued to rise promptly at eight o'clock each morning to breakfast with her husband before settling down to a day's work at her crowded, business-like desk. She saw her various officials as usual, dealt with her correspondence and state papers as usual, and went through to the Audience Room at the far end of the royal corridor to receive an ambassador or bestow a knighthood.

If anything, it seemed that she was trying to crowd more and more into her ordinary working day, as though by so doing she could compensate for the fact that she was no longer carrying out public engagements. There was one morning when, despite a routine examination by the royal physicians, she insisted upon carrying out four separate audiences in the period remaining before lunch. The audiences over-ran and she was a quarter-of-an-hour late for lunch when the last visitor took his leave.

Like so many expectant mothers, she found her tastes changing. Normally, the Queen prefers savory dishes to sweet ones, drinks her tea without sugar. But now she developed an unaccustomed sweet tooth, a fondness for honey, ice cream and cream pastries.

Gifts for the expected baby began to trickle in . . . a fifty-six piece layette from old ladies in a home at Derby, bootees and coatees from as far away as Germany and Japan, a set of feeding bottles and a manual on *Infant Care* from the United States. By the time Andrew was born, the trickle had become a flood, part of which was syphoned off to hospitals where they found good use for gifts of clothes abundant enough to have outfitted a regiment of babies.

At Christmas that year the Queen went to Sandringham as usual, though she returned to the palace slightly earlier than normal in anticipation of the baby's birth in early February. From Sandringham, during that Christmas stay, Philip traveled alone to the wedding of his cousin, Lady Pamela Mountbatten. He had arranged to stop off for some duck shooting on the way back and this excursion lasted somewhat longer than he had anticipated. He was late back at Sandringham, and the Queen, the birth of the baby now fast approaching, was noticeably worried and restless until his return.

Philip stayed on at Sandringham for a few more days after the Queen returned to London. Daily he telephoned through to the palace to talk to her and check that she was well and happy. And every morning, sharp at ten, the telephone would ring in the Queen's private sitting room. It was the Queen Mother calling her from Clarence House, keeping in touch as mothers do at such times in their daughters' lives.

III

It was Wednesday, February 17, 1960. With the birth of the new baby confidently expected within the next twenty-four hours, the Queen moved out of the royal apartment and downstairs into the Belgian Suite which she had originally occupied when she first moved back into the palace as Queen.

Prince Charles was born at the front of the palace, in the Buhl Room, where the exuberant rejoicing of the vast crowd outside, insistently singing *Go to Sleep, My Baby* far into the night, had hardly helped his mother to get the extra rest which is so essential following childbirth. This time the Queen decided to have her baby in that part of the palace furthest removed from any public celebrations that might take place around the Queen Victoria Memorial.

The next day, however, the Queen was up and about again as usual, tackling the business of monarchy from a desk looking out across the palace gardens. The royal physicians came and went at intervals. Anne, fully recovered from her recent cold— on medical advice, she had been kept away from her mother until she was well again, though the two of them had chatted animatedly over the telephone—popped in to see her mother from time to time. So did Prince Philip, by now wearing the slightly harassed look of all expectant fathers. He canceled his visit to the National College of Food and Technology, and that evening, as the Queen rested in her canopied bed, he ate dinner with her from a bedside food cart.

At eight o'clock that evening, the royal physicians took their leave, with the exception of the gynecologist, John Peel (now Sir John). Peel stayed the night in a room at the palace. When Philip finally went upstairs to his bedroom in the royal suite he left strict instructions that he was to be called immediately if there were any further developments.

There were, however, no further developments that night, and it was not until half-past three the following afternoon that Philip came dashing out of the Belgian Suite, excitedly proclaiming, "It's a boy." Ignoring the electrically-run elevator, he bounded upstairs, taking the stairs two at a time, to pop his head round the door of the day nursery and pass the news to a delighted Princess Anne.

He telephoned to Clarence House to give the Queen Mother the good news, and arranged for bottles of champagne to be opened so that the royal staff could join in "wetting the baby's head" in the traditional fashion. Then he returned to his wife's bedside bearing a huge congratulatory bouquet of white roses and carnations which he had been storing in a refrigerator to keep them cool and fresh-looking for this joyous occasion. He found the Queen sitting up in bed and quietly sipping a cup of tea.

There was no shortage of visitors to see the new baby, the first to be born to a reigning monarch for more than a century. At five o'clock Princess Anne came downstairs and tiptoed into the Belgian Suite for a peep at her new brother, not yet two hours old. A royal car was dispatched to Cheam to fetch Prince Charles. By six o'clock that evening the Queen Mother, Princess Margaret, Princess Marina (then still the Duchess of Kent) and Princess Alexandra had all arrived at the palace to see the new arrival. Members of the Queen's personal staff, too, were later accorded the privilege of tiptoeing in for a glimpse of little Prince Andrew.

But even in those first few days of renewed motherhood the Queen did not relinquish the reins of monarchy. The very day after Andrew was born she was again dealing with the contents of her leather dispatch boxes, a bedside telephone linking her with her private secretary and, through him, with the outside world.

For several days after the baby was born, the Queen stayed on in the Belgian Suite, with its portraits of Queen Victoria's grandchildren, before moving back upstairs to the royal apartment. Whenever opportunity served, Prince Philip would slip in to have his meals with her, sitting in an armchair beside the bed, eating from a tray on his lap. Anne, too, was in and out all the time, racing downstairs from the nursery as soon as her lessons were over to take another peep at her baby brother as he nestled in his canopied cot with its pink frills and blue ribbons . . . the selfsame cot that Charles and Anne had occupied before him.

CHAPTER THIRTEEN

THE SECRET ROMANCE

I

"IT IS WITH the greatest pleasure that Queen Elizabeth The Queen Mother announces the betrothal of her beloved daughter The Princess Margaret . . ."

Few events in her by no means uneventful life have brought the Queen Mother greater happiness than the engagement of her younger daughter, and her happiness showed through even the stilted wording of the formal announcement, issued from Clarence House only seven days after the birth of her third grandchild, little Prince Andrew.

The least-talked-about royal romance in history was a secret no longer. For weeks past the possibility that some enterprising newsman would sniff romance in the air between the Queen's younger sister and an energetic young photographer named Antony Armstrong-Jones had been growing steadily. So as not to clash with the Queen's own happy news, the official announcement had been held back until after the birth of Prince Andrew. Now, despite family mourning for Lady Mountbatten and the Marquess of Carisbrooke, it could be contained no longer if rumor and speculation in the gossip columns were to be avoided.

Ever since the bitter-sweet ending of Margaret's attachment to Peter Townsend, the Queen Mother had longed for the day when her younger daughter might find lasting happiness elsewhere. Even the knowledge that Margaret's marriage would mean she would be living alone at Clarence House in the future, no pleasant prospect for a woman whose greatest happiness had always been found in family life, the Queen Mother could not minimize the joy she now felt for her daughter.

The announcement took everyone but a privileged few completely by surprise. Even the staffs at Clarence House and Royal Lodge, Balmoral and Sandringham, all of which the bridegroom-to-be had visited in the course of that secret courtship, had difficulty in remembering how he had looked and what he was like until newspaper photographs jogged their memories. They recalled him then as a rather inconspicuous, inoffensive young man with a tendency to lie late abed in the morning. "Who would have thought it?" they asked each other, for the young man they now knew was to marry the Princess had seemed hardly more attentive to her than any of the other escorts so constantly around her.

There had been sound reason for that. Years before, when the Queen as a young Princess had been worried and upset by gossip and speculation concerning her romance with Prince Philip, it was Margaret, for once the wise and motherly one, who had sympathized with her, "Poor Lilibet, nothing is your own . . . not even your love affair." In the years that followed, Margaret's own attachment to Peter Townsend had run its course against an even harsher, more glaring background of rumor and gossip. The Princess wanted no repetition. This time her love affair was going to stay hers . . . and hers alone . . . until she herself decreed otherwise.

II

It was six months after she issued her statement of renunciation that Princess Margaret met Antony Armstrong-Jones for the first time, though to say that she "met" him is perhaps to employ too emphatic a word for the chance and fleeting encounter which actually took place. The date was April 21, 1956. The occasion was the marriage of Lady Anne Coke, a daughter of the Earl of Leicester, to the Hon. Colin Tennant, heir to Lord Glenconner, in the flint-built church of St. Withburga on the Leicester ancestral estate at Holkham in Norfolk, only a few miles from the Royal Family's country home at Sandringham.

Bride and bridegroom alike could describe themselves as friends of the Royal Family. Lady Anne had been one of the Queen's maids-of-honor at the Coronation. Colin Tennant had stayed several times at Balmoral for the shooting.

Princess Margaret and her mother flew from London to the wedding, lunching at Sandringham, driving over to Holkham for the marriage ceremony and subsequent reception, and flying back again immediately it was all over. It was noticeable that the Princess, leaving St. Withburga's after the ceremony, looked rather more serious than was usual for her, even perhaps a little sad, and there were those among the wedding guests who wondered why.

After the wedding ceremony came the wedding pictures . . . on the broad terrace where the fountain was playing, in the Marble Hall with its slender alabaster columns and flanking galleries with their busts and portraits. A dynamic young photographer with rumpled fair hair, a boyish grin and what seemed to be a slight limp, posed the wedding party and took the pictures. His name was Armstrong-Jones.

He was, at the time, a very up-and-coming photographer who took pictures for newspapers, magazines, advertising, a quick and restless young man with a background no less impeccable than that of the socialites whose weddings he so frequently captured for the glossy magazines and the family albums . . . Eton and Jesus College, Cambridge, Birr Castle in Ireland and Womersley Hall in Yorkshire.

Almost as far back as he could remember Tony had wanted to take photographs. As a youngster he was given a microscope which had once belonged to his grandfather and promptly swapped it with a school-fellow for his first camera. After a photographic apprenticeship with Prince Philip's friend, the famous Baron, he decided to branch out on his own. Friends found him premises suitable for his first studio. But he complained that the rent of £10 ($28.) a week was "too dear" and finally settled for alternative premises in Pimlico Road which were going at half the price.

He painted the front door himself, fixed up a door-knocker fashioned in the shape of a lion's head, and converted the basement into living quarters in the contemporary style. He ate in pubs, visited coffee bars, took his laundry along to a nearby launderette each week in a pillow-case, wore black jeans and bulky sweaters. He once bought himself some riding boots for ten shillings in a secondhand store. They were not a pair, but Tony didn't mind. "When you're on a horse, nobody sees both sides at the same time," he said, grinning. To him, the important thing was that he was doing what he most wanted to do . . . taking photographs.

He pictured such contrasting personalities as Marlene Dietrich and Salvador Dali, Eartha Kitt and Harold Macmillan, Bud Flanagan and Jean Anouilh, Brendan Behan and Christian Dior, Mike Todd and Sir Laurence Olivier. He photographed cathedrals in Malta, street scenes in London, and Lady Lewisham at the hairdresser's with her hair in curlers.

He was once ejected from the Viennese State Opera because he lacked a press pass, but successfully talked his way back inside and took his pictures. He took wedding photographs, news pictures, theatrical stills, pictures for advertisements. Photographs he took for a series of advertisements for toilet soap were still being published even after the official announcement of his engagement to Princess Margaret.

He designed ski outfits and stage scenery with equal facility, a young man very much in a hurry who was always reaching out after some fresh interest, to whom time meant nothing if he had some new idea to communicate.

Once, when a new idea came to him, he got out his motorcycle and tore straight round to the home of some married friends although it was then one o'clock in the morning. The flat was in darkness, the friends in bed, but Tony rapped on the window until they were awake and let him in. Tony poured out his idea and the stimulating conversation which ensued went on until daybreak.

He first broke into the highly privileged realm of royal photography when he wrote to the young Duke of Kent seeking permission to take his portrait. The Duke gave permission, went round to the studio in Pimlico Road for a sitting and finished up by selecting one of the resulting pictures as the official photograph to be issued on his 21st birthday.

Soon, Tony was taking photographs of Charles and Anne. The Queen had seen some photographs he had taken of the children of Lord Rupert and Lady Nevill, her close personal friends. She liked them so much that she invited the young photographer who had taken them to do the photographs of Prince Charles which would be issued in connection with his eighth birthday.

It was Tony's big chance and he took it with both hands. He racked his brain for some way of introducing a new dimension into stylized royal portraits and ended up by ransacking a succession of antique shops until he came across the big globe of the world which appeared in his final pictures of the royal children. Compared with his predecessors, with their masses of lights and drapes and scurrying assistants, the young photographer from Pimlico Road seemed rather slenderly equipped the day he turned up at Buckingham Palace to take those photographs. But the results proved to be outstanding.

III

Friendship with Princess Margaret was still a thing of the future. While they could not have avoided seeing each other at Holkham Hall on the day of Lady Anne's wedding, it could hardly be classed as a social introduction. That was to come in 1958, at a party in London at which they were both guests. Thereafter, mixing in stage and social circles which overlapped at the edges, they tended to run into each other from time to time at other parties, at weddings and theatrical occasions. They saw each other again at a Halloween Ball at the Dorchester. Then came a ball at Claridges where they danced together for the first time. This was around the time Tony was working on the huge photographic sets he did for the John Cranko revue, *Keep Your Hair On.*

Some of the sets were still damp on the night the show opened and Tony had to dash hurriedly round the members of the cast with a warning to that effect.

"Don't rub against them or the picture will come off," he cautioned a pert little blonde actress named Barbara Windsor. Years later, when Barbara was a star and Tony was Lord Snowdon, they met again at the film premiere of *Sparrows Can't Sing.*

"Do you remember—" Barbara started to say as she was presented to the now Lord Snowdon in the foyer of the cinema.

"What do you mean—do I remember?" returned Tony. "That show we did together? Of course I remember. I could hardly forget it, could I? It was a bit of a flop, wasn't it?"

Princess Margaret had planned to see the show, but it had ended its short run of life and been taken off before she returned to London from Sandringham. However, Tony's photographic scenery was generally voted an outstanding success.

In May, 1959, the names of the Princess and the photographer were briefly linked when Tony was included in Margaret's party of six when she paid her fourth visit to the American musical *West Side Story.* But no one outside their own close-knit circle gave the matter any serious thought and from then on, aware that their feeling for each other was undergoing the transformation from friendship to love, they were at some considerable pains to keep their attachment a close secret. In this, they were helped by the Queen Mother, who sensed that her daughter's happiness might be again at stake, by Ruby Gordon, Margaret's personal maid and younger sister of the Queen's beloved Bobo, and by the Princess's long-time friend, Billy Wallace.

When they went to supper parties, it was Billy Wallace who called for the Princess in his car. Tony would arrive at the rendezvous separately on his motorcycle. After all, who would suspect a young man on a motorcycle of having a date with a princess? When they went to the theater it was Ruby Gordon who booked the seats for them . . . in her own name. A headscarf and sunglasses served Margaret as a disguise for the occasional tete-a-tete meals in quiet restaurants and out-of-the-way country inns.

The two of them once spent a pleasant weekend staying with friends in the country in the course of which they roamed freely round the streets of Bath. The Princess was unnoticed and unrecognized; Tony's face was not yet familiar to press and public. Occasionally, Margaret would visit Tony's basement apartment below the studio in Pimlico Road, carefully ensuring that the street was deserted before getting out of her car and slipping across the pavement to enter the door with the lion's head knocker.

She went there on one occasion for a late-night supper party at which everyone sat around with their plates in their hands. The Princess was hardly accustomed to such free-and-easy informality and inadvertently spilled some of her food.

"I don't seem to be able to manage without a table," she confessed, ruefully. "We always have one at home, even for picnics."

Tony obligingly found one for her—a folding card table.

He was invited, in turn, to meals at Clarence House, where the atmosphere, though always friendly, was considerably less informal. Later, when she saw how things stood between the two young people, the Queen Mother from time to time invited him to spend a weekend with her and Margaret in the private, homely atmosphere of Royal Lodge at Windsor, where the Queen and Philip had done so much of their courting.

Tony arrived for such weekend visits with the back of his car crammed with photographic equipment, carefully giving the impression that he was there simply to take photographs. He resorted to the same device when he spent a brief holiday with the rest of the Royal Family at Balmoral that summer and when he stayed with them at Sandringham in the week following Christmas.

There were certainly photographic pretexts sufficient to account for his presence to all these places. He took the official portraits of the Queen and Prince Philip to mark their departure for Canada; he took the official portrait of Princess Margaret published to mark her twenty-ninth birthday.

Even in the privacy of the family circle, if there were servants and guests around, Tony and Margaret guarded their secret with care. At Sandringham that Christmas, the Princess was careful never to sit beside Tony at meal-times; always she sat beside Billy Wallace or some other guest. When the shooting party set off from Sandringham House each day, they were careful to leave separately and walk apart. Not until they were away from inquisitive eyes, with pheasants and partridges as their only witnesses, did they walk and talk together, planning their marriage and their future.

Not so much as a hint of their romance crept into the gossip columns. Other names were bandied about at intervals as suitors for the hand of the Queen's younger sister . . . Prince Christian of Hanover (a rumor quickly scotched by an official denial from Clarence House), Prince Bertil of Sweden ("the product of too much imagination," he snapped concerning rumors that he might marry the Princess), Lord Patrick Beresford, Billy Wallace (of course), Prince Henry of Hesse. But never a mention of Tony Armstrong-Jones.

Yet suspicion was growing. Models who posed for Tony in his Pimlico Road studio found their sittings interrupted by mysterious telephone calls and subsequent sittings canceled for no very clear reason. Tony, himself, was once close to letting the cat out of the bag. "The Queen Mother tells me—" he remarked in the course of a conversation. Then he bit it off quickly and as quickly changed the subject.

As a preliminary to the official announcement which could now not be much longer delayed, Tony began the process of tidying up his business affairs. To a friend who chanced on him while he was in the middle of the clear-out, he explained, perhaps with his tongue slightly in his cheek, "I may be moving to a bigger place."

His sister Susan, the Countess de Vesci, had already been let into the secret. With the official announcement now imminent, he confided in others . . . his housekeeper, Mrs. Peabody, his assistant, John Timbers. He and Susan went round together to tell the stepmother who had once nursed him through a childhood bout of poliomyelitis. Everyone found the news almost impossible to believe. "You're joking," said his stepmother when he told her that he was going to marry the Princess. "I'm astounded," said Mrs. Peabody.

The official announcement, when it finally came, left the rest of the world in exactly the same condition as Mrs. Peabody . . . astounded. By that time Tony had taken refuge from reporters at Royal Lodge, where he and Margaret posed for photographers in the gardens where water flows murmuringly among the rocks to remind the Queen Mother of her ancestral home at Glamis.

Their first public appearance together was a visit to the Royal Opera House, an evening marred by the fact that the Princess caught her silver satin gown on a projecting nail as she returned to the royal box after the interval. "Oh, Christmas," she sighed, surveying the resulting tear in the material.

Subsequently, the bridegroom-to-be moved into Buckingham Palace as a guest of the Queen until his wedding day, occupying a suite of rooms at the front of the palace normally reserved for one of the royal ladies-in-waiting. Tailors came and went as Tony, like Philip before him, outfitted himself in accordance with his new station in life. Gone, at least as far as public life was concerned, were the days of tight jeans and bulky sweaters.

IV

"I hope I keep in step," Prince Philip quipped in an effort to ease his sister-in-law's tension as they commenced their long, slow, solemn walk up the aisle of Westminster Abbey on Princess Margaret's wedding day, May 6, 1960.

Sunlight illuminated the vast rose window of the abbey. The Princess was a small, delicate figure in a wedding dress of frothing white silk with a long, foaming train, the diamonds of her tiara glinting round a coil of false hair which had been cunningly contrived to secure the tiara more firmly in place.

Behind her came the eight bridesmaids headed by Princess Anne. It was no coincidence that the puffed sleeves and Peter Pan collars of their dresses were modeled on the first evening dress Margaret had ever worn. That evening dress had been a special favorite of the father who was no longer alive to see her married.

Seldom can there have been such a varied guest list at a royal wedding . . . princes and princesses, dukes and earls, model girls and actresses. Tony's housekeeper, Mrs. Peabody, had not been overlooked. Nor had John Cranko, for whom he had once designed stage sets, and Jacqueline Chan, who had posed for so many of his earlier photographs.

The bridegroom's divorced parents were among the guests, as was his stepmother as well as the young third bride his father had married only a few days before the betrothal announcement, with protocol neatly sidestepping the issue by explaining that the wedding was an essentially private affair which the Queen was attending in a personal capacity.

There were the inevitable comments that the Queen looked solemn, but those who said this overlooked the tendency for personal emotions to be concealed behind the iron mask of royalty when in public. There was certainly nothing solemn about the Queen later, as she ran across the inner quadrangle of the palace in company with Prince Philip, the Queen Mother and Princess Anne, chasing excitedly after the royal car and showering bride and bridegroom with imitation rose petals as they set off on their Caribbean honeymoon.

The newlyweds were twenty-five minutes later than planned in leaving Buckingham Palace and it was this fact which caused their car to encounter a wildly cheering crowd swollen to huge proportions by the five o'clock rush hour by the time it reached Cannon Street. For once, not even London's stalwart and imperturbable policemen could cope with a press of people so dense and enthusiastic.

Pressing forward with good-natured relentlessness, sweeping the policemen bodily before it, the crowd succeeded finally in bringing the honeymoon car to a complete and utter standstill. So great was the pressure as those closest to hand struggled to glimpse the Princess and her husband that the glossy paintwork of the royal car was scraped by buttons and scratched by brooches to such an extent that it had to be re-sprayed when it finally arrived back in the mews at Buckingham Palace. And long before the car was on the move again, those aboard the royal yacht *Britannia*, which the Queen was loaning to her sister for her honeymoon, were fretting that they would miss the tide.

Gradually, London policemen contrived to force an opening through that dense, happy, excited London crowd. Slowly the royal car moved on again, edging its way almost foot by foot to where the waiting royal barge was moored. The Princess and her husband hurried aboard, still brushing palace rose petals from their clothes as the barge took them out across the Thames to the waiting *Britannia*.

The strain of the wedding ceremony, and those excited crowds in Cannon Street, had combined to slightly unnerve the Princess. She was visibly tense as she went up on to the bridge of the royal yacht. Once there, the signs of tension eased as she kicked off her high-heeled shoes, sighing in evident relief as she stood in her stockinged feet, waving happily to the people massed along the banks of the Thames while the royal yacht headed majestically downstream, outward bound for those far-away places with strange-sounding names . . . Trinidad and Tobago, Antigua and Dominica . . . to which the Princess has conceived such deep attachment.

V

That weekend, with her younger daughter now married and off on her honeymoon, the Queen Mother motored alone to Royal Lodge, that intimate and homely pink-walled royal residence at Windsor where her own desk still faces that of the late King across the open space of the french window in the elegant main saloon with its paneled walls, stone fireplace and gilt-framed portraits.

In the years since her husband died the Queen Mother has always kept his desk set out exactly as it was in the days when he was king. On it still stands his leather blotter, his silver inkstand and silver-cased traveling clock, the family photographs he always liked to have around him as he worked . . . photographs of Lilibet and Margaret when they were children, of the Queen Mother as she was in the days when her hair was still done in a fringe and her husband had not yet succeeded to the throne.

The fringe had long since gone, and now, in 1960, with her sixtieth birthday only three months away, the wavy, dark brown hair was flecked with grey. But her blue eyes retained all their warm friendliness, as they still do, and her fine complexion was as flawless as ever.

Photographs of the Queen Mother, restricted by their ability to deal in only two dimensions—and seldom capturing anything of that fourth dimension which is character and personality— invariably do the Queen Mother rather less than justice. Few photographs reveal the full warmth of her smile or the magnificence of her complexion, which owes so much to an emphasis on soap and water instilled into her during childhood. Her husband, in his lifetime, never tired of telling the story of the Texas senator who was presented to the two of them in Washington.

The Texan eyed the Queen, as she then was, for several seconds in undisguised admiration. Then, quite unable to contain himself, he burst out, "You sure are a thousand times prettier than your portrait, Ma'am."

The Queen Mother is quite aware that she photographs badly and once commented on the fact to the photographer who was taking her latest portrait. As a result, the photographer, determined to do her justice on this occasion, submitted a selection of proofs which had clearly been carefully re-touched. But such re-touching did not appeal to the Queen Mother's innate honesty. She sent the proofs back with a message that she did not want people thinking that she had come through her years on earth completely unscathed.

Her life, indeed, has been an exceptionally eventful one. Neither she nor her husband ever expected to come to the throne. When they found it thrust so unexpectedly upon them, she said, simply, "Well, we must take what is coming and make the best of it."

When one of her servants lamented, "Everything will be so different now; I feel quite shy with you all," the Queen Mother replied, characteristically, "Only circumstances change. People remain the same."

As her daughter was to do, in turn, she set about making a home out of a palace. She introduced her own favorite recipes into the palace menus, had flowers everywhere about the royal apartment, personally supervised the redecoration of the rooms, picked the materials for new bed-covers and window curtains. She had the carpenters build a hutch so that the Princesses could keep rabbits in the palace gardens; installed a tortoise in one of the summer houses.

She did everything she could to bolster her husband in his new and unexpected role of monarch. "You made a King of a man who never expected to become one," a friend was to say to her years later. But the Queen Mother only smiled her warm smile and shook her head. "I was just a good wife," she replied.

Her husband himself once acknowledged the debt he owed her when he said, "There have been times when my task would have been almost too heavy but for the strength and comfort I have always found in my own home."

From the very start of their marriage she had helped her husband to combat the speech impediment which had long dogged him. Cures had been tried and failed. But the Queen Mother heard of a new treatment devised by the Australian, Lionel Loguc. She begged her husband to try it; cheerfully encouraged him to persevere with the monotonous and strenuous daily exercises which the course of treatment demanded. And when the time came for him to open the Australian parliament in Canberra, she was overjoyed that he came through that undoubted ordeal without a trace of a stammer. Oblivious of those around, she caught his hand delightedly in hers. "You were splendid, darling," she murmured to him. "I'm so proud of you."

World War II, when it came, found her as unflinching as ever in her triple roles of wife, mother and consort. A suggestion that her daughters would perhaps be safer on the other side of the broad Atlantic brought the characteristic retort, "The children cannot go without me and I could not possibly leave the King." There was no need for her to add, "And the King will *never* leave." It went without saying.

Several times Buckingham Palace was bombed. One bomb crashed down in the courtyard, shattering the windows, while she and her husband were in the sitting room. Walking through the rubble afterwards, the Queen Mother observed, calmly, "In a way, I'm glad we've been bombed. Now I'll feel I can look the East End in the face."

She did more than look East Enders in the face. During one tour of the blitzed areas she helped to rescue a trapped dog. At another bombed home she found an injured mother struggling awkwardly to dress her small child. "Give him to me," said the Queen Mother, and finished dressing the child herself.

As the King and his wife walked through the smoking, bomb-scarred streets, one Londoner burst out with impetuous loyalty, "You're a good King, sir."

George VI turned. "And you're a good people," he said . . . and, saying it, there was not the slightest trace of his old stammer.

In the years following the war, as the King's health slowly failed, his wife was constantly at his side, helping him, encouraging him, calming him when his temper failed . . . just as, in turn, she was to help and encourage her elder daughter through the

first difficult years of a new monarchy . . . just as she was to help
and comfort the younger during those emotion-torn years before
she finally found happiness.

Who knows what memories came crowding back on the Queen
Mother that weekend as she called her dogs to her and walked
out on to the stone-flagged terrace of Royal Lodge, across the
lawn, past the big elm tree and on towards the miniature Welsh
cottage in which her two daughters, now grown up and married
with their own lives to lead, had played together so happily as
children.

CHAPTER FOURTEEN

GROWING UP

I

ONCE AGAIN IT was the Queen's official birthday. Back at the palace, after the colorful annual ceremony of Trooping the Color on Horse Guards Parade, the Queen sat her horse like a statue, a scarlet-clad, small, slightly serious figure, taking the salute as her troops marched past.

She rode her horse through the central archway into the inner quadrangle, dismounted, passed through the King's Door and went upstairs to the Balcony Room with its walls of yellow silk and its silk brocade Chinese curtains framing a view of the Victoria Memorial. Around the memorial and in front of the palace railings the waiting crowd wedged itself more tightly in anticipation of the Monarch's traditional one o'clock appearance on the balcony.

Big Ben struck the hour, the tall glass doors of the Balcony Room were flung open and the Queen came out. A burst of cheering greeted her appearance . . . a cheer which became a sudden lusty roar of approbation as it was seen that she was holding little Prince Andrew in her arms.

It was the first real glimpse the public had been bestowed of the baby prince since his birth nearly sixteen months earlier. Desirous as always of giving her children as normal an upbringing as is humanly possible for youngsters occupying such special positions, the Queen had decided that news and photographs of her third baby should be kept to an absolute minimum. Photographs of Andrew were accordingly released for publication a month after he was born, and there were to be no more for six months until the sixtieth birthday of his "Granny" was marked by a charming photograph of the Queen Mother with her small grandson.

Even photographs taken at the private ceremony in the Music

Room at Buckingham Palace, when Andrew, wrapped in a robe of Honiton lace which had once been worn by Queen Victoria, was christened at the silver lily font brought from Windsor Castle, were not issued for publication, though similar ones of Charles and Anne had been.

Her decision to keep Andrew's christening as a purely family affair emphasized the distinction the Queen likes to draw between her personal and public lives, though, inevitably, there are areas where the two overlap and merge. Particularly is this so where the royal children are concerned. On the one hand, there is an understandably loyal and seemingly insatiable public demand to know every smallest particular about them. On the other, is the Queen's natural desire, as a mother, to bring her children up as normally and naturally as possible.

For Charles, as heir to the throne, a considerable amount of publicity had been unavoidable earlier on and would be equally unavoidable later. Anne, too, had hitherto come in for a larger share of the public spotlight than her parents might have wished, though this might yet adjust itself of its own accord when she, in turn, went to boarding school.

And with Andrew, their third child, the Queen and her husband were clearly starting as they hoped to go on, keeping his upbringing as much their own personal affair as was humanly possible. Their resolve in this direction remained quite unaffected by the huffing and puffing of those who wanted to know more about the baby prince. Nor was it weakened by the nonsensical rumors concerning him which started to go the rounds.

Such rumors about royal children are nothing new, of course. Somewhat similar unkind rumors were circulating at one time about Princess Margaret. One rumor insisted that she was deaf and dumb, and strange as it seems now all these years later, it was not completely dispelled from the public mind until that childhood broadcast made in 1940 by the fourteen-year-old princess who was destined to become the Queen.

"Come, Margaret, say goodnight," Princess Elizabeth urged her sister at the end of the broadcast, and there was proof positive that Margaret was by no means dumb as she piped up, "Goodnight, children" in her childish treble.

Now, on a June morning in 1961, any rumors about Andrew were dispelled equally quickly. Barefooted against his mother's scarlet tunic as she held him on the balcony, he pointed first towards the cheering crowds with obvious interest before craning his tiny neck round to stare up at the Javelin fighters roaring overhead in salute.

For the first few months after the baby was born, the Queen carefully kept her official engagements to a reasonable minimum. Like a mother, she wanted to spend as much time with the new baby as she could possibly manage. Each morning he was brought down from the nursery by Mabel Anderson so that his mother could nurse him for half-an-hour or more in the privacy of her sitting room.

If friends came to call, down would come baby again for their admiration. Different people saw him in different ways. Some saw in Andrew a likeness to the Queen Mother. Others thought there was about him a fleeting resemblance to the Queen's uncle, the Duke of Gloucester. But there could be no denying that he had inherited his mother's nose, mouth and high forehead while the shape of his head was undeniably a miniature of Prince Philip's.

Everyone who saw Andrew complimented his mother on his looks, sturdiness and abundant charm. "A fine little boy you have there, Ma'am," commented the Queen's old friend, Dwight D. Eisenhower, on a day when he lunched at the palace and Andrew came down at the end of the meal. The ever-popular "Ike" had been succeeded now as President of the United States by the young John F. Kennedy . . . and Andrew was big enough and strong enough now to sit on his mother's lap and reach out to help himself to big handfuls of sugar as the Queen and the ex-President finished their coffee.

Her work over for the day, the Queen would take the elevator to the nursery floor to join in the pleasant daily ceremony of checking Andrew's increasing weight on the nursery scales and share in the fun of baby's bath-time. Often enough, she would put on an apron and undertake to bath the growing baby herself, powdering him with a fluffy pink powder-puff from the same padded baby basket she had used for Charles and Anne when they were tiny, and fluffing his silky blond hair with the same silver-backed hairbrush which had been used on her own hair in childhood before carrying him through to the night nursery and settling him down for the night in his canopied cot.

The baby's nurse, Mabel Anderson, always slept in the same room at night, while a newly-engaged assistant nursemaid now shared Anne's room. Charles, the schoolboy, was sufficiently grown

In June, 1961, Queen Elizabeth gave a dinner party at Buckingham Palace in honor of the late President John F. Kennedy.

The Queen, followed by her husband, leaves for the traditional Trooping of the Color at the Horse Guards' Parade. This ceremony was the first event to be transmitted by live television from Great Britain to Russia.

RAY BELLISARIO

Prince Charles skiing on Mt. Cairgorm, in Scotland near his
school, Gordonstoun.

Princess Anne arrives at Westminster Abbey for the wedding of
Princess Alexandra of Kent.

Princess Alexandra and Angus Ogilvy walk down the aisle of
Westminster Abbey after their marriage.

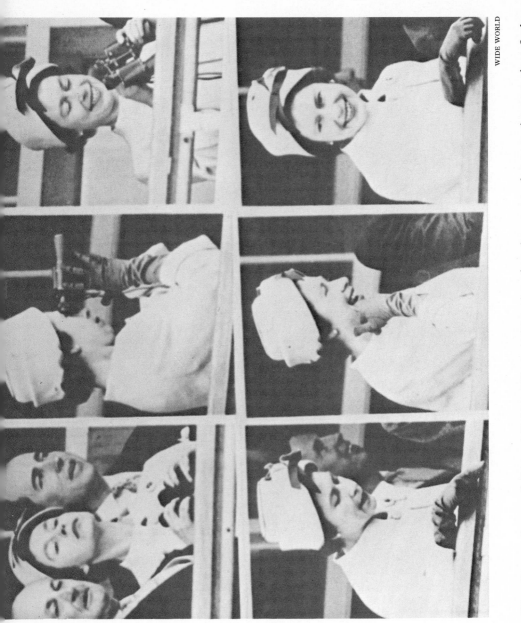

The Queen shows obvious delight while watching her favorite sport—horse racing—at the 184th

Princess Margaret and her husband, Lord Snowdon (Antony
Armstrong-Jones), visit the Acropolis in Athens.

Queen Elizabeth with her two youngest children, Prince Andrew and the newly born Prince Edward. (Photograph by Cecil Beaton)

up to move out of the nursery entirely and he was given a room of his own at the front of the palace. Utterly devoted to the new baby, Miss Anderson could scarcely be persuaded to take so much as an afternoon or evening off duty in those first few months after Andrew was born.

Whenever his work permitted him to spare the time, Philip, too, would go bounding up to the nursery to watch Andrew bathed and weighed at bed-time, picking him up and tossing him into the air as fathers will, caring not a bit if his baby son smeared his white shirt with fingers fresh from nursing a chocolate cooky. Inevitably, there came the evening when a childish mishap saw Philip hurrying downstairs again to change into a fresh suit before going out to fulfill an evening engagement.

Anxious not to uproot or unsettle the baby any more than was absolutely necessary, the Queen did not take Andrew with her when she went to Windsor at weekends. He stayed behind at the palace with his nurse, his routine undisturbed. But he went with his mother to Windsor for the long stay over Easter, to Balmoral in the summer and to Sandringham for Christmas, where there was now an extra stocking for the Queen to fill before tiptoeing into her children's rooms on a Santa Claus visit on Christmas Eve. The Queen has never bought ready-made Christmas stockings; she prefers to buy the individual toys and sweets, games and novelties, and make her own, one for each of the children, and one each, containing a new rubber bone and some dog biscuits, for the pet corgis.

Much of the new baby's time, that first summer of childhood, was spent outside in the palace gardens, lying in his carriage with only a single light blanket to cover him and a patrolling policeman to keep watch on him. On wet days the carriage was drawn up under the glass canopy of the garden entrance so that Andrew still benefited from the fresh air while sheltered from wind and rain. If ever he cried, a telephone call from the police lodge would bring Mabel Anderson hurrying quickly down from the upstairs nursery. But Andrew was a happy, contented baby, who chuckled and gurgled much more than ever he cried. And with the dawn of recognition, his happiest laughter was reserved for the young woman whose sometimes somber face was illuminated by a dazzling smile as she forgot the duties of monarchy for a short time while wheeling her baby across the gardens and round the lake.

For the Queen, busier than ever in her twin role of monarch and mother, time seemed positively to fly in those months following Andrew's birth. In no time at all, it seemed, he was lifting himself up, greeting mother and nanny alike with a big, beaming smile of recognition, doubling his birthweight ahead of schedule, graduating from milk and orange juice to strained baby foods, cutting his first teeth on a boned ring with a silver bell which had once belonged to Princess Anne.

There were times, of course, when the joys of motherhood and the duties of monarchy were directly in conflict. Such was the time when the Queen's forty-seven-day tour of India, Pakistan and Nepal made it quite impossible for her to be with her baby son on his first birthday. But "Granny" did duty for her, helping her grandson celebrate the occasion with a sponge cake baked in the royal kitchens, while his mother, six thousand miles away in Madras, was cutting an iced cake with one candle which had been thoughtfully prepared by the Madras State Government so that she should not feel too removed from her son on his first important milestone through life.

But there were compensations for even such a long absence as this, and the Queen, returning to London, was delighted to find that Andrew had gained several more pounds in her absence and was in the process of cutting another tooth.

Soon Andrew was beginning to toddle and his mother, whose ideas of motherhood are far from staid or old-fashioned permitted him to roam the palace gardens in his bare feet. As he grew older, he inherited the toy wheelbarrow which had once belonged to Charles and did his best to help the palace gardeners, though his help was sometimes a childish hindrance.

On fine afternoons there were picnic teas in the garden, with Anne hurrying down from her schoolroom to join in. Like all big sisters, she enjoyed nothing so much as wheeling Andrew round the gardens in his carriage, and later, as he outgrew it, she would play with him in the garden sandpit and in the miniature caravan with its imitation sink and cooker which had been a gift to her and Charles some years before.

Her deep affection for her baby brother was never more clearly seen than the day Andrew fell while toddling along one of the paths, grazing his knees and bursting, child-like, into tears. Anne tore across the garden towards him, almost in tears herself as she picked him up and consoled him.

To his mother, as all children to all mothers, Andrew seemed to grow up all too fast. He certainly grew straight and strong and sturdy. By Christmas, 1961, when the family again went to Sandringham, he was big enough to walk the length of Liverpool Street station instead of being carried, a sturdy, bright-eyed young man in a cream coat and gaiters, who, returning to London some weeks later, was sufficiently grown up to shake hands in dignified fashion with officials waiting on No. 9 platform to greet the Royal Family's return.

He was still too young, that second Christmas of his life, to join the rest of the family for Christmas lunch, but he came down from the nursery towards the end of the meal to sit on his mother's lap and share in the fun of pulling the crackers.

The Queen missed no opportunity of savoring to the full the joys of motherhood at this most absorbing period of Andrew's life, the transition from a baby to a small boy, even to the extent of having him with her during what she regards as her working hours.

While his mother sat at her desk, coping with the endless flow of state papers and official correspondence, Andrew would sit nearby on the carpet, playing happily with his toys. Inevitably, toys and balls and building blocks tended to become scattered across the floor and there was one occasion when a royal page, failing to observe a ball underfoot as he entered the Queen's presence, executed an unexpected ballet leap.

Andrew was growing up a happy, laughing, active, sometimes mischievous youngster. There was one mealtime when articles vanished from the table as fast as they were set out in an apparently deserted nursery. A chuckle betrayed the culprit. Andrew was found crouching behind one of the chintz-covered armchairs with the missing articles distributed around him.

A nursery hearth brush became a "bat" for improvised games of cricket in the corridor, once with Philip's mother, Princess Alice of Greece, consenting to act as bowler. That same corridor also formed an excellent proving ground for a pedal tractor which Andrew was given as a present.

With the coming of another Christmas, Andrew, now nearly three, was old enough to appreciate the heavy downfalls of snow which cloaked Sandringham in a crisp white mantle from Christmas onwards. He helped Charles and Anne with the construction of a magnificent snowman, complete with hat and pipe; joined merrily in their snowball fights on the terrace.

But again duty called the Queen away and Andrew's third birthday, as his first, was celebrated in the absence of his mother who was making another royal tour of Australia and New Zealand. But February 19—Andrew's birthday—brought an exciting telephone call to the royal nursery. His mother and father were calling all the way from Australia to wish him a happy birthday and find out how he was enjoying the gifts they had bought and wrapped in readiness for his birthday before leaving London.

II

As soon as he was old enough, the Queen began teaching Andrew to count, tell the time and say his ABC during half-hour lessons which she gave him each day in the dining room immediately after breakfast. The major problems of his education were still in the future.

The big decision concerning Prince Charles's upbringing had already been taken. He was following in his father's footsteps at Cheam and Gordonstoun. It was the question of Princess Anne's upbringing which was currently exercising the minds of the royal parents. She, too, would be going to boarding school in the future and meantime it would be beneficial to widen her horizons.

Unobtrusively, without publicizing the fact, her parents allowed Anne to go out and about far more than was generally realized at the time. She went to the Bank of England and to the House of Commons at question time. Along with her brother, Prince Charles, she paid an exciting visit to Scotland Yard. They were shown over the information room and the fingerprint department, and, as a special treat, allowed to summon police car Alpha One-Five over the radio call system and go out briefly on patrol.

She learned tennis from Dan Maskell and went ice skating at Richmond in black tights and a pleated skirt. When Colonel Glenn's space capsule was displayed at the Science Museum, she went there to see it. She went to the ballet and to Wimbledon for the tennis championships on more than one occasion, arriving there once in a helicopter flown by her father. She went to the theater and the circus. She saw *Oliver*, the Crazy Gang, the Black and White Minstrels and the Italian Piccoli Puppets, where she was taken backstage to see how the puppets were operated.

At the circus at Olympia she rode on the dodgems, the switch-

back and the ghost train and bagged several imitation ducks on
the miniature shooting range. She went to the movies with her
brother to see *Ben Hur* and when they came out the two of them
walked along the street until they could hail a taxi to take them
back to Buckingham Palace.

The palace Brownie Pack was re-born, and weekly meetings of
the Brownies, and later of the Girl Guides, brought the Queen's
daughter into contact with girls from less regal walks of life. As a
Brownie, Anne gained a proficiency badge for swimming as well
as both her second and first-class badges, passing a test which
included cooking a breakfast of bacon and sausages and knitting a
pair of woolly bootees. If she came later in life to some of the
things which children in more ordinary walks of life take for
granted, there were still other things in which she was considerably
advanced for her years.

By her eleventh birthday she could already handle a car sufficiently well to drive the Queen part of the way to Birkhall along
the private roads of the Balmoral estate when the family went
over to spend a day with the Queen Mother. She was growing up
fast and that year, for her birthday, she had a new bicycle in
replacement for one she had now outgrown. That earlier bicycle,
in turn, had been a replacement for a previous one which had
collapsed under the weight of Philip's manly frame.

The family had been for a picnic in the hills around Balmoral,
Anne going along on her bicycle. But she was too tired to cycle back
when it was time to return. Her father lifted her into the Land
Rover and volunteered to ride the bicycle back himself. But the
combination of Philip's weight and the rough going proved rather
more than the small machine could take. It collapsed under him so
completely that it could not even be pushed further, let alone ridden.
With the Land Rover out of sight by now, there was nothing for it
but to hoist the bicycle on his shoulder and carry it back.

Anne enjoyed cycling. But horses still remained the big, all-
absorbing passion. When her father played polo at Smith's Lawn,
the Princess, sensibly clad in slacks and a windbreaker, would
help to look after his polo ponies, polishing saddle and stirrups
until they gleamed in the watery sunlight. At the age of eleven
she made her first appearance in a public riding event, winning
a rosette for second place in a jumping contest for under-fourteens.
A few days later, at Ascot Gymkhana, she had a clear round in
another jumping event for which she entered, but collected four

faults in the jump-off. She presented the awards in the children's class at the Royal Windsor Horse Show, one of the very rare occasions on which the Queen has relaxed her rule against her children carrying out public duties until they are considerably older.

"They'll get plenty of that soon enough," Philip once told a man inquisitive enough to inquire why the royal children were not at a palace garden party. And the Queen has said, "We want our children to grow up as normally as possible. We believe that public life is not a fair burden to place upon them."

She declined to permit Anne to present the prizes in a much-publicized children's cookery competition. She turned down a suggestion that Charles might open a new bridge linking Devon with Cornwall, and she has banned the use of Andrew's portrait for commercial purposes. All this is part of her wish that her children should lead as normal a life as possible and few will quarrel with her views.

Anne graduated from the role of an angel in a nativity play staged by the Brownies in the Throne Room at the palace, to the title role in a seventy-five minute version of *Cinderella* performed by the palace Guides. Her mother, watching her as Cinderella, must surely have thought back to the time when she, herself, was Prince Charming in the same pantomime at Windsor Castle with Princess Margaret as Cinderella. Almost unnoticed, twenty eventful years had slipped away, and now here was her daughter as Cinderella while the part the Queen had once taken was now being played by twelve-year-old Gillian Huish, whose father worked in the royal stables.

The Queen's daughter went camping with the Guides, sleeping under canvas, taking her turn at helping with the cooking and washing up. She took part in a Guides swimming gala, beating the gun in her eagerness to plunge into the water at the start of her thirty-yards free style race. She swam to the side, climbed out, lined up afresh and finished third.

Her trip on *Britannia* to Tobruk for reunion with her parents at the tender age of three must by now have passed into the limbo of half-forgotten memories. Now, at the age of eleven, she had her first real experience of foreign travel when she journeyed to France on an ordinary cross-Channel steamer.

Shipping officials had received no advance notification of what was intended to be a purely private visit, a combination of holiday and education, but the news inevitably leaked out with the sort of consequences which have so often marred the ordinary upbringing the Queen and her husband try to achieve for their children.

What could have been an exciting visit to the colorful village fair at Chapelle-sur-Oudon was largely spoiled for the little princess by the dense crowds which thronged round her and the thrusting photographers with their all-too-candid cameras. Anne had hoped to buy something at the fair to take back for Andrew, but she became so nervous and upset by all that was going on around her that she had to leave without it. However, she did manage to buy gifts for her family in a small town some thirty miles from the Chateau de la Lorie, where she was staying with the eleven-year-old daughter of the Marquis Louis de Saint-Genys.

"Please don't tell anyone what I've bought," she begged the shopkeeper, "or the newspapers will print it and that will spoil the surprise."

With her brother for an escort, Anne went to her first real dance. It was the Garth Hunt Pony Club ball, held in the White Hart Hotel at Windsor. The dancers were predominantly young people, the Twist was all the rage, and the Queen's daughter thoroughly enjoyed herself, dancing with enthusiasm until it was time to go home again at fifteen minutes after eleven. She helped her father and brother to crew the family's newly-acquired racing yawl *Bloodhound* on an adventurous cruise of the Western Isles, and the girl in blue jeans, a windbreaker and a woolly cap who darted about the deck, handling fenders, ropes and boathooks with familiar ease, seemed a very different person to the girl in a dance dress at the White Hart Hotel.

For her birthday portrait, that year of 1962, the Princess posed in a new sweptback hairstyle, and by the following year, when she flew with her father to visit his relatives in Germany, ankle-socks had given way to teenage nylons. Though her thirteenth birthday was still some months away, the Queen's daughter was growing up fast, turning from a rather coltish girl into what promised to be a tall and assured young woman with something of the same happy-go-lucky nature as Princess Alexandra.

III

Like his sister, Prince Charles, too, was growing up fast during these all-important, formative years. When he first went to Cheam, he stuffed his pockets, as boys will, with all manner of odds and ends dear to the schoolboy heart. He read boys' comics, played with water pistols and raced about with hair so tousled that his mother, glimpsing him in this condition on one occasion, teased him with looking rather like a Shetland pony.

Once he had overcome his initial and understandable nervousness at leaving the quiet and ordered existence of his palace home for the noisy, brash, extrovert world of a boys' boarding school, he proved himself an average schoolboy in all respects. He tied for first in one of the end-of-term swimming races and a well-finished bookshelf which he had made was displayed in the school handicrafts exhibition.

He quickly revealed a very considerable aptitude for handicrafts and there was seldom a term when he did not travel home with some new gift he had made in the workshops at Cheam. He gave the bookshelf to his mother. He made a small stool for Princess Anne, a pen and pencil stand for Mabel Anderson, and a sturdy rocking elephant with a leather saddle for his baby brother Andrew.

His years at Cheam wrought a big change in Charles. He became more assured, less shy, more active, much more of the real boy in every respect, which his father had anticipated when advocating a boarding school education. More than once he proved he could stand up for himself and hold his own in boyish scuffles, though the nursery training of earlier days did not permit him to descend to such schoolboy habits as shouting and name-calling.

Almost imperceptibly, schooldays began to slim the puppy fat from him. At school he continued to wear the short trousers which were part of the regulation uniform, but at home, during the holidays, he graduated to long trousers. Then came the Christmas when suddenly he had outgrown such childish things as pantomimes. He wanted to go to something more grown-up. The show his parents picked for him was *The Sound of Music*.

At Cheam he gained his proficiency badge for cycling and took the part of Richard, Duke of Gloucester, in a school play dealing with the War of Roses. He twisted his leg in a fall on the school stairs and ended up hobbling around with it in plaster for a short time. "Here comes Hopalong," Anne would cry, teasingly. There was one term when he topped his class in geography, and his final winter at Cheam saw him captain of the school soccer team, just as his father had once captained the cricket and hockey teams at Gordonstoun.

It was during his final term, only a few weeks before he was due to leave Cheam for the more rugged environment of Gordonstoun, that he awoke one morning "feeling queer," as he explained to the school matron. He was seen by the school doctor and it was deemed advisable to call in Sir Wilfrid Sheldon, the tall, arrow-straight physician who has watched over the health of the royal children since they were born. The diagnosis was appendicitis. The Queen was informed and a cable sent off to Prince Philip, away on his South American tour.

Late that night it became evident that an immediate operation was imperative. An ambulance rushed the thirteen-year-old prince the fifty-eight miles from Cheam School to the Great Ormond Street Hospital for Sick Children in London. He arrived there shortly after midnight and at two o'clock in the morning the hospital's resident surgeon, summoned from his home at Isleworth, dealt with the offending appendix.

When his mother drove to the hospital to visit him the following afternoon he was already recovering satisfactorily, if slowly, from the effect of the operation.

The young prince's upbringing was by no means confined to the academic studies of schoolboy life. Outside school hours, there was tuition in the manly arts from Prince Philip. The two of them went sailing together, with Charles learning to manipulate a sail and handle a tiller. A bicycle gave way to a pony for practice at polo. Despite his previous practice on a bicycle with a miniature mallet and a tennis ball, Charles experienced understandable difficulty when it first came to striking a moving ball from the back of a moving horse. "Never mind," his father said consolingly. "It takes time to get the knack."

In the shooting field, however, Charles was more successful. Gone were the days when he was forced to content himself with merely counting the day's bag with the questionable help of a teasing younger sister. Now he had his own gun and gun-dog, a black labrador named Flash from the kennels at Sandringham, and a new relationship to experience . . . the relationship between master and dog. It was a relationship, initially, with its own problems to be solved.

There was an occasion at Balmoral soon after he first had the dog, when he wanted Flash to get into a Land Rover. But Flash took not the slightest notice of his young master's commands. When Charles went after him, Flash treated it as a great game and darted away. The Queen, coming out of the main entrance at that moment, was just in time to witness the sight of Flash bounding round the front lawn with Charles dashing after him. Making no bones about it, she pursed her lips and gave a shrill whistle. Obediently, Flash came to heel.

At Sandringham and Balmoral alike, veteran gamekeepers watched the way the young prince handled a gun with shrewd and expert eyes. "A likely lad," was the general consensus of opinion among them. "One of these days he'll be a very good shot."

This side of the boy's upbringing brought repeated and much-publicized protests from the League Against Cruel Sports, even to the lengths of sending the Queen a resolution of protest when Charles was reported as having shot a stag at Balmoral. But the Queen, who had stalked deer herself from the age of eighteen, was not prepared to let others dictate the type of upbringing she accorded her son.

There was another side to out-of-school activities to which no one could object. For a king-in-the-making, ordinary schooling is not enough, and side by side with his academic studies Charles was also being trained by his parents towards the high position that is his destiny. In his free time, he was taken to such places as the Houses of Parliament and Westminster Abbey, where, significantly perhaps, one of the things he asked to see was the coronation chair in which he will one day sit.

On one occasion he joined his parents at the large, oval, mahogany table in the 1844 Room for one of the informal luncheon parties which have become a feature of palace life in recent times. These palace lunches, attended by such varied guests as politicians and painters, scientists and pop singers, businessmen and footballers, play their part in helping the Queen keep in touch with the vast and changing world outside the palace. With Charles developing gradually from boyhood to manhood, she felt that his horizons should begin to widen too.

Since before the age of five Charles has been imperceptibly trained to know who he is and what he will one day be. In him, as he has grown up, prince and schoolboy have been inextricably mingled. It was surely the prince rather than the boy, who, passing through one of the compartments on the royal train, told members of the staff who were sitting there, "Please don't bother to stand up." But it was the schoolboy rather than the prince who felt suddenly peckish on the way to Sandringham and asked for the royal car to be stopped so that he could pop into a shop at Knebworth to buy something to eat. He decided upon a pork pie and a packet of crackers.

"Do you think you should?" said the detective with him, referring to the cocktail biscuits. "They've got cream in them."

But Charles knew better. "It isn't cream. It's cheese, isn't it?" he appealed to the shopkeeper.

The shopkeeper agreed and the boy got his cocktail biscuits.

IV

It was the beginning of the 1962 summer term at Gordonstoun, that much-talked about and somewhat unorthodox school in the Scottish Highlands which owes much of its recent fame to the fact that Prince Philip was once The Guardian there or head boy. Now boys of another generation, returning to Gordonstoun that term, found a police car parked prominently outside the main gates. A uniformed policeman inquired their names before they were permitted to pass through into the school grounds. Boys being boys, some of them thought it amusing to give false names, causing the unfortunate policeman some fruitless searching through the printed lists he had been given before the sly grins on the boys' faces betrayed the fact that they were pulling his leg.

The reason for the security check became plain later that day when the school's most famous alumnus arrived at Gordonstoun to see again the granite-walled buildings within which he had absorbed those principles which are still today so much a part of him. Accompanying him was his son, Prince Charles, now thirteen, changing rapidly from boyhood to manhood. Looking very grown up for his years, there was much about the son that was reminiscent of the father that day at Gordonstoun.

Charles's hands were clasped behind his back, duplicating his father's famous pose, as he walked over to be introduced to his headmaster and housemaster. His hands were dug deep in the jacket pockets of his lounge suit as he was shown round Windmill Lodge, his new home for some years to come. He looked assured and confident, every inch a prince.

Later, after his parents had gone, he reverted from the prince to the schoolboy, changing from his long-trousered lounge suit to the Gordonstoun uniform of dark blue short trousers with no side pockets, gray-blue open-neck shirt and accompanying sweater.

The decision to send Charles to his father's old school on the windswept shores of the Moray Firth had been taken some time before, while newspapers and public alike were still speculating as to what would happen to him after his years at Cheam. It was, as all such decisions concerning sons should be, patently the father's choice, and all the more acceptable to the Queen on that account.

Once again the royal parents appealed for their son to be allowed to grow up and be educated like any other boy. They fully understood the very natural interest in his education, said the statement from Buckingham Palace. "They feel," the statement continued, "he will only be able to derive full benefit from his days at school if he is not made the center of special attention."

Where the upbringing of their children is concerned, the Queen and her husband are in an unenviable and difficult position. As much as the royal parents may wish it, it is quite impossible for them to treat their children as ordinary youngsters. If special safeguards are not taken, then the children are harassed by crowds of enthusiastic sightseers and stalked by enterprising photographers, as Anne was on her visit to France. If extra precautions are taken, such as the tall detective installed at Gordonstoun with instructions to accompany Charles wherever he goes, then the boy inevitably comes to be regarded as "someone special" by his schoolfellows.

The detective apart, from the outset Charles was treated at Gordonstoun like any other boy. He was listed as Prince Charles in the school handbook, but he was simply Charles to the masters in class and to the boys with whom he lived and worked. He shared a dormitory with several other boys, undressed in the adjoining locker room, made his own bed, cleaned his own shoes.

He turned out stripped to the waist for the early-morning jog-trot or alternative physical exercises which are the Gordonstoun method of getting its boys thoroughly awake for the day's work. Afterwards, he lined up for the morning shower. He negotiated the school's tricky commando course in safe, if plodding, fashion, even to swarming across a rope without coming to grief in the lake below.

He tried his hand at everything, uncomplainingly, seeking no special favors. He did his share of menial duties, sweeping floors, weeding flower beds, raking gravel paths. He took his turn in waiting on table at meal-times. Each Tuesday and Friday, for part of his first term, he even helped to carry the ash barrels of Windmill Lodge out into the roadway for collection and emptying.

For a minor transgression of the school rules, he was awarded the regulation punishment of running and walking alternately in circles for a fixed period. He played cricket that summer and rugby the following winter, emerging muddy and bruised from a strenuous game against boys from Aberdeen Grammar School on a rain-soaked pitch.

He flew home to London tourist-class at the end of each term, and his parents were scrupulously careful to telephone, write and see him no more than the parents of any other boy. Their only visit to the school during their son's first year was when the school staged a handicrafts exhibition in the local hall at nearby Duffus. Charles had found a new outlet for his undoubted aptitude for handicrafts—the school pottery shop—and several articles he had turned on the potter's wheel were included in the exhibition.

When he was asked once how Charles was coming along at Gordonstoun, Prince Philip gave the sort of grinning answer fathers invariably do. "Well, he hasn't run away yet," he said.

In fact, all along Charles has made steady, if unspectacular, progress. The Gordonstoun system in this respect is considerably unorthodox. A new boy, though he already has his school uniform, must earn the right to it by satisfactory progress and the general pattern of his behavior. Charles had done this by the end of his first term. Soon afterwards he qualified for the school training plan, under which supervision is somewhat relaxed and a boy is trusted to do the things he is supposed to do, and is on his honor to accord himself minus marks if he slacks in any direction or commits any breaches of the rules. He is on his honor, too, to carry out any punishment he may be awarded in consequence of his own marking.

Charles's right to his school uniform was celebrated in traditional Gordonstoun fashion when he was seized bodily by a group of other boys, carried shoulder-high to the nearest washroom and dumped fully clothed into a bath of cold water. All new boys, sooner or later, undergo this cold and watery ceremony, and the school authorities made no attempt to intervene in the case of Charles. To have done so would have been contrary to the Queen's wish that he should be treated like all the other boys.

He joined the school choir, went swimming at Elgin baths, where he gained, first, an elementary certificate and, later, a bronze medallion for life saving. He bicycled over to Hopeman Harbor, where the school's cutters and schooners are moored, for lessons in seamanship. He learned how to capsize and right a canoe. Between seamanship lessons, along with his school-fellows he invaded the village shops in Hopeman in search of buns and tarts to satisfy the pangs of hunger created by sea air and physical exercise.

Initially, as at Cheam, many of the boys tended to keep their distance. After all, this was their future King and there was the inevitable awkwardness of knowing how to talk to him and how far to treat him like any other boy. But this stage passed as Charles settled down to his new life at Gordonstoun, and the other boys settled down to Charles. His own unassuming manner and do-as-you-would be-done-by attitude to school life soon won him friends. When the boys of Windmill Lodge began practicing for the school's annual sports, it was Charles who produced a stop-watch and obligingly lent it to whoever wanted to borrow it.

He studied English and history, French and Latin, science and Scripture. He learned to hurl the javelin and put the shot. In his free time, he went swimming in the indoor baths at Elgin, skiing at Cairngorm. He learned to ski during a winter sports holiday in Switzerland, another step in the big royal experiment of living as ordinary a life as possible. But like his sister's visit to France, Charles's stay in Switzerland was partly spoiled by the persistence of photographers and the enthusiastic curiosity of the general public.

"Please leave the boy alone," begged Princess Louis of Hesse, at whose holiday villa he was staying. "He has only eight days' holiday in which to learn to ski and have some fun at it."

To a large extent, her plea fell on deaf ears. Continental photographers went so far as to invade the private grounds of the villa where Charles was staying in their determination to get better and more candid photographs, an intrusion halted only by threats of imprisonment and expulsion from the Swiss authorities.

Despite such harassing conditions, Charles, warmly clad in black stretch trousers and a blue jacket, picked up the rudiments of skiing sufficiently quickly to obtain twenty-five points out of a possible twenty-eight in his first test.

His enthusiasm for handicrafts found yet another outlet during a visit to Elgin. In a local scrapyard he and some school friends unearthed a rusty, dilapidated four-seater tandem. They persuaded the owner of the scrapyard to let them have it, took it back to

Gordonstoun with them and set to with a will to restore it to working order. They cleaned away the rust and grime of years, painted it, oiled it and, finally, used it around the school grounds, the four of them, pedalling in furious unison, hurtling along at perilously high speeds.

In another of the more unorthodox sides of Gordonstoun education, Charles learned how to read a map and box the compass, how to operate an oil stove and cook a meal in a mess-tin. He was taught how to treat wounds and burns, fainting and electric shocks, and successfully passed an examination in elementary first-aid which included treating a supposedly fractured arm with splints and bandages. He qualified for the school cadet force. Warmly clad in long trousers and a tartan shirt, thick sweater and windproof jacket, stout walking boots on his feet, he took part in a number of hill-climbing expeditions, his newly-acquired knowledge of mess-tin cookery coming in useful in the preparation of a meal of bacon and beans after a night spent in an isolated hut high in the Cairngorms.

His seamanship improved to the stage where he was included in the schoolboy crew of one of the school's two schooners for a training cruise of the Western Isles. But it is the idiosyncrasies of royalty that make the headlines rather than the normalities, and Charles's undoubted ability as a schoolboy sailor attracted considerably less attention than the fact that he walked into the bar of a Stornaway hotel and ordered himself a cherry brandy. Even then, the incident might have attracted less attention than it did if it had not at first been denied by Buckingham Palace.

It was, of course, a breach of the licensing laws—Charles was only fourteen—and presumably he was suitably punished on his return to Gordonstoun at the end of the cruise. Even so, one can picture his father's quizzical grin when he heard what had happened. It showed, after all, exactly the sort of initiative he had sent his son to Gordonstoun to acquire.

Gordonstoun is a school where a boy is judged not so much on the marks he obtains in examinations or the success he achieves on the playing fields as on the way his character develops in the face of such obstacles as boredom and mockery, discomfort and hardship. Charles had yet another obstacle to overcome—the specialness of his position—and the way he has shaped so far must surely have delighted his father, obviously so eager for his son to show himself to be a real chip off the paternal block.

CHAPTER FIFTEEN

A ROYAL "THANK YOU"

I

"I AM DELIGHTED," the Queen said when she learned that her cousin, Princess Alexandra, was planning to marry the Hon. Angus Ogilvy. Unhesitatingly, she gave her royal consent to their formal betrothal.

Between these two royal cousins there has grown up over the years a bond of affection that goes deeper and is more enduring than mere relationship, and the Queen could not have been more pleased than to see her tall, Junoesque cousin marry into an ancient Scottish line whose members had been close to the Royal Family through successive generations.

The prospective bridegroom's grandmother, the Dowager Countess of Airlie, had been lady-in-waiting to the Queen's own grandmother, Queen Mary, and a close friend. His father, the Earl of Airlie, held the post of Lord Chamberlain to the Queen Mother's Household. His brother, Lord Ogilvy, had acted as escort to the Queen's sister, Princess Margaret, in the days when both were unmarried.

In the years since the Queen ascended the throne, no one, Prince Philip apart, has helped her more untiringly or unstintingly than Princess Alexandra. With so many royal tours bursting out in all directions, so may state visitors to be met and welcomed, so many public functions of all kinds to be attended, with Prince Philip busy in his own directions, Princess Margaret not always available, the Queen Mother and Princess Marina getting no younger, and the Duke of Gloucester feeling the need to be relieved of some of his own share of the royal burden, it has been Princess Alexandra who has helped to ease things to a considerable extent.

In the four busy years which preceded her own betrothal, the Princess visited Latin America, Siam and Cambodia, Sweden and

Australia, Hong Kong, Burma and Japan, as well as standing in for the Queen at the independence celebrations in Nigeria and fulfilling scores of engagements throughout the length and breadth of Britain.

Like the Queen herself, Alexandra takes her royal duties with painstaking seriousness. Before visiting Sheffield, she assiduously read up all about the steel industry. As president of the Guide Dogs for the Blind Association, she insisted upon being blind-folded and led along by a newly-trained dog to discover for herself exactly what it felt like to be entirely dependent on a four-footed friend. Before going to Australia she spent weeks doing her "homework," reading books, pamphlets and specially-prepared memoranda to familiarize herself with life down under.

Before she went to Hong Kong she practiced Chinese phrases each day while taking her morning bath.

And wherever she has gone, at home or abroad, she has im-printed the indelible informality of her own refreshing per-sonality. When she launched the frigate *Jaguar* there was a hitch in the proceedings when the vessel obstinately declined to move down the slipway. But Alexandra was more than equal to the occasion. To the cheers of the crowd, she ran forward and pre-tended to push . . . the sort of unrehearsed royal gesture which has become her hallmark.

In America, a young man in the crowd called out, loud enough for everyone to hear, "You're a swell girl, Alex." She did not pretend she had not heard, as more reserved members of the Royal Family would have done. She smiled in his direction and called back, "Thank you very much."

In Australia, her first solo tour overseas, she climbed into her car outside Brisbane cathedral and sat plop on the glossy top hat of Queensland's Governor, Sir Henry Abel Smith. With so many people watching, it could have been a moment of acute embarrass-ment. But not for the irrepressible Alexandra. Smiling gleefully, she picked up the battered top hat and waved it at the laughing crowd.

That Australian tour—ninety-eight official functions crowded into six weeks of time and 8,000 miles of travel while the Queen was at Balmoral, resting from her strenuous Canadian tour and in anticipation of Prince Andrew—could have been a considerable ordeal for a young woman of twenty-two. If it was any sort of an ordeal for Princess Alexandra, she did not let the fact show other than on two quite exceptional occasions. There was one occasion when she was crushed against the side of her car by over-enthusiastic students in Sydney; another when she was completely hemmed in by milling crowds at Healesville with the flash-bulbs of amateur photographers popping almost in her face. Even the Queen, so much more experienced at such things, has been known occasionally to become tense and nervous when the enthusiasm of a large crowd threatens to get out of hand, and no one would fault Princess Alexandra for behaving in the same fashion.

Such isolated incidents apart, Alexandra's progress across Australia was a complete triumph. Her youth, her looks, and, more than anything else, her informality turned a schedule which was labeled "stuffy and pompous" at the outset into an "accent on youth" tour which met and matched the breezy, uninhibited outlook of the Australians themselves.

At one point of the tour there was a buffet lunch for young people at which everyone seemed to sit around in tongue-tied awkwardness. Then the Princess came in, sizing up the situation at a glance. "Oh, what a dreadful silence," she exclaimed, and the very naturalness of the remark served to break the ice and ensure the success of the function.

In Brisbane her attention was caught by two students standing by the roadside with a blackboard on which was lettered, "See you in Maryborough." Sure enough, she did see them again in Maryborough. Now their blackboard was inscribed, "Here we are." Alexandra had them tracked down and invited to the royal ball, where she specifically sought them out to dance with them.

In Brisbane, previously, she had asked for four airmen from her guard-of-honor to be invited to the royal ball. She, herself, extended invitations to four young farmers she met. And in Rockhampton, at yet another royal ball, she danced with a bank clerk and a journalist, a solicitor's clerk and a young businessman. About such behavior, on the part of a royal princess, there was nothing that was either stuffy or pompous.

So successful was Alexandra's Australian tour that the following year, with Princess Margaret seeking to be excused because of her recent marriage, the Queen asked her cousin to fly to Nigeria to represent her at that country's independence celebrations. The visit turned into another triumph which even the Nigerian rain-fall could not damp down. Alexandra drove through the rain with the top of her car down, dye from her hat trickling down her smiling face, so that people should see her. At a garden party, despite a cloudburst, she insisted on squelching around under an umbrella until her shoes and dress alike were thoroughly soaked.

In 1961 she was off again, this time to Burma, Thailand, Japan and Hong Kong, where she ate with chopsticks, had a trip in a sampan and drove a diesel. Informal as ever, she also went for a trip on the famous Suzie Wong ferry, buying her ticket with a borrowed Hong Kong dollar, and for a ride on a tram, during the course of which she skillfully fended off the joint efforts of three U.S. sailors to date her.

It is perhaps as well that the tall princess has a natural flair for handling such un-royal situations for her royal travels have brought many such her way. She has watched native girls diving for pearls, seen snake-charmers at work at close quarters, talked with Geisha girls, visited a harem and, in Aden, squatted shoeless to eat with her fingers at an Arab banquet.

"I mustn't play the giddy goat," she had told Australian newsmen before leaving London. Nor did she. But she brought her own special brand of youthful breeziness to the stuffiest of functions. Time and again, she ignored the rule that there should be no unofficial roadside stops. She even stopped her car, in a rural area some twenty miles from Brisbane, to talk to a solitary twelve-year-old girl who was standing by the roadside to watch her pass, and gave her some sweets before driving on. She chatted with all manner of people not included in the official line-ups . . . choir girls and waitresses, Red Cross girls and schoolchildren.

At a state fair she halted her tour of inspection to pose for a small boy with a box camera . . . just as, opening a nurses' school in Britain, she had obligingly popped her head in through a window of the men's chest ward and kept it there while one of the pyjama-clad patients fetched his camera and took a picture.

On a trip down the Brisbane River, she gleefully tooted the siren of her launch again and again in response to the cheers of the crowd lining the banks, and, showing the same thoughtfulness that the Queen always shows, before leaving Brisbane she went along to a farewell party for her drivers and baggage men.

Princess Alexandra is like that . . . thoughtful, considerate, essentially human. Photographers rate her as the most co-operative of all the Royal Family, and leaving Australia she found a magnificent bouquet awaiting her from the photographers for whom she had provided such worthwhile pictures. Characteristically, she turned round and blew them a thank-you kiss.

II

Princess Alexandra has large, gray-green eyes, a warm, clear complexion, an oval face framed with honey-brown hair. She shares the Queen's enthusiasm for horses, though not for racing, and the two of them ride together frequently when on holiday at Balmoral or Sandringham. But like her mother, she does not share the general royal enthusiasm for the great outdoors.

While the Queen, the Queen Mother and even Princess Margaret will cheerfully endure wind and rain, snow and sleet, tramping round at the heels of the menfolk as they pursue pheasants and partridges, grouse and hares across the wide acres of Balmoral or Sandringham, Princess Marina and her daughter will slip away unobtrusively at the first opportunity to seek the shelter of the house and the warmth of the fireside. "It's much too cold for me out there," Princess Marina has observed, sinking thankfully into a big armchair in front of a crackling log fire and ringing for tea.

Alexandra takes after her mother in other ways, too. She has inherited both Princess Marina's figure and impeccable dress sense, her fondness for antique furnishings and her appreciation of music. Asked once what she would like for a gift, she replied promptly, "Some Scarlatti sonatas, please."

But she does not share her mother's dietary determination. "I do wish Mummy wouldn't diet so much," she sighed at a royal reception after Princess Marina, feeling faint, had summoned her car to take her home. "Then this sort of thing wouldn't happen."

Alexandra's own dieting is usually limited to simply foregoing potatoes, but even then temptation is sometimes too much for her. There was an occasion at Balmoral when she firmly refused a helping of potatoes to go with the grouse at dinner. But a few minutes later she was enviously eyeing the succulent, crisply-fried potatoes on the neighboring plate of Prince Philip. "May I steal one?" she asked, and did so.

The story of how the Kent family lived in the years following the then Duke of Kent's tragic death when his seaplane blundered into the side of a Scottish mountain . . . of how his widow disposed of the lease of their London home, sold some of her dead husband's paintings, antiques and art treasures, cut down on servants, entertaining and travel has become part of royal history.

But though they may not have been over-affluent by royal standards, the Kents were not as poor as all that. When five servants were paid off, more than that number still remained. When three cars had been sold, there were still two to call on. Later, there was a royal rent-free apartment at Kensington Palace, renovated, close-carpeted, centrally heated and furnished with fine antiques, and an unspecified allowance at the Queen's discretion.

Yet there was a need to be careful for royal outgoings are heavy, and Alexandra's upbringing brought her into touch with ordinary life in a way the Queen's never did. By the same token, her life was free in a way the Queen's never can be. She could board a bus in Kensington High Street to visit her bank in the Strand or go shopping in Oxford Street. In 1960, when she passed her driving test after some five years of spasmodic instruction, buses were superseded by an easily-parked compact car.

Once, shopping for men's sweaters at a chain store in Oxford Street, she gauged the size she wanted by the simple expedient of holding them up against herself. There was another occasion when she walked into a shoe department at a time when the only assistant was already serving someone else. "Don't worry about me," said the Princess. "I don't mind waiting."

Only a few days before her Westminster Abbey wedding to Angus Ogilvy she dropped into a supermarket, emerging again with a shopping bag containing chops and frozen peas.

III

The Royal Family was getting better and better at keeping its personal secrets. Not a whisper of Princess Margaret's attachment to Tony Armstrong-Jones had leaked out until the official announcement. Alexandra's brother, the young Duke of Kent, had carefully sidetracked speculation as to his feelings for Miss Katherine Worsley by allowing himself to be seen out publicly with a succession of other young ladies. So careful was he to cover his tracks when meeting her in the Tyrol during a period of leave from his regiment in Germany that he left camp without signing out . . . an omission for which he received the traditional army reprimand upon his return. Not until two weeks before the official engagement did that particular cat start to slip out of the bag when the Duke hurried off to his duties at the War Office leaving a diamond and sapphire ring on the table behind him at Kensington Palace.

Now, in turn, Princess Alexandra was to keep her attachment to Angus Ogilvy a closely-guarded secret until the official announcement of their engagement in November, 1962. They had, in fact, known each other for a considerable time. They had met at a house party at Luton Hoo, the home of Sir Harold and Lady Zia Wernher, close personal friends of the Queen, where they found themselves partnering each other on the tennis court and, later, on the dance floor. Subsequently, Angus asked the Princess to several of his own cocktail parties, to one of which she went along early to help with preparing the snacks. They met secretly for dinner, on her return from each successive overseas tour. They went to the movies together and to the celebrated 400 Club. But not a whisper of their growing friendship trickled through to the gossip columns, most of which had their attention firmly riveted on Lord O'Neill as the most likely suitor for the hand of the Princess.

Once the secret was out with the official announcement, a leather-framed photograph of his royal fiancée appeared on Mr. Ogilvy's desk at his office in Old Broad Street, and he made no bones about giving her an enthusiastic kiss in full public view on Perth station when she visited his ancestral home.

Half-an-inch taller than Prince Philip, with blue eyes and a crinkle-faced grin, Angus endeared himself to the public by his obvious and openly displayed affection for the Princess and by his reaction towards the royal occasions in which he inevitably found himself caught up.

At the Royal Film Show he darted straight towards Jessie Matthews with outstretched arms and an eager cry of "My old pin-up."

Between the betrothal and the wedding, he found no necessity to retreat into the privacy of Buckingham Palace. He was out and about as usual, went back and forth to his office in Old Broad Street. Even on the day before the wedding, which was also the morning after a night-before reception and ball at Windsor Castle from which he did not get back until 4 A.M., he was up at eight o'clock as usual to go to the office.

The Queen and Prince Philip acted as hosts to a whole regiment of European royalties, crowned and uncrowned, throned and exiled, converging on London for the wedding ceremony. By way of entertainment in keeping with the general informal character of the occasion, they hired two coaches, filled them with their guests— kings and queens, princes and princesses, counts and margraves— and took them on a day's trip of the English countryside.

They stopped for a light lunch at the Hind's Head Hotel in Bray, where Philip had sometimes dropped in for a drink on his way from Corsham to London to court the girl who was then Princess Elizabeth.

In those days he was a young naval officer driving a small M.G. and with no more money than any other young naval officer. Now, in 1963, the M.G. had given way to an Alvis and his income was steady at £40,000 ($112,000.) a year. But he went back with his tastes unchanged, calling for a pint of bitter "in a pewter tankard, please" before sitting down with his royal guests to a meal of lobster and lamb, molasses tart and Stilton cheese.

The Queen's affection for Princess Alexandra, and her gratitude for all that Alexandra had done in recent times by way of royal duty, was clearly shown by the reception and ball given at Windsor Castle in honor of the royal bride-to-be and the tall, handsome company director she was to marry. It was easily the biggest party held in that old, gray castle by the Thames since the far-off days of Queen Victoria . . . and a good deal livelier than any party of Victorian times. There were 1600 guests, two bands, 125 extra servants.

In St. George's Hall, which Prince Philip uses as a badminton court sometimes on wet weekends, tables groaned under a buffet supper of lavish proportions . . . smoked salmon and caviar, turkey and chicken, ham and duck, fruit and cream, with bacon and eggs later for those who stayed on until almost time for breakfast.

In the neighboring Waterloo Chamber, location of the traditional annual dinner celebrating Wellington's victory, the huge mahogany table, large enough to seat 150 guests, had been removed, the vast Indian carpet made for Queen Victoria rolled back and stored away, and the floor was given over to dancing which ranged from the sedateness of a Strauss waltz to the uninhibited liveliness of the Twist.

For Charles and Anne, it was their first real taste of a royal ball and naturally they made the most of it. They filmed some of the dancing from the vantage point of the gallery which overlooks the Waterloo Chamber, and, later, looking exceptionally grown-up for their years, joined in themselves. Charles partnered his grandmother, the Queen Mother, while Anne, as principal bridesmaid at the coming wedding, danced with the prospective bridegroom.

But it was essentially Princess Alexandra's night. As the Queen and her dinner guests entered the Waterloo Chamber and the band struck up a Strauss waltz, everyone waited for the Queen and Prince Philip to lead off the dancing, as is customary on such royal occasions. But, smiling, the Queen stood aside, motioning Princess Alexandra and her fiancé to take the floor first with a gracious gesture which said plainly, "This is for you."

Only when the two of them had circled the ballroom, the focus of all eyes, did she and Prince Philip follow suit as a sign for the general dancing to commence.

IV

Alexandra's brother, the Duke of Kent, flew home from Hong Kong, where he was stationed with his regiment, to give his sister in marriage. Princess Anne was chief bridesmaid. Not yet thirteen, she could easily have been taken for sixteen in a dress of creamy satin, her blonde hair upswept in a very sophisticated chignon. Her brother, Charles, looked equally grown-up in a charcoal-gray business suit, his voice, which had broken since going to Gordonstoun, now a mature and masculine version of the Queen's own clear, carrying tones.

Princess Alexandra wore a wedding dress of magnolia-tinted lace, and Philip, as always, managed to ease the strain of the occasion with a joke about the weight of her twenty-foot bridal train, so long and trailing that there was one point during the marriage ceremony when she had to check herself rather abruptly to prevent it wrenching her tiara from her head.

That tiara was the same one Alexandra's mother had worn twenty-nine years before for her marriage to the happy-go-lucky prince whose life was to end so tragically in a war-time air crash. Watching her daughter marry, Princess Marina would have been less than human if her thoughts had not gone winging back over the years, and there were times during the wedding ceremony when her face wore an expression as if, momentarily for her, Westminster Abbey was peopled with the ghosts of that other wedding.

"It reminded me so much of my own wedding," she confided in a friend, later.

CHAPTER SIXTEEN

THE CHANGING PRINCE

I

IT WAS EIGHT o'clock in the morning . . . almost any morning not long ago when Prince Philip was at home at Buckingham Palace and not overseas in Montreal or San Francisco, South America or Australia, not braving the biting cold of the Antarctic or paying a flying visit to his sister in Germany.

At the same time that she called the Queen, Bobo MacDonald also took Philip the small pot of tea which he always likes to start the day. The Queen has nothing until breakfast. In the adjoining bathroom, one of Philip's two valets—Joseph Pearce and that same James MacDonald who was valet to the Queen's father—ran the Prince's bath and then went through to the dressing room to lay out the clothes Philip would be wearing that day.

His bath over, Philip wrapped himself in a dressing gown and went through to breakfast in the dining room of the Royal Family's private apartment. He and the Queen breakfast together, occupying adjoining places at the oval table of highly polished mahogany, the day's newspapers between them on the breakfast table, a transistor radio playing as they eat.

For a man who consistently consumes so much energy in both his work and his play, Philip is a comparatively small eater. A single course of bacon and egg and one cup of coffee—black, with sugar—is usually sufficient for him at breakfast. For lunch, a main meat course with a side plate of salad, followed by cheese and crackers, an apple or a few grapes, usually suffices. He seldom bothers with afternoon tea. For dinner he has perhaps a small portion of fish, a small portion of meat, a side-plate of salad and a light sweet such as ice cream. He is a quick, disinterested eater who prefers his beef rare, his game aged and his cheese strong.

"I never see any home cooking," he confided once to some schoolgirls during a visit to Birmingham. "All I get is fancy stuff."

Perhaps it was said whimsically, intended as a joke. While it is true that the Queen does not do the family cooking any more than she does the washing and ironing—nor would one reasonably expect her to have the time for such tasks, even assuming the inclination—palace meals, with the exception of official banquets, are seldom exotic.

There was a time, earlier in their marriage, when Philip liked cooking his own breakfast in an electric frying pan and preparing his own salad dressing. But those days have gone. His crowded working day no longer permits him the time for such culinary niceties, and his own cookery exploits these days are limited to the portable barbecue outfit which accompanies family picnics in the hills above Balmoral in summer.

Philip's working day starts over breakfast, as he skims rapidly through the daily newspapers while eating, sometimes drawing his wife's attention to some item in the papers which concerns the Royal Family. He is more sensitive than is the Queen to newspaper comments and criticism, and items which she will shrug off, smile over or simply ignore can rouse him to indignation. Gossip about their private lives, and candid camera shots of themselves or the children taken with long-range lenses are particularly irritating to him and he was moved to indignation over an article entitled "Does England Really Need A Queen?" which appeared in a leading U.S. magazine at a time when he and the Queen were actually visiting Canada and the United States.

"If they must print this sort of thing, surely they could at least do it when we weren't here," he commented.

Breakfast over, Philip leaves the table, pausing perhaps for a few words of father and son conversation with little Prince Andrew who has popped into the dining room on his way back from a morning walk with his nurse in the palace gardens. While the Queen spends the next half-hour giving her small son his daily lesson, teaching him to read, count and tell the time. Philip heads for his dressing room. He is a lightning dresser. With his clothes laid out ready for him, he can be dressed and on his way through to his gadget-laden study in little more than two minutes flat. To him, clothes, like food, are simply essentials to the business of living. He has never been one for dressing up, for setting or following fashion.

In the days when he was courting the then Princess Elizabeth he thought nothing of turning up to spend a weekend at Royal

Lodge with a change of clothes crammed haphazardly into a naval-type valise. Nor has monarchy made any great difference to his attitude in this direction. Britain's tailors and hatters, who hoped that the Queen's husband might boost business for them by setting a succession of new trends, as the Duke of Windsor did in the days when he was Prince of Wales, have been doomed to disappointment. Except when he is wearing uniform, as often as not Philip will go around bareheaded, often wrenching his suits out of shape by his trick of stuffing his hands deep into his jacket pockets.

But however shapeless he may render his suits, however much his hair may have thinned with the passage of time, his quick, boyish grin, slim build and perennial well-scrubbed, athletic appearance make him still a Prince Charming to dowagers and debutantes, office girls and factory workers the world over.

II

Whatever criticisms may be leveled against Prince Philip— and there have been not a few over the years—no one can deny that he is a hard and tireless worker. "I am quite used to an eighteen-hour day," he told the mayor of San Francisco when he visited the city in 1962. So many different tasks does he tackle, and so thoroughly does he tackle each one of them, that he is seldom at the palace for lunch and, often, an evening engagement will keep him away from the palace for dinner.

Even if there is no evening engagement to take him out and about, he will not infrequently work in his study until midnight or later. "If he takes on much more," the Queen once confided in a friend, "he won't even have time for breakfast."

Wherever her husband has gone in the course of the world-wide travels he has undertaken in recent years, he has left a trail of harassed industrialists and exhausted mayors behind him. They find it difficult to keep pace with both his quick-striding walk and his seemingly endless succession of sticky questions. "I don't want him at my factory again," one irate industrialist was over-heard to fume after Philip had been and gone.

His questions, like his speeches, are highly intelligent, sometimes pointedly blunt, always carefully prepared. "He does not know a great deal about science, but he knows enough to ask sensible questions and be interested in the answers," a top U.S. scientist said of him after his visit to San Francisco.

The extent of his knowledge comes from thorough research. Whenever he is preparing a speech or getting ready for a visit— and there is seldom a day when he is not doing either one or the other—he bombards his private secretary, James Orr, with a constant stream of requests for books, pamphlets, memoranda, more answers to more questions.

When he has been and gone, industrialists and mayors alike sink back exhausted into their chairs. But for Philip there is little chance to sit down. He is usually on his way to the next stopping-place, where the questions and speeches are due to start all over again. But, sensibly, he realizes that not even a man as physically fit as he is can go on indefinitely, and, on a tour of any magnitude, whenever time and circumstances permit, he will stretch out on the nearest available bed or sofa between engagements, cat-napping with the Churchillian facility of waking to the minute without the aid of an alarm clock.

No matter what time he finishes his working day, even if it is midnight or later, Philip is always up promptly at eight o'clock the following morning to start another busy and energetic round of engagements. He is not a man to fritter time away, and even at weekends, when he and the Queen are supposedly relaxing at Windsor, or when they are on holiday at Balmoral or Sandringham, he seldom relaxes completely. Certainly he never lounges around or lies late abed.

Indeed, such vacation periods sometimes find him rising earlier than ever. There was one winter's morning when two wet and chilled duck hunters turned up at a small hotel not far from the Lincolnshire marshes and asked to be served with breakfast. It was Philip and a friend, film actor James Robertson Justice. They had risen as early as five o'clock and been out on the frosty marshes in windbreakers and boots when the wild duck flew high at dawn.

Philip moves on from work to play, from sport to hobby, with scarcely a moment's pause in between. There has been more than one occasion at Balmoral, after a day's brisk sport on the moors, when the rest of the shooting party have been more than content to sit around, healthily tired, discussing the day's kill, until it was time for dinner. But not Philip.

He would take a bath, change his clothes and hurry along

to the small room he has had converted into an amateur workshop. Surrounded by vise, lathe and electric drill, he worked happily away until dinner on the elaborate scale model of Balmoral Castle which he has been constructing, on and off, for some years.

Philip is a doer rather than a watcher, and it is this side of his nature which does not permit him to share the Queen's abounding enthusiasm for horse racing. Even the annual spectacle of Royal Ascot, where horse racing and traditional pageantry go hand in hand, holds little appeal for him.

Once, riding in an open landau with the Queen, the Duke of Gloucester and the Duke of Beaufort, Master of the Queen's Horse, at the head of the traditional procession from the entry gates to the royal box, his attention was clearly elsewhere. He was listening to a cricket commentary emanating from a small transistor radio held in his hand. Reaching the royal box, he made the briefest possible public appearance before vanishing into the inner room where he promptly switched on the television set to catch up on the cricket.

Yet even cricket on television he finds a poor substitute. He would far rather be playing himself and more than once he has disappeared from the royal box soon after arrival at Ascot to get in some polo practice or take part in an actual game. "I hate watching other people," he confessed once at the races. "I want to be out there doing things myself." There is plenty of time for him to adopt a purely spectator capacity when he is older, he has said. And that time is clearly still very much in the future.

III

There are few forms of sporting endeavor at which the Queen's husband has not tried his hand at one time or another. Cricket and rugby, hockey and athletics, yachting and swimming, fishing and big-game hunting, deer stalking and grouse shooting, duck hunting and water skiing, gliding and falconry, public house ninepins in his naval days, polo, aqua-lung diving in the heated swimming pool at the Palace and the chilly, unheated waters of Scotland's Loch Muick. Golf is a notable omission from his long list of sporting pursuits and he has given as a reason that to hit a stationary ball from a stationary position would seem tame after hitting a fast-moving ball from the back of a galloping polo pony.

Determinedly, he has mastered every sport to which he has ever

put his hand. When he first went shooting with the Queen's
father at Balmoral and Sandringham he was neither a particularly
good shot nor especially enamored with the idea of shooting
grouse and pheasants. But shooting was a basic part of the royal
way of life and Philip was resolved to master it. There was one
day when he was noticeably missing for several hours during a
house party at Sandringham and it transpired that he had been
out on his own with a gun, testing his rapidly improving marks-
manship against the zigzag flight of the woodcock, among the
wiliest of birds.

So proficient has he become since that in Denmark once he
brought down twelve pheasants in thirteen shots. He has shot
stag and grouse in Scotland, partridges and pheasants at Sandringham, wild duck in Canada, pheasants in Italy, wild pig in
Holland, wild boar in Germany, crocodiles in Australia and
Gambia, mountain goat in Pakistan and a tiger in India, though
the death of this particular tiger created such widespread controversy that Philip cannot have been other than content when a
whitlow on his trigger finger prevented him from taking part in a
second tiger shoot subsequently arranged.

Nothing has roused certain factions of the public to such fury
as his apparent addiction to shooting. His deer stalking at Balmoral has been termed loathsome by an irate Member of Parliament. Italian newspapers screamed "butchery" after he had
accompanied sewing machine tycoon Vittorio Necchi on a day's
shooting which ended with around 500 pheasants and 150 wild
duck in the bag. The League Against Cruel Sports, angrily denouncing what it called his "trigger happy exploits," labeled his
decision to accept the presidency of the World Wild Life Fund
"humbug," while an Australian politician, furious when Philip
condemned that country's practice of shooting kangaroos, hit back
with the retort: "Perhaps he will likewise denounce the organized
and cruel slaughtering of animals in the United Kingdom—
children taught to shoot stags and coverts beaten so that pheasants
fly over hidden sportsmen to their deaths by the bagful."

Philip himself apparently saw no contradiction in terms between
his own shooting exploits and his presidency of the Wild Life
Fund, and in a speech in New York he roundly denounced the
shooting of elephants "because people want chessmen or a new
set of billiard balls," rhinoceros "to get its horn for export to
China where for some incomprehensible reason they think it acts

as a sex stimulant," the North American golden eagle—"it is smart to have their feathers and claws"—and the Arabian oryx—"so that they will inherit its legendary courage and virility."

As with his shooting, so with his polo, flying and yachting. In the years since he first learned to fly—he had his first lesson at White Waltham nine months after the Queen ascended the throne—he has piloted an amazing variety of machines from that first Chipmunk trainer to the new-style Hovercraft.

Philip put the Hovercraft through its paces faster than had ever been done before, rounding a headland at high speed in a rough sea and a twenty-knot wind and handing it back to its makers with two rather large dents in the bows. Whether flying or driving, he is a man who likes to be at the controls himself. When he first decided to make use of helicopters to speed up his ever-increasing round of public engagements in Britain, nothing would satisfy him until he had learned to pilot a helicopter for himself, and in 1962, on his airborne South American tour when he covered 36,000 miles and visited no fewer than eleven countries in sixty whirlwind days in one of the new Handley Page Heralds, he took over the controls personally for ninety-nine of the hours the machine was in the air.

As a polo player, he has improved tremendously since those early days at Malta in 1950 when he barged about the polo field with considerable daring if little skill. He has a natural eye for the ball and that, combined with diligent practice, has made him one of the foremost players in Britain. For a fortnight prior to the start of each new polo season he will vanish at intervals into one of the stables in the royal mews, specially converted into an indoor practice arena. Straddling a wooden "pony," Philip gets into trim for the coming season by methodically hitting the ball into a series of nets cunningly devised to return it to him at varying speeds and from every conceivable angle.

Philip is as enthusiastic about polo as the Queen is about horse racing. He once slipped away from church at Sandringham towards the tail-end of morning service to be on time for a game at Cowdray, scoring three goals. Even more spectacular was the occasion when he was visiting Holy Island with the Queen at the time his team was due to play in the Royal Windsor Cup. Unobtrusively, he slipped away from the official party and went back to the royal barge, which was waiting to whip him along the coast to Seahouses. Here a car was standing by to take him to Acklington

R.A.F. station, from where he flew to White Waltham and then drove to Smith's Lawn at Windsor. He helped his team to win the cup by scoring two goals, flew back north and finally chased the royal yacht by motor-boat in order to rejoin his wife.

Just as the Queen really relaxes at the races, hopping excitedly from foot to foot, pounding the rail with a white-gloved hand, giving vent to excited cries of "Ride him! Ride him!" so Philip is at his most informal on the polo field. He thinks nothing of changing his shirt in the open with only the glossy bodywork of his car as a screen, and once, feeling the need for a shower in the heat of a game he contrived one by the simple expedient of up-ending a bottle and pouring the contents over his head.

His polo breeches are designed with a zipp-fastener below each knee to make for speed of changing. The zipp-fasteners are Philip's own invention, as is the electrically-heated, swivel-operated silver kettle with which the Queen brews her own cup of tea at break-fast each morning. He has a quick and inventive brain. He de-signed the silver dog collar which he presented for a greyhound race run in aid of his Duke of Edinburgh's Award scheme, the per-sonal monogram which adorns his bottle-green notepaper and black leather dispatch cases, and the bronze fountain forming the center-piece of the rose garden at Windsor Castle. And when the rose garden was laid out afresh it was Philip who constructed a model complete with sponge-rubber evergreens and rose trees to show how the finished layout was required to look.

His polo game, vastly improved though it is, is still a hell-for-leather one and he once confessed publicly that he had had the greatest difficulty in refraining from punching the umpire in a game the previous day "when he whistled me up for some in-fringement of the rules I hadn't committed." The occasional mishap is an almost inevitable result of the dash and daring which characterizes his play.

During the 1960 polo season he tore a thigh muscle. The following year found him hobbling among the guests at a Buck-ingham Palace garden party with a broken ankle. Yet another year saw him so badly bruised after a fall from his horse in a game against the French team, Laversine, that he was unable to play the following week, while during 1963, in another game against Laversine, he had to have stitches inserted in his left arm after it had been gashed by the bridle of another pony with which he was in collision.

Such incidents visibly disturb the Queen if she is watching. Her face pales and momentarily she goes tense until she is assured that her husband's injuries are not of a serious nature. Philip knows that the Queen worries for him and more than once, remounting after a fall at polo, he has cantered over to her before resuming the game to assure her that all is well.

Philip himself is unconcerned by the element of personal risk, unbothered by either a spill at polo or a soaking at sea . . . and he has experienced both in recent times. He was racing at Cowes during the summer of 1962 when his Flying Fifteen *Coweslip* heeled over and capsized. Treading water, Philip managed to right the craft with the aid of his old friend and sailing companion, the grizzled Uffa Fox, who was with him at the time, and they were subsequently towed in by a photographer's launch, bailing as they went.

Then, as *Coweslip* was being winched up onto the jetty, came a second mishap. The crane being used for the winching snapped suddenly at the base. Philip heard the sharp crack as the crane gave way, looked up . . . and sprang nimbly aside as the heavy, thirty-foot arm thudded down precisely where he had been standing no more than a split-second before.

"That was a close shave," he remarked coolly to Uffa Fox.

IV

It was Mrs. V. L. Pandit, the Indian High Commissioner, who described Prince Philip as "a young man in a hurry, anxious to put the gains of knowledge and science to work for the welfare of mankind." Speaking in July, 1961, Mrs. Pandit told the Queen's husband, "You represent all that is modern and progressive. In a very real sense you are the spirit of the age in which you live."

Her words were not merely idle flattery. They were basically true. In every way, Prince Philip has shown himself to be "a young man in a hurry," eager and anxious to get things done, and few things irritate him so much as when people decry the inevitable march of progress. "If anybody has a new idea in this country," he fumed once, "there are twice as many people who advocate putting a man with a red flag in front of it."

Unhesitatingly he has introduced modern methods to speed and streamline the work of monarchy . . . production boards and intercoms, tape recorders and electric typewriters, television as a ready-to-hand medium of mass communication, fast cars, jet planes and helicopters to make for quicker travel. His helicopter, buzzing overhead to land at Suffolk when he attended the Aldeburgh Festival in 1962, disturbed the concentration of a golfer playing a chip shot to the fourteenth green. "I raised my head and missed the shot," lamented the unfortunate golfer.

More and more Prince Philip has resorted to television to spread his obvious and very real enthusiasm for projects such as National Productivity Year and Commonwealth Technical Training Week. He wrote his own narrative for the twenty-minute film entitled *Training For Tomorrow* with which the Training Week was launched. The forty-five-minute television talk he gave on his return from his South American tour was watched by an estimated twelve and a half million people and shared eighth place in the week's rankings.

By the use of closed-circuit television, in April, 1963, he contrived to open two new nuclear power stations two hundred miles apart at one and the same time. Nor was this the first occasion on which he employed the magic carpet of television to be in two places, or even more, at one time. As president of the National Playing Fields Association, a role he has consistently pursued with zeal and vigor, he once opened five new playing fields at one time in places as far apart as Dundee and Radnorshire, Liverpool, Leicester and Middlesex.

Physically, Prince Philip has changed little in the years since the Queen ascended the throne. But undoubtedly he has matured with the years. His fortieth birthday now behind him, the dashing and largely carefree young husband of pre-monarchy days has given way to today's full man, serious in his outlook, highly intellectual, eminently responsible, a man whose speeches alone would assure him a seat in Parliament if he were not the Queen's husband.

But though he could well hold his own in the catch-as-catch-can of politics, it is debatable whether he would make a good diplomat. Diplomats are not noted for their forthrightness and Prince Philip still prefers to call a spade a spade, as with his blunt and outright statement to British industrialists, "Gentlemen, it is time we pulled our fingers out." It may have been true, but it was phrased to shock. A month later, in Sierra Leone, he was saying, hardly less bluntly, "I have noticed a growing tendency in many parts of the free world for ordinary people to be pushed round by authority, supposedly for their own good."

In San Francisco, touring an exhibition of British art, he described one exhibit as looking like "something to hang a towel on" and decried another as "a coffin for a beatnik." In Australia, in March, 1963, his reported remark, "I was born in Greece, but I am not a Greek" raised a considerable flurry in the land from which his family was forced to flee into exile when he was a blond-haired toddler of no more than eighteen months. Indignant questions were asked in the Greek parliament and the newspaper *Ethnos* demanded that Philip should remove the Greek flag from his coat of arms.

Occasionally he has injected into his speeches a humorous note of nostalgic reminiscence. Addressing a dinner for Canadian war correspondents, he recalled the time when his ship was berthed alongside a Canadian destroyer at Scapa Flow. "It didn't last long," he quipped, "which may have been a good thing because we soon lost track of where one hangover ended and the next began."

It was as revealing an insight as the speech he had made years before, when the Queen was still a Princess and he was awarded the freedom of Edinburgh. On that occasion, he recalled a previous visit to Edinburgh, and a very hospitable Lord Provost.

"We were about to leave," he said, "when someone came in and said that the train was twenty minutes late. The Lord Provost rushed round and refilled our glasses. As we were finishing, someone else came in and said that the train was twenty minutes late. This continued for some time and we eventually decided that the train was one more drink late. When we came out of the hotel many of your citizens must have marveled to see their Lord Provost and myself on such extremely good terms."

For the Queen's husband, these days, to confess to a hangover or decide that a train is "one more drink late" would be almost unthinkable. Yet nothing endears Philip so much to the man in the street as the candid admission that he has been capable of such human weaknesses.

And was there perhaps a note of personal feeling in the speech he made to the Anglo-German Association in 1960. Speaking shortly before making a flying trip to visit his sisters in Germany, Philip said on that occasion, "Although forgiving one's enemies may be difficult for many people to visualize, it is much more likely to achieve a better future than stoking the fires of hatred and suspicion."

He was speaking on a subject close to his own heart. All three of his sisters, to whom he is closely attached despite the disparity in ages, married German princes. With national emotions in Britain still running high, they were uninvited to their brother's wedding little more than two years after VE Day, though Philip wrote them a letter giving advance news of his engagement and subsequently sent them photographs of the actual wedding.

Enmities stirred up by war die all too slowly and it was not until the birth of Princess Anne in 1950, with British feelings towards Germany beginning to soften a little, that any of his sisters visited him in Britain. With the birth of the baby princess, his eldest sister, Princess Margarita, wife of the Prince of Hohenlohe-Langenburg, flew to Britain to do duty as godmother. All three sisters—Margarita, Theodora, then married to the late Prince Berthold of Baden, and Sophie, the youngest, who married Prince George of Hanover after her first husband was killed in a war-time air crash—were guests at the coronation, and in the years since, happily, Philip has seen them at frequent intervals. They have stayed with him and the Queen at Buckingham Palace and Windsor, at Sandringham and Balmoral. He, in turn, has visited them, upon occasion taking his children with him to meet their aunts and uncles and numerous cousins in Germany.

V

Prince Philip's position in public life is fluid and undefined. The only certain definition is that he is the Queen's husband. No more; no less. The contents of the leather-bound dispatch boxes which arrive for his wife from the busy bee-hives of Downing Street and Whitehall are not for his eyes. Her regular Tuesday evening conference with the prime minister is not for his ears. His job as the Queen's husband is what he likes to make of it, and Philip has made industry and science, youth and education and Commonwealth relations very much his special province.

His views on all these subjects are not always orthodox. "There has been a tendency in recent years," he said in a speech in 1961, "to pick on the younger generation for their dress, their social habits and their ways of enjoying themselves. It seems about time the other side of the coin got a showing."

"For some strange reason," he said in another speech, "it is perfectly respectable to teach history and math, electronics and engineering, but any attempts to develop character and the whole man tends to be viewed with the utmost suspicion."

And in yet another: "New ideas can be bad as well as good, but whereas an intelligent man with an open mind can demolish a bad idea by reasoned argument, those who allow their brains to atrophy resort to meaningless catch-phrases, derision and finally anger in the face of anything new."

By exhortation and example he has frequently contrived to get things done which might otherwise have remained undone, and his influence on thought and life in Britain has been wide and far-ranging . . . and may yet prove wider and even further-ranging in the years to come.

Improved lighting for road vehicles, crash helmets for motor-cyclists, double white lines on dangerous bends . . . all these things have resulted from only one of Prince Philip's many roles, his ten-year presidency of the Automobile Association. Even the transformation of Britain's archaic road signs, only recently translated into reality, was foreshadowed in a speech Philip made several years ago roundly denouncing the "chaotic signposting" of British roads. Despite frequent campaigning, however, he has not yet succeeded in accomplishing anything tangible in the battle against diesel fumes. "I am sure diesel smoke is shortening my life," he has said uncompromisingly.

The changes which have been brought about by his prodding finger and forthright tongue have not always been without controversy and Philip himself is under no illusions on this point. Attending a luncheon of the Saints and Sinners Club, he was careful to wear a pink buttonhole so as to avoid being classified as extreme in either direction. "I am frequently accused of meddling in affairs that are no concern of mine," he told the assembled Saints and Sinners. "I am always told that I must not take sides."

He had much the same thing to say when addressing a gathering of architects. "I seem to have got a terrible reputation for telling people what they ought to be doing," he confessed. But un-deterred by his reputation he went on to exhort the architects, "Anything which persuades you occasionally to break away from the cigar-box and gasometer line ought to be encouraged."

As in public affairs, so in the private life of the Royal Family the progressive thinking and forward-looking ideas of the Queen's husband have had and are having their effect, and for the Royal

Family public and personal life are seldom completely divisible. The education and upbringing of their son is a matter of personal decision for the Queen and her husband, but the outcome of the decisions they take will assuredly affect the monarchy, and through the monarchy, British public life for years, perhaps generations, to come.

Charles at Gordonstoun, Anne at Benenden, the ending of the anachronistic system of debutante presentations, the in-auguration of informal palace luncheon parties . . . these things, and many more, are linked, directly and indirectly, with Philip's progressive outlook.

In the television broadcast he made late in 1962 to usher in the National Productivity Year, he revealed that time-and-motion experts were being called in to study what could be done about streamlining Buckingham Palace itself. Months later they were still there. Few of the guests who attended the state banquet given at the palace to honor King Paul and Queen Frederika of Greece can have paid any attention to the solitary figure surveying all that went on from one end of the vast and lofty banquet hall. That lone figure was one of the team of time-and-motion experts who that evening studied the progress of the food from the huge kitchens at the south-west corner of the palace, through the stone-flagged basements and up three flights of stairs to be served on gold plates at the banquet table.

Ever since the Queen ascended the throne, her husband has held the view that Buckingham Palace could be run more efficiently and more economically, with fewer servants and at less cost. He is not the first occupant of the palace to have held that view, though others before him have had to confess themselves beaten finally by this huge labyrinth of stairs and passageways, rooms and corridors.

Philip may yet be beaten too, but it will certainly not have been for the want of trying.

CHAPTER SEVENTEEN

THE QUEEN'S "IDEAL FAMILY"

I

SIR MICHAEL ADEANE, a slight, balding figure with features which might well serve as a model for a bust of William Shakespeare, turned left at the top of the stairs and walked briskly along the red-carpeted corridor of the palace, a wickerwork tray of letters and documents tucked safely beneath one arm. Cultured and essentially discreet, Sir Michael is the Queen's private secretary, grandson of the man who was private secretary, to her great-great-grandmother.

He paused before the white-painted door of the Queen's sitting room, tapped gently, turned the gilt door handle and entered, knowing that the Queen was expecting him.

But the Queen's chair, on the far-side of her cluttered, flat-topped desk standing in the big recess of the bay window, was unoccupied. Playing truant for a few moments from the manifold duties of monarchy, the Queen was kneeling on the close-carpeted floor, happily engaged in some game involving little Prince Andrew, one of the royal corgis and a brightly-colored ball.

Sir Michael gave the slight obeisance of the head which has replaced the deep bow courtiers once accorded members of the Royal Family. Smiling, the Queen rose to her feet and crossed the room to her customary chair at the desk. For the next half-hour, while Andrew remained in the sitting room, quietly and contentedly amusing himself, the Queen and her private secretary attended the business of monarchy.

Until the Queen ascended the throne, the royal study had always been regarded as a holy of holies. King George V's children entered it only when summoned by their father and then usually in anticipation of some parental correction or lecture. The Queen's father, though he humanized the monarchy in so many ways, drew a fairly rigid line between his family life and his working hours. But the Queen, as the first mother to occupy the throne since the days of Queen Victoria, has so contrived things that monarchy and motherhood go hand-in-hand.

At Buckingham Palace, the Queen's working day starts promptly at ten o'clock when she seats herself at her desk and goes through her morning mail, slitting the envelopes neatly with a paper-knife. On a royal visit to some other part of Britain or an overseas tour her day frequently starts much earlier. She has risen as early as half-past four in the morning to board her aircraft on the next leg of a long tour. She has been on dusty parade grounds soon after eight o'clock to take the salute at a march-past before the heat of the day becomes too intense. Once it was four o'clock in the morning when the royal aircraft touched down at Gander to refuel. No official welcome was scheduled in the Queen's itinerary and she was sleeping. But, waking, she learned that a crowd had been waiting all night in hope of seeing her. Quickly she dressed and left the aircraft to acknowledge their greeting.

At Buckingham Palace, normally, there is no need for quite so early a start. For the Queen, there is the opportunity for a relaxed breakfast, a glimpse at the racing news and a half-hour of personal family life before the necessity for going along to her sitting room to begin the day's work.

The sitting room which also doubles as the Queen's study is large and high-ceilinged, light and airy. It lacks the business-like atmosphere of Prince Philip's study just along the corridor. In contrast, it has a feminine, essentially homely atmosphere of comfortable furnishings, personal possessions and freshly-cut flowers. Whatever the season, a vase of pink carnations stands always among the profusion of working paraphernalia and family photographs which crowd the Queen's desk.

More flowers stand beside the gilt-handled door which leads through to the Royal Family's private dining room, and yet more on the occasional table between the mushroom-covered armchairs which flank one side of the marble fireplace in which a log fire burns to provide additional warmth and sense of comfort in cold weather.

Magazines and newspapers are ranged in neat rows on the long side-table standing behind the settee. Books on horse racing and the breeding of thoroughbreds, a few novels to be dipped into from time to time, and some well-thumbed works of reference are piled rather higgledy-piggledy on top of a small, drawered chest. On a nearby card table, most days, there reposes up to a dozen photographs for the Queen to sign with her stylized royal signature before they are dispatched to local mayors and military regiments.

With so many portraits to be so constantly signed, it was suggested once that the Queen should arrange for her signature to be artificially reproduced. She would not hear of it. If she did not sign the portraits personally they would lose their significance, she said.

Pastel portraits of the royal children stand on easels in front of the Queen's desk, where she can see them whenever she glances up. A freshly-filled bowl of water for the royal corgis stands beside the desk. Like the photographs to be signed, other items come and go from day to day . . . the leather-bound dispatch boxes from Downing Street and Whitehall, maps and itineraries for some future tour, crossword puzzles the Queen has not yet completely solved, films she has taken recently, patterns for curtains, cushions and coverings for a room she is perhaps planning to re-furnish.

When she renovated the Edward III Tower at Windsor Castle, the Queen's sitting room was littered for weeks on end with plans and sketches, paint-cards and samples of fabric, as she and Philip discussed how best to convert a medieval tower into a modern guest suite without interfering with the actual structure.

The Queen's morning mail is large and varied. Personal letters from relatives and close friends, easily identified by special marking on the outer envelope, are placed carefully to one side to be answered in her own slanting, rather hurried handwriting as opportunity serves.

The Queen sorts her mail with the same meticulousness that she once devoted to grading the coffee sugar according to size before eating it. Accounts go into yet another pile for later discussion with Lord Tryon, the Keeper of the Privy Purse, whose task it is to administer the royal household expenses. Into her wickerwork letter-basket go letters seeking her help in all manner of directions. A surprisingly large number of people write to the Queen for help when they can think of no other direction in which to turn . . . a pensioner and his wife seeking a home for their old age, a worried mother whose husband is desperately ill and whose only son is on military service in the Far East, a small businessman hamstrung in his dealings with authority. The Queen reads them all, discusses them with one or other of her secretaries before indicating her wishes in the matter.

Her correspondence sorted, the Queen rings for Sir Michael Adeane. He comes up from his ground-floor office with more letters for the Queen's attention, government documents, plans and programs for forthcoming visits, notes to brief the Queen concerning the various people she is due to meet in the course of the day. And before Sir Michael has closed the door behind him again at the end of this morning session, the Queen is already summoning one of her two assistant private secretaries—Sir Edward Ford or Sir Martin Charteris—to deal with yet more letters, requests, itineraries, documents.

By quarter past eleven, most mornings, it is time for the Queen to go along to the Audience Room with its blue and white Wedgwood decor at the far end of the royal corridor. Here she receives foreign ambassadors arriving to present their credentials, British ambassadors going abroad or reporting back, visiting sheiks and foreign princes, newly-appointed bishops and judges, freshly-honored knights and baronets. One audience succeeds another with streamlined efficiency until it is one o'clock and time for lunch.

Occasionally an ambassador and his wife will be invited to stay on for lunch. Sometimes there is a guest such as Princess Grace of Monaco or Mrs. Kennedy, the wife of America's late President, both of whom have lunched with the Queen in recent years. And from time to time up to a dozen guests drawn from all walks of life—from government and commerce, education and science, television and the press, sport and show business—will be invited to join the Queen and Prince Philip at an informal luncheon party.

These informal lunches do much to help the Queen to keep more closely in touch with all that is going on in the vast world outside the palace railings. Throughout the meal and for a short time afterwards she and her guests converse animatedly on all manner of topics until it is time for the Queen to turn to other things. She signals that lunch has ended by reaching for her handbag, suspended always beneath the table at her side by a specially-contrived hook, thanks her guests for coming and goes back upstairs to her private apartment.

Such palace luncheon parties usually run to three courses. For herself, when she lunches alone, the Queen is invariably content with a single course followed by cheese and crackers. Like

Prince Philip, she is a light eater. But light eating should not be confused with dieting. The Queen's only form of diet is what Norman Hartnell, the royal fashion designer, once termed "a diet of duty."

Her work, her love of outdoor life and, more especially perhaps, her frequent travels are more than sufficient to keep her slim and youthful. She will usually return from a tour of any magnitude having noticeably lost weight. Understandably so. One royal aide, who accompanied her and Prince Philip on their six-month round-the-world-tour early in the new reign, arrived back to discover that he had lost twenty pounds in the process.

If the Queen is lunching in her own apartment, little Prince Andrew will usually come down from the nursery at the end of the meal to spend a further half-hour with Mummy. Afterwards the Queen sees various household officials and senior servants to discuss problems which only she can settle . . . perhaps the accommodation arrangements for some overseas monarch or president paying a state visit to Britain, the menu for the consequent state banquet, the order of seating for a palace luncheon party being held the following week, staff matters and financial matters, including the many charitable organizations to which the Queen subscribes so generously. All this, of course, assuming that there are no public engagements—barracks to be inspected, housing estates and factories to see over, schools and hospitals to be visited, trees to be planted or foundation stones to be laid.

Even if there are no outside public engagements, the Queen's afternoons are seldom other than fully occupied. She is a woman as well as a monarch and mother, and once a week, at least, time must be found for her hairdresser. Twice a week, on average, she must find time for her milliners, fashion designers, dressmakers or shoe-maker. Because she must wear a different dress in York to what she wore in London, never appear at a banquet in Adelaide wearing the same gown that she wore in Sydney, the Queen must devote more of her time than other women to the tasks of selecting and fitting.

But the Queen knows the need for a break in routine and the benefits of physical exercise. Whenever possible, she finds time in the afternoon to change her high-heeled shoes for a pair of stout walking brogues and takes the royal corgis for an airing in the grounds, often joined in her walk by Prince Andrew if he is in the gardens at the time.

At five o'clock, washed and changed after his sometimes grubby exertions in the palace gardens—for royal children are no different from other children when it comes to outdoor play—Andrew again joins his mother for afternoon tea . . . though "tea" for him takes the form of a cup of milk accompanied by such childhood delicacies as jam sandwiches, banana sandwiches and sponge cake. Sometimes mother and son will sit together to watch the children's programs on television before Andrew goes back up to the nursery for bath-time and bed-time.

Regularly each Tuesday evening the Queen goes along to the Audience Room at the end of the royal suite for her weekly talk with the prime minister. This seldom lasts less than an hour. Other evenings bring other audiences, and it is surprising how many of the Queen's evenings, between half-past six when she leaves the nursery and eight o'clock dinner, are taken up with seeing returning diplomats or retiring generals who, for one reason or another, cannot be fitted into her always busy morning schedule.

The Queen and her husband have discontinued the former royal custom of changing into evening dress when they dine alone. From time to time, however, the Queen will invite relatives and personal friends to dinner at the palace and on these occasions she changes into a cocktail dress or evening gown while Prince Philip dons a black tie and dinner jacket.

The Queen Mother, as might be expected, is a frequent guest at these private dinner parties. So are Princess Margaret and Lord Snowdon, Prince Philip's uncle, Earl Mountbatten, and such close personal friends of the Queen as Lord and Lady Porchester, Lord Rupert and Lady Nevill, and Sir Harold and Lady Zia Wernher, at whose country home Princess Alexandra first met her husband.

On other evenings when she has no public engagement to fulfill, the Queen likes to relax in the privacy of her own apartment, reading the evening newspapers, tackling crossword puzzles, up-dating her stud records and racing diary. She watches television only occasionally, when there is a play of outstanding merit to be seen or some program like show-jumping, which is in line with her special interests.

She enjoys solving crossword puzzles, as does Princess Margaret and as their father did before them. Princess Margaret once entered a crossword competition and won a small prize. The

Queen is not concerned with competitions. For her there is sufficient satisfaction in merely solving a difficult puzzle and each day she will grapple meticulously with two of the cryptic puzzles to be found in the newspapers, sometimes turning to Prince Philip or her personal page for assistance if she finds herself stumped over a particular word. She is seldom stumped, however, years of experience having attuned her mind to the torturous twists of the most complicated clues and it is seldom any puzzle baffles her for long. She permits no puzzle to beat her entirely and if necessary she will keep a particular newspaper by her for days until she has successfully mastered every clue.

Occasionally, the Queen and Prince Philip go out with friends to spend an evening at the theater. Such evenings, not to be confused with command performances or charity matinees, are strictly private, completely informal. Usually the theater seats are booked by the accompanying friends in their own name with no mention of the fact that royalty is to be included in the party. One of the less conspicuous royal cars is used for the journey from Buckingham Palace to the theater and only the theater manager is given warning—and then often at the last minute—that the Queen will be in the audience that evening.

So informal were things when the Queen and Prince Philip attended the London production of the Lawrence of Arabia play, *Ross*, that they and their friends sat in the wrong seats and obligingly moved further along the row when another theater-goer showed up with a ticket for the seat the Queen's husband was occupying!

II

What is she really like, this young mother, wife and monarch who occupies England's age-old throne? Her physical attributes are self-evident. She is of medium height with a mature figure and a swinging walk. Her hair is brown and wavy, her eyes blue, her forehead high, her mouth rather wide and her complexion magnificent. Viewed as a woman, she is tremendously attractive. As a monarch, her personality is positively electrifying. There is about her a *mystique* which makes women blink their eyes when she passes by and retired colonels contend with unexpected lumps in the throat. "When she smiles," the American artist, Douglas Chandor, has said, "there is a radiance such as I have seldom seen in any face."

So often serious in public—because so many public occasions demand seriousness of her—the Queen laughs heartily and often in private, and behind the royal mask she so often wears lurks a distinctly impish sense of humor. At that royal garden party when both Prince Philip and the Queen Mother were limping—one after a spill at polo, the other following a fall at Windsor—the Queen could not resist the temptation to mimic with a mock limp.

More than once she has been known to arrive back from an evening function at the end of a day of non-stop engagements, remove her tiara with an exaggerated gesture of feigned relief, pretend to mop her brow and perform a brief caricature portrayal of mock exhaustion as she goes to her room.

Hers is a life governed always by the clock and the calendar . . . by the gilt-framed engagement card and perpetual calendar which confront her each morning on her desk, by the clock which ticks away on the marble mantelpiece across the room and the tiny gold and platinum wristwatch she wears always *over* her glove so that it is plainly visible.

The duties of monarchy which she tackles so industriously and conscientiously have increased several-fold even in the short span of time since her father's day . . . and much of the increase has been due to her own unremitting sense of royal duty. In that one world tour she undertook in the second year of her reign she traveled more miles than her father did in his entire period of monarchy. And she has not stopped traveling since.

She loves her husband, adores her children, though she refuses to coddle them. She sends Charles to Gordonstoun, Anne to Benenden, lets them holiday abroad without her. The Duke of Windsor, when he was Prince of Wales, was reluctantly compelled to give up steeplechasing because the risk of an accident was thought to be too great.

The Queen enforces no such inhibitions on her children. Anne takes part in show-jumping; Charles goes skiing and sailing and flies home from school. If the Queen ever fears, like a mother, for her children's safety, she buries her fears in the knowledge that some degree of exposure to risk is an inherent part of life and living. She shares her husband's view that the art of educating youngsters is "to combine formal training with as wide a variety of experiences as possible, including some which involve a calculated risk."

It has always been the great strength of the Royal Family that it has not hesitated to change with the changing times. Never was this more true than today when the rate of change is so vastly accelerated . . . when Princess Margaret marries a photographer and goes to Switzerland for winter sports, when Princess Alexandra parks her compact at parking meters while her husband works in a city office, and even slips away from the royal enclosure at Ascot through necessity to be back at his desk, when the Duke of Kent goes abroad as a junior army officer, living in a small flat, pushing his son ahead of him in a baby carriage as he and his wife shop in a supermarket, when Prince William of Gloucester goes to an American university and hopes for a job in the civil service.

All these things have the Queen's wholehearted approval. Yet the ordained orbit of her own life can change to only a small degree. She may send her children to boarding school, but she herself cannot shop in a supermarket or holiday in Switzerland. She would be mobbed with affection if she so much as dared to try, even in countries which have no direct link with either the Crown or the Commonwealth, as was seen in France when elegantly-gowned women clambered on priceless statues and in New York where they knocked over chairs and stood on counters to see her.

Not that the Queen has been known to evince any desire to shop in a supermarket or go skiing in Switzerland. She is well content with a destined pattern of life which continues unchanged and unchanging . . . a pattern woven around her husband and her home, her work and her children, the same leather-bound dispatch boxes piled high on her desk each day, the same ceremonies of tree-planting, ship-launching, hand-shaking, opening, visiting, inspecting. Always the same, yet always, in the finer details, different. And the Queen would wish it no other way.

Even the pattern of her private life changes little. Most of her weekends she spends at Windsor, leaving Buckingham Palace on Friday afternoons as London's rush-hour traffic begins to build up, returning on Monday mornings. At Windsor she finds relaxation and enjoyment in the outdoor life to which she is so firmly attached . . . riding in Windsor Great Park, walking her dogs along the quiet reaches of the Thames, unnoticed by the occupants of passing pleasure craft, watching her athletic-looking husband play a vigorous game of polo, accompanying him when he goes shooting, visiting her mother at Royal Lodge, taking her children to see the pigs and cows at the Home Farm, going to church on Sunday mornings as she has done every Sunday of her life.

Each summer finds her at Balmoral, each Christmas at Sandringham, just as her father and grandfather went to those places at those times before her. After the crowds which hem her in for so much of the year, there are times when she finds her own company all that she requires. Stalking a stag in the heather-clad hills with sandwiches as her only food and a hunting guide her only companion . . . long hilltop walks in head scarf, raincoat and stout shoes with only her dogs to pace her . . . riding a horse along remote and lonely paths . . . family picnics far from the madding crowd . . . these are her pleasures.

At Sandringham at Christmas, she finds happiness enough in such simple, homely tasks as filling her children's stockings with toys and sweets, in family games of charades and hide and seek, carols sung round the grand piano, long walks through a windswept countryside painted with frosty fingers, the happy laughter of her children as they toboggan down snowy slopes or pelt each other with snowballs.

III

It was at Balmoral Castle towards the tail-end of the summer of 1963 that Sir George Middleton, the bespectacled Scots doctor who holds the ancient and quaintly-named post of Surgeon Apothecary to the Royal Household at Balmoral, confirmed the Queen's hopes that she was expecting another child . . . her fourth.

Of course, the Queen did not go to the small, granite consulting room adjoining the stables where Sir George attends to the aches and pains of royal servants. Instead, he went to see her in her tartan-carpeted private apartment with its travel-folder views of the heather-clad hills.

The Queen was overjoyed at what Sir George had to tell her at the end of his examination. Years ago, at the time of her marriage to Prince Philip, she confided to a close friend that her dearest wish was for a family of four children. Her first child, Prince Charles, was born within twelve months of marriage. Twenty-one months later Charles was joined in the nursery by a baby sister, Princess Anne. In those days Elizabeth was still living at Clarence House, where her mother lives now; still a princess, not yet the Queen.

Had the Queen remained a princess there can be little doubt that she would have had other children at intervals enabling them all to grow up together. Then fate took a hand. With Charles no more than three years old and Anne still a flaxen-topped toddler of some eighteen months, the princess became the Queen.

Monarchy is a hard taskmaster, demanding its own special type of sacrifice from those who serve it. From Philip it demanded that he surrender his nationality and religion and even a father's right to have his son reared in his own name. Its demands upon the young woman who is now Queen Elizabeth II were heavier still . . . and reluctantly, for a time at least, Elizabeth was forced to forgo her personal desire for more children.

Eight busy, travel-packed years, crammed with official tree plantings and ship launchings, bouquets accepted and hands shaken, foundation stones laid and speeches made, were to pass before the Queen could again feel free to place personal happiness ahead of royal duty . . . and even then, as we have related, her third pregnancy was to clash with a royal tour of Canada.

To the Queen, the birth of Prince Andrew, close on the heels of the eighth anniversary of her accession to the throne, was like starting a family all over again. Between Anne and Andrew there was a gap of almost ten years. The gap between Charles and Andrew was wider still. Indeed, Charles had already started his years at boarding school. With Anne soon destined to follow suit, the Queen's desire for a family of four children was reinforced now by the knowledge that Andrew would otherwise be brought up virtually as an only child.

"Now we must see about a little playmate for Andrew," she remarked, once, in the months immediately following his birth.

She said it with a smile, but, as subsequent events have shown, she was not entirely joking.

Prince Philip was out on the heathery moors, shooting grouse, when the Queen learned from Sir George Middleton that she was expecting another baby. Philip's own delight, when she told him the news on his return, was reflected in a display of husbandly concern and a characteristic succession of witty quips.

Philip, in turn, passed the news on to Charles and Anne during a stroll with them on the castle lawn. Charles took the announcement phlegmatically, as teenage boys are apt to do. But the more volatile Anne turned excitedly on her heels, raced back across the lawn, dashed up the broad granite steps of the castle and burst in on her mother.

"Is it really true, Mummy?" she wanted to know. "Are you really having another baby?"

It was the Queen herself who told little Prince Andrew about the new baby. Soon, she said, he would be having a baby brother or sister to share the royal nursery with him. At three years old, Andrew could hardly be blamed if he found such exciting news also a little confusing.

"I'm going to have a little baby brother *and* sister," he told everyone he met that day . . . the servants in the castle, the gardeners on the grounds, the milkmaids in the royal dairy. He even announced the news in a loud voice to his pony, Valkyrie, when he went for his daily ride.

During the weeks which remained of her summer stay at Balmoral, the Queen began her preparations for motherhood. Every day she went for long, beneficial walks across the Scottish hills. Even the rain—and it rained a lot at Balmoral that summer—could not deter her. With a raincoat over her tweeds, her hair protected by a scarf, she walked for miles in the rain, sometimes with Philip, sometimes with only her dogs for company.

As a brief interlude in her Scottish holiday, she boarded the royal train and made a round trip of 1,000 miles to take Princess Anne to her new boarding school at Benenden, a few miles south of London. There was a hasty re-shuffle of more formal royal engagements. Plans for the Queen to visit the University of Sussex and a number of northern towns were postponed. Her participation in the traditional Armistice Day service at the Cenotaph in Whitehall was cancelled.

Back at Buckingham Palace at the end of her holiday, she continued to rise promptly at eight o'clock each morning, spending the greater part of each day working at her desk as usual, going through to the elegant blue and white Audience Room at the far end of the royal apartment from time to time to receive ambassadors and diplomats. Her last audience was held only five days before the baby was born, when she received the new Viet-Namese ambassador, Professor Vu Van Mau, and the departing High Commissioner of Tanganyika, Mr. Sam Ntiro. For ten minutes she talked with Professor Mau, mostly about his five children.

On the morning of March 10 the Queen rode down from her second floor apartment in her private elevator for her customary walk in the palace gardens. Her pet corgis went with her. While she was out walking, her personal belongings were to be moved down to the first-floor Belgian Suite, which she would occupy for the baby's birth, and as the Queen walked out by the garden entrance, Sister Rowe, the royal midwife, entered the elevator to help with the moving.

By chance, the elevator selected that precise moment to break down, trapping Sister Rowe between floors. Workmen were hastily summoned, but it was a further forty-five minutes before the elevator was restored to working order so that Sister Rowe could be rescued and proceed with her mission.

"A good thing that Queen wasn't in it," was the general comment . . . a remark with which the Queen was in smiling agreement when she returned from her walk and heard what had happened.

She spent what was left of the morning working at her desk in the sitting room of the Belgian Suite, where Philip, calling off a Variety Club luncheon at which he was due to make a speech, joined her for lunch. A few hours later—at 8:40 in the evening—the baby was born.

At five pounds seven ounces, little Prince Edward was easily the smallest of the royal babies at birth, nearly two pounds less than either Charles or Andrew, nine ounces lighter even than Princess Anne, his tiny nose and rather wide mouth stemming undeniably from his mother.

Prince Philip promptly telephoned news of the birth to the Queen Mother and Princess Margaret, herself expecting another baby, as well as to Charles and Anne at their schools. Andrew was already in bed and asleep. But first thing the following morning he was taken along for a peep at his baby brother, taking his mother a nosegay of snowdrops he had gathered for her in the palace gardens.

The Queen Mum and Princess Margaret also dropped in at the palace to see the new arrival, the Queen Mother not yet fully recovered from the emergency appendectomy for which she had been rushed into hospital only a short time before. Like a mother, she had postponed the convalescence which should have followed until she was assured that all was well with her elder daughter and latest grandchild. Only then would she fly out of London for a convalescent cruise aboard the royal yacht in Caribbean sunshine.

As always, the royal birth made world news. United States radio networks broke into their scheduled programs. Messages of congratulation streamed into the palace, among them a personal message from President Johnson and a cable from the Governor General of Canada expressing "great joy" on behalf of the Canadian people.

That weekend, with Charles having traveled south from Gordonstoun, Anne home from Benenden, Philip back from Athens where he had been attending the funeral of King Paul of the Hellenes, the Queen gathered around her the "ideal family" for which she had longed so long . . . Charles, mature and manly at fifteen; Anne, a thirteen-year-old schoolgirl; Andrew, a bright-eyed, mischievous four-year-old; and little Prince Edward, asleep in the satin-covered cot which has held every royal baby since the Queen herself was born.

More than twelve years had elapsed since Sir Martin Charteris, shocked by news of the King's death, was moved to utter that poignant phrase, "My poor dear lady." Nobody, seeing the Queen with her family around her, could conceivably think of her in such terms today. She has won the respect and affection of millions, not only in Britain, but around the world. In terms of human happiness, she is secure in her husband's love and the pleasure she derives from her home and her children.

She is the Queen. But she is also a wife and mother . . . and the strength she draws from marriage and motherhood is perhaps, in the final analysis, the monarchy's greatest asset.

THE AUTHORS AND THEIR BOOK

GRAHAM AND HEATHER FISHER *are internationally known authors and magazine writers. Born and educated in England, they have written or compiled three books besides* ELIZABETH: QUEEN AND MOTHER—Historic Britain, Best After Dinner Stories, *and* Blackshirt. *In addition to having their stories syndicated in twelve countries, the Fishers have written articles for* Punch, Coronet, McCall's, Saturday Evening Post, Redbook, *and* Cosmopolitan, *including stories on Princess Grace of Monaco ("The Prince and I") and Hayley Mills ("The World's Favorite Teenager") for* The Ladies' Home Journal. *The Fishers have traveled all over the globe doing research for articles on personalities such as King Hussein of Jordan, Princess Grace of Monaco, Charlton Heston, and, of course, Queen Elizabeth.*

ELIZABETH: QUEEN AND MOTHER/The Story of Elizabeth II and the British Royal Family (*Hawthorn, 1964*) *was composed by Westcott and Thomson of Philadelphia, printed by Universal Lithographers of Baltimore, and bound by The Book Press, Inc. of Brattleboro, Vermont. The typeface used is Imprint, a typeface based on William Caslon's Old Face and designed in 1912 by J. H. Mason and the staff of the English magazine* The Imprint.

A HAWTHORN BOOK